Faith, Freedom

Beyond
the
Boundaries

Edited by
Janette Bredenoord Elliott
& Berise T. Heasly

COVENTRY
PRESS

Published in Australia by
Coventry Press
33 Scoresby Road
Bayswater VIC 3153

ISBN 9781922589224

Catalogue-in-Publication entry is available from the National Library of Australia
http://catalogue.nla.gov.au

Cover design by Ian James – www.jgd.com.au
Cover photograph by Louise McMahon
Text design by Coventry Press
Set in Tex Gyre Pagella

Printed in Australia

Table of Contents

Reflection on the Gospel Theme for our Project

Michael Elligate

John 10:10
'I have come that you may have life – Life in plenty.'

How deep is your well?
How rich is your wine?
How devoted is the Shepherd?

The measure that John glimpses in the words and actions of
Jesus are summed up in the remarkable word – plenty.

Plenty assures us that his gifts never run out:
Always remain fresh
And are always there for our taking.

Acknowledgment of Country

The contributors to this volume wish to acknowledge the Aboriginal and Torres Strait Islander traditional owners of the land on which we live, act and learn. We pay respect to their Elders – past, present and emerging – and the place of Indigenous knowledge in the academy and in our community. We acknowledge and respect that Aboriginal and Torres Strait Islander people have always used resources of this country, from the land and from the waters, for nourishment, medicine and healing.

About the front cover

The cover photograph highlights the Australian context of *Beyond the Boundaries*. The red soil draws our attention to the Aboriginal influence. The plants highlight ideas of growth, freedom and identity in place. Just noticeable are the tyre marks in the soil, pointing, so that the traveller, the pilgrim, the believer is beckoned to look forward and to look backward on the spectrum that represents the journey of life and lived experience.

Prologue

Janette Bredenoord Elliott
Berise T. Heasly

In the fourth Gospel, John has Jesus say that he came so that we may have 'life to the full'. What does that mean in the 21st century?

Lived experience: it is so vital to understanding how the Holy Spirit connects with each one of us: 'Go back! There is something I want you to do'. My story was one that mystified me for at least ten years. The problem and the experience are still alive and present with me today: I was looking down on my body, worrying as my mother, my father, the resident doctor who saved my life, Dr Fox, and one nurse surrounded my bed. There was one other person present, hazy but vitally present, and I was conscious of never wanting to go back to the boarding school in Warracknabeal, when a loving arm encircled my shoulders. I tried to turn and walk down a large corridor towards a warm and golden light, but the gentle voice just said, 'Go Back! There is something I want you to do'.

Reluctantly I agreed, and found myself back in my hospital bed, telling my Dad that I was ok, and not to worry. I have spent my life ever since, being involved in family life, Catholic education, music and liturgy, gardening and travel; wondering whether the current project is the 'something I want you to do'. Responding to needs of those around me has been the central focus of my life and the only thanks or appreciation I seek is that from my 'partner', the Holy Cosmic Mystery of the Trinity: the mystery of our creator, teacher and fount of wisdom, emanating from the source and energy that sustains this planet, the vastness of the Cosmos, and the lived experience of each individual. This is according to the mystery of a divine plan beyond the complete understanding of the People of God – the 'people in the pews' (*Call No One Father*, 2019).

Then over the years, after 10 am Mass in our parish, there grew a remarkable 'coffee group' – up to 25 people at any Sunday after Mass, as we caught up with each other, and tried to eventually come to terms with the reports of the Royal Commission into Institutional Responses to Child Sexual Abuse in the Catholic Church. We listened together, we worried together, we pooled our lived experience from so diverse our range of academic and lived expertise. And so, the prompt from one of the group to write on whatever clericalism was, became *Call No One Father*. And *We Too: the Laity speaks* followed. Now, we review our lived experience in the face of the pandemic and its aftermath, of devastating invasion of war, of the worry of climate change, and much more. It seems important, therefore, to look beyond the present, as Pope Francis is showing us, to chart our course of lived experience.

When the scandal of child sexual abuse in the Australian Catholic Church was brought intentionally to my attention, I was part of an enclosed Benedictine community. As a community, we watched a documentary on the scandal. I watched a deeply sobering and long list of names of priests and religious who had been convicted of child sexual abuse. As if the scandal wasn't shocking enough, the knowledge that I knew five of the names rocked me. That night as I tried to

8

sleep my mind flitted between profound gratitude that I had not known such devastating abuse, and great distress. I could not fathom that, children of my age – both boys and girls – had suffered at the hands of those who represented and professed to be agents of God's care and compassion.

One of the names I recognised was of a parish priest who facilitated the 'Renew Program' in my deanery during the 1980s. I was a young adult at the time. The other name was of a priest who had visited my home with his brother priests, one of who was a close musician friend of my mothers. It sickens me to recall this since I was a young pre-pubescent girl and remember him coming to my bedroom – along with others who were looking for the bathroom. It is scary at times to think of the situations that appeared so innocent while wondering if other forces were at work that were not of God. Still, this memory serves to remind me how lucky and protected I was.

I grew up in a small parish community cared for by the Servite Order, and we also had a close family connection with the priest who founded the parish. In fact, he was probably the source of my unequivocal trust in priests and religious as a child. He was incredibly kind to mum and me at a time when my parents' marriage was falling to pieces. There were times when mum and I escaped late at night from my dad drunkenly lost in the pain of his P.O.W experiences, and we were 'rescued' by this priest. At other times, his assistance of food, and or funds helped mum make it over the poverty line. They were extraordinary days, and the kindness of this self-less priest stands out as the best of what the priestly vocation represented – at least to a vulnerable child. I was always protected. The Church represented safety and compassion to me as a child.

Then I grew up and discovered that this was not everyone's experience. Further, this had nothing to do whether we were good or bad, but the best or worst use of positions of power, opportunity and distorted sexuality. Once the bubble of safety in the Church was well and truly broken by witnessing that documentary, I have grieved and continue to grieve for the lives and innocent souls trampled on still. The knowledge that disclosure of child sexual abuse may not peak until the early 2030s due to the average time it takes for victims to feel safe enough to disclose, means that there is still much to be done.

I admit to feeling guilty about the blessings of faith and love I have known, the opportunities I have been given through the generosity of others in my own lifetime. This is not to say my life has not had its quota of challenges, losses, failures and pain. It certainly has had all these through my rather different life's journey. However, as a result of all I have received, I have sought to live with and from deep gratitude by sharing these blessings with others in the capacity I can, or by the sometimes more challenging call to accept the invitation to move out of my comfort zone. The recent exhortation of Joan Chittister on 12 May 2022 at Melbourne Town Hall, to embrace a spirituality of engagement for a rediscovery of the place of religion in society is timely. We can all respond to such a spirituality of engagement and this project represents a response to this call.

It is fair to say that 'the love of Christ compels me' in taking up this call – and not just because of Joan Chittister. Her words speak into my conviction that the empowering of laity is at the heart of the Church's future. My deeper hope through this conviction is that the healing of our individual and communal, as well as ecclesial soul, is something we share responsibility for. If ever there was a moment in our history to claim our baptismal dignity as children of God it is now. The Easter Christ calls us forth to the new shores of hope and healing, awareness and forgiveness, of mercy and of grace, of courage and of justice. Whatever holds us back from the recognition of the Easter Christ, whose wounds like ours remain visible, let us cast it into the ocean behind us, that we may run to Christ on the shores of welcome, inclusivity, transparency, accountability and a re-imagined God of Life.

Where does Julian of Norwich fit into all of this? My first introduction to Julian was in Chatswood, N.S.W. I was enjoying the hospitality of the Missionaries of God's Love – a relatively new and pioneering religious order in Sydney. I was taking part in an informal vocational 'Come and See' experience. In the mid to late 1980s when I was starting out as a Primary School teacher, I felt a strong vocational 'pull' to a life of dedication to God that asked no less than everything. In this particular 'Come and See' phase, I came across the Penguin Classic edition of *The Revelations of Divine Love*. I could not put it down because I was so thoroughly delighted by it. Other spiritual reading I had read in the course of my vocational seeking did not convey, as Julian did, the overwhelming fact and intimacy of God's love for us – body and soul, even toward the 'lowest of our needs'. That God is closer to us than our own soul touched the core of my being, finding harmony with my deepest desires for life and happiness. Julian's theology was positive yet it took account of our wounds and our desires, our longings, our love for the Church while all steeped in God's love – God's for us and ours for God.

While my life has been a weaving in and out of varying experiences of religious and/or communal life, as also people's lives, Julian has remained a constant and wise guide encouraging open and engagement with Christ. Julian's engagement with Christ has captured my interest and energy to the extent that I am now finishing a doctoral thesis on her engagement. The point here is that I recognise a dynamic at work in Julian, that was also part of my dad's search for inner peace and healing. This link between my dad's experience and Julian convinces me of how significant a role the Mystics can play in our lives today. Julian on her sickbed took a heartful of desire, of trauma due to the Black Death, of devotion, of concern for sin and the pain it causes, and all her longings to Christ Crucified and Risen. My dad took his heartful of desire and restless seeking, of his trauma from the camps and of surviving the experience, of his despair and his hope to the Crucified Lord. The image of the Crucified with wounds exposed – laid bare, vulnerable and alone – symbolised all that dad felt in the death and labour camps as a young man of seventeen. So like Julian he had his own version of the question Julian asked: 'How can all be well because of the great harm done to creatures?' Dad's question directly to Christ on the Cross was 'Did you suffer as much as me?' For the non-discerning person and even priest, this question may seem presumptuous. Yet it was dad's question coming out of a trauma too real to weigh up against the sufferings of Christ's Passion. Dad was looking for empathy of a depth only Christ could know, and such a question could only be put to Christ. This was dad's question which he engaged with in prayer, with me, through his flashbacks and low times, and eventually to those I was able to introduce him to able to hold those questions with respect.

Julian received her answer initially through her Vision, but more especially in the fifteen to twenty years in which she consciously reflected on those Visions setting them down in her Long Version while most likely then an anchoress. The key is in their openness – Julian's and Dad's to the questions inside them, and their preparedness to engage with those questions before Christ, ultimately wrestling for God's blessing of peace. Julian desired an illness to come into knowledge and empathy for Christ's sufferings. Dad towards the end of his life and following heart surgery, identified with Christ in his prayer of Abandonment on the Cross. The cruelty of the flashbacks at that time, brought dad to his knees in the re-traumatization of that moment. Yet both Julian and Dad let Christ answer them in the means available, six hundred years apart. Both took their real sufferings and real questions of their life to engage with their faith, to engage with Christ who became the answer in his own body Crucified and Risen.

We the laity, the people of the pews – whether in churches, on the margins, whether virtually, or hidden in the silence of trauma, woundedness, sufferings, indifference or irrelevance, now wrestle for a blessing. The blessing we seek is to be free to live in freedom of the children of God beyond the boundaries of wherever our lives, choices and sufferings have led us through the faith we have received, the freedom we desire and the identity we share in the spirit of the Risen Christ. This is not about seeking a forced unity, or a coercively procured faith. It is about standing where we are before Christ Risen yet also Wounded Healer, who meets us on the shores of our hearts where life, where hope, where healing and where prophetic action for change is welcomed, encouraged and supported.

God wants us to pay attention to his gracious touch, rejoicing in his unconditional love rather than sorrowing in our own failings. For all of the things we could do it is our surrender to live with our burdens in joy and gratitude that brings him the most glory... The greatest penance of all is our natural longing for him. He himself creates this yearning in us, and he helps us to bear it. His love makes him long for us... Our trials will continue until the time when he makes us whole and gives us himself as our reward. As so he wants us to set our hearts on our

13

transition, that is, from the pain we feel to the joy we trust.
(LT 81)

It is from this place of trust that we seek to embrace a new
future in our Church. Yet, to re-build that trust is perhaps the
prophetic action required at this moment – after listening to
the voices of the people in the pews as presented in this Third
Book of the Trilogy, that is, *Beyond the Boundaries: Faith, Freedom
and Identity*.

Introduction

Berise T. Heasly

Looking forward: looking back

So today 'WE TOO, the Laity...', (2020) of the 21st century Catholic Church, are critiquing and evaluating how to bring the whole institution of the Catholic monolith towards a realistic understanding of the historical truth of the flaws, the ugliness, the trauma experienced by the Laity. Trauma is the daily fare of the 'people in the pews'. Life is hard in the secular sphere and made almost impossible by the confused and sometimes dismissive or vicious voices and behaviour of some in the hierarchical branch of our global church.

Sources of trauma arise out of the secular and the religious spheres in individual daily lived experience and they clash and cloud, confuse and crush an individual whose conscience is often sidelined by unforgivable authoritarian decisions made in a distant and distorted manner. It is especially noticeable that when a copy of 'WE TOO: The Laity speaks!' was given to a leading Australian archbishop, he responded in an airy dismissive way that he had given it a 'quick read' but did not like the use of the word: 'must', which appeared in the text. He missed so much of the interweaving and complex detail within the work of individual contributors.

He did not discover the *tensegrity* which held the whole together by the underlying faith and wisdom of the contributors.

15

He assumed that the whole was a light grizzle by people he could dismiss, rather than the deep intensity of authors who were working in Practical Theology for the 21st century. MUST is not synonymous with demand; it is the expression of desperation by 'people in the pews', whose lifelong lived experience and wish has been to contribute as we were invited to do by the hierarchical arm of the Australian Church to prepare for the Plenary Council, in two sessions beginning in October 2021.

We need to register the role of science, all of it, not cherry-picking what we can control and dismissing what we chose to ignore. This is especially so in disciplines where understanding of the human condition has advanced: psychology; psychiatry; psychotherapy; neuroscience; medical, nuclear and robotic science; artificial intelligence; medical surgery and associated disciplines within orthodox medicine. It is important to make room and to study all the allied health disciplines often ignored by 'orthodox' medical authorities as suspect. This applies also to management of some historically authentic alternative medicine from the First Peoples of our world. Much for theologians to develop here is indicated by such a wide arc of disciplines!

Historically, we need, (MUST?) to register that despite all these deeper sources of knowledge, we do not see enough development in Curia or Bishops' Conference circles. The struggles that dog the efforts of Pope Francis, as he tries to bring in a change of paradigm, are a case in point. The wilful censorship of his work must cause him trauma on a daily basis: witness the work of Mickens, Faggioli and others in reporting the Pope's efforts to update the machinery of administration by introducing the concept of synodality (Brian Roewe, *La Croix*, May 2021) and his re-titling of the Curial departments.

Consequently, we, the Laity, have a responsibility to source, to search, to seek and to coordinate in order to understand the various strands of uncertainty facing the whole church. It MUST be done at the deepest level, to respect and acknowledge the human condition in its diversity and creativity. The possibility that 'dadirri', from our own respected Aboriginal people, may add deep and compassionate notes to the concept of discernment (a term which has gained currently the status of a Facebook jingle). Our appointed Senior Australian of the Year, 2021, Miriam Rose Ungunmerr-Baumann, described very carefully the depth and breadth of 'dadirri' in the Autumn edition of *The Swag*, 2021. Whatever the term discernment initially meant, it is being bandied around too much today, as an ideological concept, and seems to have lost its impact.

It is almost fashionable today in some Catholic circles to register defiance, resistance, exclusiveness, and harsh judgmental responses to new knowledge, under the dubious banner of *knowing* the mind of God! Witness those whose political ideologies include the haughty insistence that single issue policies about abortion and euthanasia allow them to decide that Holy Communion is to be actively withheld. So too, those who try the same tactic for divorced people or gay people, whose daily lives they do not know! The emergence of a body of people whose best efforts have resulted in an Australia-wide, nineteen groups of reform-minded expertise is our best hope to address, in a spirit of parrhesia, the difficulties which face us now, during the second session of the Plenary Council, and well beyond.

And so emerged another, the third in the trilogy, collaborative effort of contributors. Their brief, like the second in the trilogy, was to think deeply, write compassionately in the spirit of both parrhesia and truth. No constraints were applied, and the resultant work then and now has been a process of keen observation, personal lived experience, balanced academic learning, eventually equalling a telling manuscript in this book which contributes to our thinking, our prayer, and our concern for the future. The title: **Beyond the boundaries – faith, freedom and identity** addresses the confusion, the compassion and the need for clarity needed to face the future.

Research explored earlier (*Call No One Father*) and the undeniable quality of Gideon Goosen's *Clericalism* (2020) leads us to further expand the work of those now twenty reform groups in Australia, who wish to highlight the need to consciously promote the reality of the message of Jesus. The aim here is to distinguish regeneration and reform from ideological and inappropriate and steely use of binary thinking, and the assumption of cultic medieval behaviour as somehow close to 'the mind of God', so that clear thinking skills and evaluation of practical theological issues and considerations can contribute regularly to the conversation. Relational community groups, whether parish-based or prayer-oriented, allow for maturation of individuals and release us to follow Jesus, not the uncomfortable institutional arm of the church at this point in time.

And so, we need to become aware of the enormity of the various overwhelming sources of trauma like slave labour, globalisation, sexual abuse, asylum seekers' conditions, human trafficking, despotism, as well as the current difficulties of pandemics of poverty, racism, war, domestic or institutional or communal violence, famine, flood, drought and volcanic eruption, climate change, massive wildfires, and escaped viruses. All these become unbearable without the mercy and compassion of our God which is promoted by our current pope. We need every clerical member of the Curia out working daily in the 'field hospital' mentioned by Pope Francis. We need release from the strong-arm tactics of a hierarchy, scared to move beyond the familiar authoritarian requirements of Pope John Paul II, shown in the stormy bishops' responses during the second session of the Australian Plenary Council (July 2022).

It is possible to move carefully and sensitively from being overwhelmed by the tragedies of trauma, towards a growing trust. If we can earn authentically the trust of the 'people in the pews' by constancy, truthfulness, careful research, much prayer – together and alone – it seems possible for a change of paradigm to emerge, based on a refreshed understanding of the Jesus message, and supported by our general positive faith in the existence of a Cosmic Creator, also referred to as The Trinity. So much practical theology can make for fascinating lived experience as we move together further into the third millennium. The first millennium seems to be that in which humanity historically tried to understand the person of Jesus; the second millennium seemed to have broadened our exploration of our Cosmic Father-Creator, and the third millennium seems to be that we have become more deeply aware of the Spirit of God, as the breath of the Godhead, stirring the waters of our times, disturbing our comfortable beliefs, drawing us on towards the nearness of that Cosmic Creator. Who knows where the Spirit will direct us (Treston, 2018)?

Is it possible, therefore, to worry that the rigid outright denial of modernity, of recent times and some recent popes of Rome, have possibly enabled some of the various dreadful chaos, depravity and brutality at large in the world today? Would it be that today's ills may well be the result of unbridled, unleashed will to go to extremes – without the cool voices of reason and goodness (not pious pontificating) being allowed to emerge?

Professor Brian Cox, in the BBC Earth series about the history of the Universe titled 'Human Universe', teaches us that Climate Change has happened on a planetary scale twice before; that the ensuing outcome for humankind has been a massive stride forward each time in the intellectual understanding of humankind of our daily lived experience; that the response of humankind each time was a massive increase in intelligence because of a doubling of the size of the brain size of human species; and that this may be what we face in the third millennium. This evolution in response to climate change stimulated the ingenuity of humankind to make instruments to adapt to the ever-changing conditions – to the tune of 80 billion neurons in one brain. The implications of such a massive proposition show us that there is much that will provoke, bemuse, bother, and mystify us. As we face all the uncertainties implied here, we can see, sometimes dimly, but with increasing clarity, that we will face the requirement to TRUST! Because the alternative choice will be extinction! Seemingly, that Trust will be in the presence and at the behest of Sophia-Spirit, as we learn, adjust and appreciate the urgency of regeneration, refreshment, reform that is emerging, despite our reluctance to face changes that will happen on a massive scale everywhere.

The contributors

It is our pleasure to introduce the contributor's articles. We are proud to have the expertise, the courage and the transparency which is displayed in this volume:

Morag Fraser, in **Encounters**, gives us a sensitive and enlightened understanding of the value of faith and the enduring pride of her encounters with remarkable people in her life's journey. We glimpse the insightful and intelligent response of a woman of active faith in today's world. She teach us with a gentle hand the subtlety and insight which emerges from the daily lived experience of modern response to living 'life to the full'.

Hugh McGinlay, in **Second Vatican Council: morning star or false dawn?** has courageously tapped into his lived experience, particularly his remarkable life story, and allowed us to see his honest wrestling with questions about the event we call Vatican ll. His exploration of the outcomes of the Ecumenical Council and the events that followed is a succinct way of highlighting the confusion caused by hierarchical responses, leaving him with a life question.

Janette Elliott has given us the benefit of her very long association and research into the life, life experience and sayings of Julian of Norwich, in **Words for Life: Wisdom Distilled from Julian's Window'**. She applies Julian's thinking and prayerful responses to the questions of faith, of freedom, and of identity as Catholic Christians, in 21st century conditions of pandemic and the post Royal Commission climate today. Her attention to the era of Julian allows us space to recognise the place of Tradition in the living out of the Jesus message, with the aspiration that Julian used: All shall be well' – her daily lived experience included trauma, just as ours does today.

Gideon Goosen, in typical terms of clarity and the wide lens of learning, has titled his paper **Promises and Pitfalls**. He refers to the quality of insight needed to address so much of the vexed questions surrounding definition of Faith, of Freedom and of Identity in the institution of the Catholic Church in the 21st century. Gideon has shown us that we need to analyse our daily lived experience to respond to those Promises and Pitfalls he mentions, allowing us to respond to the message of Jesus today.

Ian Hamilton, in his inimitable style, has pointed his academic lens towards **A Question of Authority**, which we need to address in our lived experience in this disrupted period in the life of the Australian Church. His cool assessments are balanced and lend us opportunity to think carefully about our own responses. The second session of the Australian Plenary Council has been a dramatic example of how misuse of authority can be tediously used to stonewall the Spirit. We need his analysis, so that we can decipher subtleties and nuances as we delve deeper into vexed questions.

Adrian Hubbard has courageously taken up the challenge to move beyond the boundary set up historically in the practice of faith according to the Curial dictate. In **Tensegrity – the basis of created life today**, he has explained in careful language (and given us real knowledge) in the scientific fields in which he works. We need to be patient as he takes us through many scientific conundrums not fully understood by so many of us still mired in the constraints of clericalism. His method of recognising the new information and knowledge of various forms of medical and quantum knowledge, allows us to address just what we mean today when we use language familiar in medieval times, to describe Creation, and relevant sub-questions. He does not provide answers, just raises the relevant questions which must be the realm of 21st century theologians. Otherwise, we live with unresolved questions which impede our progress towards learning what Jesus meant when he apparently indicated that we as humankind were to aspire to live 'life to the full'.

In Part 2 of the volume, we find the voice of knowledge and experience. In **Liturgical Seasons Across Australia** by *Michael Elligate*, we read how discussing the value of good liturgy is built. His 48 years of successful parish leadership shows sensible insights on preparation of liturgy, gives value to the imagination which informs such preparation, and allows us to think positively about how we experience liturgy in our eucharistic lives. He allows for our own relationship with Jesus to develop as we encounter the mystical hand of Jesus in reflection emerging from good eucharistic liturgy, in the celebration of many different prayer rituals, not distinguishing only the Mass.

He is followed by a vivid and eloquent auto-biographical account: **'I, Naomi'** (*Naomi Wolfe*), of the lived experience of a remarkable and courageous Aboriginal woman, initially from Tasmania, explaining her experience in melding her Aboriginal culture with both Anglican and Catholic traditions, as she has been taught. There is beauty, compassion, understanding and insight beyond the boundaries we normally discover, as she responds to our brief, which asked her to tell us her story from her own unique perspective. Her daily lived experience highlights the effort to find the mystical depths of Aboriginal belief in Creation, with its reverence for Country, its rituals celebrating the beauty that surrounds us, and finding the depth too of what she already understands of Anglican and Catholic lived experience in her life.

Peter Johnstone has provided us with a balanced, considered, insightful, honest response to his experience within the workings of both the Reform movement in Australia as well as his experience within the life and process of the Plenary

Council. In **Synodality, Inclusion and Good Governance – beyond dysfunction**, we have the benefit of expertise in relevant areas of transparency, accountability and truth-telling in governance in the marketplace. All this he has offered to the Australian Church. We would do well to study his paper thoroughly. He has so far survived the trauma and the daily lived experience of the formal two sessions of the Australian Plenary Council and the immense mountain of work that took place between the two formal sessions. We could be forgiven for wilting under the weight of his and other members of the Australia-wide Reform groups, for thinking that what he is analysing is too difficult. His strength and clarity is helping us to find our way.

Maree Stanley was asked to teach us about the effects of trauma from a professional stance. It is noticeable today just how uncertain and unpredictable our world has become, and how mental stress finds so many of us facing trauma. Her kind, compassionate and insightful paper titled **Addressing Trauma in our lives in an Age of Uncertainty** warns us about the long-term effects of trauma, especially when all kinds of abuse are likely to damage the whole life of a person too young or too vulnerable to survive an overwhelming experience not understood. There is deep value and insight here that points to a glimmer of hope, allowing us to aspire to that 'life to the full'.

Finally, *Berise Heasly*, in **From Trauma, to Trust, to Trinity**, takes the dreadful effects of trauma and tries to make sense of how we manage the lived experience of trauma in our own and others' lives. We need to find ways through faith, through freedom and through the building up of personal identity, to survive and thrive. In this way, it may be possible to learn what Trust is. For a Catholic Christian, it also can lead us towards some knowledge, some awe and wonder, and some appreciation of the mystery we call Trinity.

Finally...

It is to be hoped that readers will have the patience and the goodwill to read this volume at leisure, rather than 'just a quick read', and that some of the content will resonate positively and help us as we negotiate the years ahead.

Acknowledgments

We wish to thank each contributor whose paper appears in this book. Each person accepted the brief to speak from lived experience, in a spirit of parrhesia, with an eye on the 'signs of the times' within the church and taking account of widespread difficulties globally.

Part 1

Encounters

Morag Fraser

'Epiphanies' is too grand a word for the experiences, the encounters, that have kept me Catholic. Much of what has happened during my life, some of the people I've met, and aspects of the natural world, have edged towards an inkling, an intimation of transcendence, or a dimension of wonder that I cannot explain. Let these encounters speak for themselves. They are not nostalgic reflections: they are portents, expressions of hope in a dynamic future for the church and the world that has nurtured me.

The first priest I remember knowing (apart from gruff Father O'Hanlon who terrified me as a shy primary-school confessant) was Leo Curran, parish priest of Newport in Melbourne. In those days, the 1950s, I called him Father, but I could sense that to my mum and dad he was a man, a companion, someone who had an eventful life behind him, not all of it spent in a presbytery. I did hold him and the church in the same space in my young head, though he never uttered a word of what you might call theology to me. But I also absorbed the family story about him, and set it alongside – or perhaps against – what I was supposed to think about priests.

My mother had met Leo Curran when she was on her honeymoon in Werribee with Jim, her first husband. An Adelaide girl, mum loved the bush. On the track to the bridge across the Werribee River she used to see an old bloke whose daytime entertainment seemed to be tossing his bike over the bridge and into the water. A tall, strong, silver-haired man in an open-necked shirt would clamber down the bank, drag the bike back up and restore it to its owner. The routine went on for days. Finally, mum asked the man why he persisted. The old fellow was probably drunk most of the time. What was achieved?

Incorrigible wasn't a word I knew then, and mum wouldn't have used it anyway. But that – an intractable circumstance – was how she met Leo Curran, and how, at a generational remove, I learned, imperfectly, about patience, and unstinting compassion.

I learned other things from Leo Curran: he let me drive his Dodge (in a paddock) and taught me how to do a Rolls Royce stop (very smooth, very pro.). He used to shoot at the Werribee rifle range. I have a memory of the weight of the wooden stock against my shoulder, and of his trying to teach me how to aim, if not fire. I know he saw my parents through sorrow, transitions and adjustments: mum's loss of her first husband (an RAAF wartime accident, over Inverness, on their first wedding anniversary); later, a new life in Melbourne with my father, a Scot, a widower, merchant seaman and very much skipper of his own ship. Dad was Presbyterian, a Wee Free, though I never knew him in a church except for family weddings and his own funeral in the once-was Little Sisters' chapel in Adelaide. Dad knew we'd send him off him from there. Monsignor Brendan Bowler, my aunt's brother-in-law, celebrated the Mass, and never, not for a second, appropriated my Protestant father into anything more than a blessed fellowship of love and wry affection. You can learn ecumenism by example.

Leo Curran was dead by then. Had he outlived my father, he would have been there in the chapel, up on the altar. Family... Leo understood about death, and bereavement. I guessed from his occasional bouts of malaria that he'd seen war, somewhere up north. In October, 1970, he was one of the first to reach the site of Melbourne's Westgate Bridge collapse, to give comfort where he could, and last rites to men who died there. Never one for heroics, he served, simply.

It is as a man that I remember him, vulnerable (adenoidal, so no pulpit rhetorician), smiling, witty, restrained. I am sure he loved all of us. When we had to make hard decisions, he was there, never judging, gently wise. The words 'clerical, or 'lay' were not part of our shared vocabulary.

I was reminded of Leo Curran when I saw the cover photo on Bishop Geoffrey Robinson's recent, posthumously published book, *Towards the end of my days*.[1] Another silver-haired man with a gentle smile. But steely determination. It has been from Geoffrey Robinson (and from Sister Angela Ryan CSB, who for a time worked with him), that I have learned most, and best, about clerical sexual abuse, about just and loving dealings with those abused, about damage, about healing, about recompense, and ways of attending to the great rent that abuse has made in our beliefs and institutional trust. And always given by Geoffrey Robinson in such clear, unvarnished terms, free of jargon – legal, psychological, or theological. I was reminded of that salutary directness when I read his chapter sixteen, called, simply, 'The Seeking of Goodness'. Here is some of it: 'Throughout human history people have related to

---

[1] Robinson, Geoffrey (Bishop), *Towards the end of my days, Theological and Spiritual Reflections*.Coordinating editor, Seamus O'Grady. Garratt Publishing, Australia, 2022.

other people largely on one of two bases: either the usefulness of others to themselves or the essential dignity of others' (page 188).

What follows may seem an odd instance of 'the essential dignity' of another, but it is a radiant memory, one I treasure. It was lunchtime, at a 'religious identity' conference (more like religious travails, not that it was called that) in Canberra, on Anglican land. The morning's emphasis had been on people (victims, yes, but people first) who had suffered from abuse – on their stories rather than analysis of the ways churches were going to manage their respective moral and reputational crises. Geoffrey Robinson had spoken lengthily, and now looked wan as he waited, tray in hand, in the lunch queue. Standing behind him (we'd just been introduced) I watched, intrigued, as he spooned small portions of meat onto his plate. 'No vegetables?' I asked. He turned, smiled (I like to think conspiratorially) and said, 'No *white* vegetables', then continued, 'Since my mother died, no one is *ever again* going to make me eat white vegetables. I *loathe* cauliflower'.

We never met again, but that bright moment of connection, of personal disclosure – a man, not a bishop, smiling with a stranger, a woman – has stayed with me. It's been a beacon, like the lighthouse that welcomes sailors (my father among them) into the shelter of the harbour.

There have been other conferences, other lunches. Once, at a yearly gathering of the priests of the Melbourne diocese, I was invited to speak, following Helen Garner (the priests were a welcoming, inclusive lot). I can't remember now what I said but I do recall that the Archbishop arrived late, while Helen was speaking, and sat up in the back row. When lunchtime came, his food was carried up and served to him. There was no mingling.

On my study wall, I keep sellotaped a copy of a poem written by another prelate, Hélder Câmara, Archbishop of Olinda and Recife in Brazil. It has carried me through very many fractious board meetings, legal proceedings, arguments about governance, and moments of dark disillusionment. I heard him speak once, and every time I say his lines over now, I remember that his smile was broad and infectious. Here is the poem:

> We must have no illusions.
> We must not be naïve.
> If we listen to the voice of God,
> > we must make our choice,
> > get out of ourselves and
> > fight non-violently
> > > for a better world.
>
> We must not expect to find it
> > easy;
> > we shall not walk on roses,
> > people will not throng
> > > to hear us and applaud,
> > and we shall not always
> > > be aware of divine
> > > protection.
>
> If we are to be pilgrims
> > for justice and peace
> we must expect the desert.

◇◇◇

Easter week, and it is Autumn in Canberra. The trees are laying down a jewelled carpet. I gather some leaves and count eight shades of red. ('We shall not walk on roses.' But we shall skip through nature's glory.) The bare twigs of the Manchurian pear already show the swelling of next season's blossom. On the university campus there are two giant eucalypts, carefully conserved, wearing their great age with a scarred, stately grace that lifts my heart as I drive slowly past them. In Melbourne, amid the chaos of outer suburban roadworks, there stands an ancient River Redgum, fenced about with cyclone panels. Cockatoos perch there, and poke nonchalantly about in its hollows, as they have always done. On Good Friday, I hear a fine performance of Bach's St Matthew Passion. Beauty and death, sorrow and exultation – all within Bach's mighty scope.

I was educated (thirteen years in the one Brigidine convent) by women who would never have used the word feminism. 'Fortiter et suaviter' – strength and gentleness – was the injunction. But gentleness did not entail docility. Not for us the example of (was it?) the Little Flower who, although keen on art, and good at it, insisted on using the worst tools. Some self-denial looks like perverse pride.

I won't attempt to universalise (or sentimentalise) my experience of convent schooling. For some of my contemporaries it proved stifling, even alienating. I was young, avid and insouciant – spurred by a talented mother whose formal education had ended too early, and a father who had absorbed every skerrick of Scotland's dominie spirit. Education, for him, was a sacred duty (and a right). Also, I lived so much inside my head and books that I simply didn't understand how to be repressed.

What I took away from those thirteen years was an experience of women who made their own independent decisions and who, however gently, exercised power. They were generous women (not all of them nuns), and, in some signal instances, were as excited by music, literature, drama, thinking, science, religion, history – the whole beckoning world – as I was. When three of us Matric girls were finalists in a public debating competition (on television!), our Principal, Mother Margaret Mary Bourke, packed us off to the Melbourne University Philosophy Department to be tutored in argument. Argument, not doctrine. We were to debate that 'Might is Right' – and on the affirmative side. One of our intellectual crammers was Fr Eric D'Arcy, later to be Archbishop of Hobart. I often wonder if he remembered aiding three young women to behave like aggressive QCs – and win.

Independent women – isn't that what women's religious orders have cultivated for centuries? Always the church's loyal opposition, but proving grounds at the same time for women who have had to make decisions, lead, give succour, educate, and build functioning communities. Yes, there were abuses in those communities. But it is vital, surely, that in our collective chastisement, we do not lose sight of the good, the sterling example, the dedication and commitment to education that characterised women's (and men's) religious communities.

I watch now as Australian religious orders – of women and men – diminish, close off recruitment. But I also watch, and, in a small way, participate, as they reshape, and reconstitute themselves – metamorphosing into new institutional structures (via, for example, Public Juridic Person arrangements), ones that are able and equipped to sustain the spirit of commitment that animated their founders, and infuse others with it. In education particularly, the line between lay and religious has become blurred in ways which, I believe, can only be positive for the church, and for us all. Lay women and men – we are many, and many of us are willing!

In school governance meetings, we often refer to the prophetic function of education. Catholic schools (I would add all good schools) have a long history of nurturing the mind and spirit of young people, of providing space and time for them to grow, to enquire, to shape their conscience and develop a sensitivity to that 'essential dignity of others'. If this sounds rosy, I'll plead experience – many years of classroom teaching in which I saw my share of selfishness, ego, brutality, pettiness, and insecurity manifesting as a yen for power. But the counterbalance was always that spark in young people that could, through trust (and some professional skill), blaze into a passion for learning, for understanding how the world works, and how our companions, our neighbours, our fellows, fit alongside us into a great scheme of discovery. Anyone who has been around Catholic school principals during these past two years of pandemic will have been witness, as I have, to extraordinary feats of leadership, endurance, pedagogical adaption and spiritual strength. I don't mean to praise only Catholic principals, it is just that they are ones I see at close quarters, and they have been inspiring. I only wish our political leaders could understand (and adopt) the practice of leadership for others, servant leadership, leadership based in integrity, that is modelled so powerfully in our schools.

There is something else that I must add here: learning is exhilarating. It has no boundaries. Instrumental thinking about education (making students, or graduates 'job ready') is limited thinking. Of course, I would want all young people to be equipped, even credentialled for life, to have skills that will enable them to support themselves and others, and to contribute to society. But I also want them to be given the chance to sparkle in their own way – to make, to build, to compose, to break ground, to connect fresh ideas and categories of received thought together, and to experience the effects, for themselves and others, of intellectual bravery and an unwavering commitment to truth.

When I was twenty-two, luxuriating in the lengthy 'adjustment' time that Adelaide's Calvary hospital then afforded young mothers, I was visited by Monsignor Robert Aitken. My memory is that he was Vicar General at the time (though perhaps that came later, as with the title Monsignor). He came as a family friend, neither confessor nor chaplain. As I quickly made myself (almost) seemly, pushing the cumbersome breast-feeding apparatus under my blankets, he launched into a conversation about the background to *Humanae vitae*. (I couldn't do anything about the pink rollers in my hair and I doubt he noticed them – a serious man always). I call it a conversation because that is exactly what it was. Certainly, we argued, but my strong sense, even now, is that he genuinely wanted to know what a young, fertile woman thought about an issue that was roiling Catholic circles at the time (and goes on doing it). We didn't agree, but I was struck then by the expression on his face – open, probing – as he talked about the importance of consistency in argument. It was a look of genuine enquiry. I remember our talk as an exchange between equals. That is not arrogance on my part: it is a tribute to the man's respect for the dignity of another.

Catholic circles at Melbourne University in the 1960s were places of a related openness and intellectual ferment. The Newman Society eased the entry of a tall, diffident young woman (with that deceptive, apparent confidence that convent education could inculcate) into a life very different from that of her childhood and youth in a seaside Melbourne suburb.

Like so many young women of my time, I was the first in my family to go to University. I remember that in some quarters universities were feared – regarded as places where one could lose one's faith. If that was not my experience, it was because I had been well prepared in the rigours and exactitudes of independent thought by my parents and by the women who had taught me. Thinking was an exciting, clarifying enterprise. And university life, then so much less pressured, less vocation/qualification driven, was full of interesting people who enjoyed arguing, reading, discussing and acting (in life and on stage) as much as I did. Some of them were young men – intellectually challenging in ways I had not experienced before.

I will never forget the courtesy and patience with which Peter Steele, Jesuit priest and poet (and at the time a tutor in English), answered my questions when I rocked up, unannounced, to his room in the Old Arts Building and asked if he would explain irony to me (Jonathan Swift was his research preoccupation at the time).

Peter's influence, his generosity and intellectual example (stringent and formidable as it was) did not end with his death in 2012. What I understand about the incarnational nature of my Catholic faith has been refined and expanded by him over the many years I've been blessed to know him as friend, and for a brief, almost comical period, as my boss. He was the Jesuit Provincial. I was the (unexpected) editor of the Jesuit magazine, *Eureka Street*. Neither of us, I think, was adept at the boss/employee dynamic.

One indelible moment: winter, in Mildura, the grape vines pruned back to their twigged starkness. Peter was speaking at the annual Mildura Writer's Festival, following his acceptance of the Festival's literary award, a sculpted Memorial Medal named for the late poet, Philip Hodgins. Yes, Peter spoke and answered questions about his poetry. But the audience wanted something more: they wanted to hear how a poet could also be that (to them) exotic creature, a Catholic priest, and indeed, how a poet could have been the leader, the provincial of a religious order, even one with the intellectual reputation of the Jesuits. This was eight years before the 2017 handing down of the report of the *Royal Commission into Institutional Responses to Child Sexual Abuse*, and Peter's audience were more intent on the man, the poet, than on clerical accountability.

But institutional tarnish and individual suffering were nonetheless realities of which audience and speaker were both aware. What I remember best were Peter's answer to questions about the responsibility of holding and exercising power (I had flashes of all the blustering motivational speeches about leadership I've heard – though never from him). Someone asked what had been the personal cost, for him, the man, the poet. Peter answered, succinctly, without self-regard, or anything resembling self-pity. The burden of authority, of leadership, of responsibility had, for him, been onerous, something to be borne. When he finished speaking (and, as was his way, quickly disappeared from the congratulatory throng), I watched the expression on the face of Stefano De Pieri, one of the patron/founders of the Festival. Stefano, usually an irrepressible man, just shook his head in wonder, and smiled with a kind of proud, shared gladness that has no verbal equivalence

Another moment: America in Fall, on one of our yearly one-semester sojourns to a college town, and I was in the Princeton University Chapel when a baptism took place. I say 'the Chapel' because that is where I went each Sunday. I'd tried my old 1990's Jesuit haunt, where the welcome had always been warm and the sermons thought-provoking. But by 2007, everything had changed. I don't know whether the Jesuits had vacated the house, but I do recall the frost with which my presence was greeted and the frankly fundamentalist and prescriptive tone of the sermons. Soon after, I was at a friend's wedding, and happened to be seated, afterwards, next to the celebrant, Dr Alison Boden, the Dean of Religious Life and of the Princeton University Chapel. Our newly-wed friend was born Catholic and guessed I would find Alison's company stimulating. I did, that night, and for the decade after when I went to the Chapel every Sunday and on many days in-between. The Princeton Chapel was a model of inclusion, of intelligent, open-minded seeking after truth and justice in faith, in politics, in society.

Princeton is a very privileged place. It is also only a short train ride from Trenton, New Jersey, where life is not privileged. I learned much about America and its disparities of wealth and opportunity from Alison and from the preachers she invited to speak from the high pulpit in the Chapel. Together we shared stories, music, meals, books (two of them volumes of poetry and homilies by Peter Steele). Alison came from Chicago. I could tell her that Chicago was one of Peter's favourite cities. Once there, he would go and sit in the public gallery of a Chicago courtroom (the equivalent of Melbourne's Magistrates' Court), to watch, to be silent, to absorb something of the human tragedy that is regularly played out in such a place.

I learned about the potency and importance of women in priestly ministry by watching Alison. The highlight – the revelatory moment for me – on that baptism day, came when, having performed the rite, this graceful, unassuming woman in her beautiful, sprigged vestment, carried the swaddled child in her arms, all the way from the altar font, down the full length of the Chapel aisle to the great doors and then slowly back again to the altar. The symbolism hardly needs to be unpacked.

There was such music in that Chapel, of all kinds – Baroque, Jazz, Gregorian, Palestrina, Appalachian folk hymns, Spirituals from the American South, from England's great store of sacred songs. Its unifying feature was the quality and zest of performance, the evident delight and skill of the young people (and older townsfolk) in the choir, of the conductor, the organist and the visiting musicians. The students who came (and sang, and read, and played and talked) participated in a model of church that couldn't fail to uplift, console and sustain them.

The Princeton Chapel is non-sectarian. It welcomes all comers – students, townspeople, strangers like me. Sitting there, always in the same spot in the middle of the second row (from where I could see the minor miracle of the jazz pianist's fingerwork), I would often reflect on the scandal, but, even more, on the tragedy of Christianity's divisions. As I write this, the Russian and Ukrainian Orthodox Churches are in conflict, exactly at a time when religion should appeal, not inflame.

Not for a moment would I dismiss or disparage the specific history, tradition and practice of (most) Christian denominations. I know how necessary, how sacred, time-sanctified rituals, traditions and modes of praise are to human beings. But I am also descended from a tribal people, a people of clans, and I know how blood-soaked is my ancestral soil. Scotland's maps are dense with tiny black crosses that mark battles, too often the sites of religious conflict, or of territorial disputes that used religion as a mask for voracious acquisition or tribal ambition. Holy war? Has there ever truly been such a thing?

I've referred principally to signal moments, for me, in Christian places, Christian institutions. But some of the most sacred experiences I've had have been moments of inter-faith encounter. One of the writers I cherish most, and learn from best, is the American novelist, essayist, teacher and Calvinist, Marilynne Robinson. Some years ago, at a gracious Passover Seder in Melbourne, to which we had been invited, Robinson's name came up. Someone quoted a passage from one of her novels, and immediately, across the table, the rituals briefly suspended, we discovered how much we had in common, how literature, like music, art, or manifest integrity, can mediate, can transcend difference. It was too precious a moment to analyse, but I shall never forget it.

In India, as a young woman, I was often driven around Bombay (as Mumbai was then called, and not just by colonial incomers) on the back of a motorcycle by an infinitely patient, dignified young man who took seriously his obligation to be hospitable to strangers. I was alone, potentially vulnerable, innocent and precocious simultaneously. One can be blessed sometimes with an unexpected friendship (the adjective I'd have used then was platonic) that is honest, searching and enriching. This was one such. Bulbul (the name I knew him by, though I can't now guarantee either the spelling or the accuracy) was a Sikh, deeply engaged in politics. Indira Gandhi was about to be elected, but the turmoil that had followed the death of her predecessor, Lal Bahadur Shastri, was evident across the city.

Perhaps it was part of my friend's religious commitment or perhaps his pride as a citizen, to keep this tall, wide-eyed, sari-clad Australian safe, and to educate her about his country, its food, its caste system, its customs, its taboos. I will never know which now, but when I saw him years later on an

Australian foreign affairs program, playing a statesman's role in Indian politics, I was not at all surprised. Moved, and grateful, certainly, and so glad that integrity and goodness shine even in a world torn by sectarian strife. Now when I see and admire the community spirit and efforts of the Australian Sikh community during fires and floods, I smile and remember my long-ago initiation into another tradition of love and kindness – thy neighbour as thyself.

The Catholic church, the Christian world indeed, has been in various stages of transformation and reform since the time of Jesus Christ. We can expend our good energies and many more millions of words listing, documenting, questioning, berating, curtailing, disciplining, objecting, protesting. As we should, and must. But sometimes we need also to pause, to celebrate what is around us, what is in the good hearts of our fellows and in the splendour of creation. After all, we have the music – that other glory of creation and humankind. We should stop for a while, and sing.

Bibliography

Robinson, Geoffrey, *Towards the end of my days, Theological and Spiritual Reflections*. Coordinating editor, Seamus O'Grady. Garrett Publishing, Australia, 2022.

Second Vatican Council: Morning Star or False Dawn?

Hugh McGinlay

All in favour?

November 1965: The fourth and last session of the Second Vatical Council is meeting in Rome. The Scottish bishops have invited a special guest to the Scots College to give us the benefit of his insights and expectations. During dinner, he leans across the table and tells us solemnly that, before the Council, there had been a cancer in one limb of the Church but because of the Council, the cancer had spread to the entire body of the Church.

The visitor was Archbishop Marcel Lefebvre, Superior General of the Holy Ghost Fathers, and later a prominent critic of the Council that led to his founding the Society of St Pius X and eventual excommunication for ordaining bishops against the wishes of the Pope.

What is extraordinary about that memory is that his opinions seemed to us so unexpected and exceptional. Among those of us living and studying in Rome at that time, there was a papabile sense of excitement and enthusiasm for the renewal that was at the heart of the Council's deliberations and declarations. Views like those of Lefebvre, it seemed to us, were much those of a tiny minority whose most vocal representative was Cardinal Alfredo Ottaviani of the Holy Office within the Roman Curia.

In the years since, we recognise that not everyone shared our enthusiasm and that Marcel Lefebvre and Alfredo Ottaviani were not lone voices but perhaps only the most vigorous of many in the church who shared their misgivings and worked ever since to undo the Council's tradition and teaching. They represented the views of many who looked back to times when the teaching authority of bishops was respected; when theological opinion was more constrained; a time when liturgy was mysterious and comforting; and structures were more clerical and commanding. A time, perhaps, when we all knew our exclusive place in God's eternal plans, happy within a system that had served the church well for four hundred years since Trent and searching for a return to the certainty that the centralised authority of the papacy had ensured for more than a century and a half.

Times of change, times of loss

So, what changed over all those years? From the perspective of lay people, the obvious changes were liturgical: Mass in English, creation of lectionaries with a new emphasis on preaching gospel themes, new programs in Religious Education, fresh sacramental initiatives, an openness to other Christian traditions, attempts to involve lay people in pastoral planning through parish and, occasionally, diocesan councils.

Like Archbishops Lefevre and Ottaviani, not everyone rejoiced in the changes. Understandably, many regretted that former ways of worship and piety and identity were being discarded for what was unfamiliar and challenging. And, in hindsight, many of the changes were introduced without adequate education or preparation. And some violently. In many parishes, priests – with more passion than sensitivity – replaced (sometimes destroyed) altars, statues and other structures that had not only sustained people for centuries but had also been reminders of the struggles of their ancient families to pay for the very structures and fabric that were now disappearing, mostly with no consultation.

Other, more pastoral clergy seemed to manage fruitful change, often incorporating the former liturgical architecture to accommodate the new expressions of worship. But often, resentments were left unaddressed, especially among the clergy, and these misgivings about change gradually led to a silent polarisation between those who welcomed the reforms and those who longed for former times when the function of clergy was more defined and authority structures unchallenged.

Many younger clergy failed utterly to understand the sense of loss among older, faithful Catholics. Traditions and practices that had sustained them for generations were now sometimes mocked for their sentimentality. In my former city of Glasgow, at least one priest in the pulpit publicly destroyed rosary beads and threw them away as symbols of a discarded piety, failing to notice how offensive and insensitive this was. Forms of prayer that had sustained generations of Catholics – rosary and benediction, devotion to the Sacred Heart, First Fridays and First Saturdays, Stations of the Cross, Forty Hours, exposition of the Sacrament – gradually disappeared; familiar hymns (admittedly of a more sentimental kind) were replaced by (often equally sentimental) allegedly Bible-focused offerings, now accompanied by guitarists whose musical skills were often indifferent at least.

And a personal note: These devotions, prayers and practices sustained my own parents, grandparents and ancestors over many years and I imagine that the very depth of their sentimentality comforted and assured them in their life's journey, often in times of migration, poverty, world wars, loss, insecurity and ill health. But society too was changing over those fifty years and if there was a gradual decline in church attendance and devotional practice, changes in society played more than a little part. Even in those Council years, church – for most Catholics – was at the heart of their social as well as religious lives. The church culture was where you met your friends, played your sports, joined your clubs; often the only approved, safe environment for discreet courting. In the absence of what we now take for granted – television, mobile phones, internet, mass entertainment, ease of travel – gathering at church for services, devotions, seasonal practices were often the main focus of 'entertainment' and diversion. The only place where you would regularly meet friends and enjoy company outside the home.

Change of identity

So, for a variety of reasons, church belonging and identity was changing. Priestly ministry was changing too. The once common practice of regular visits by priests to parishioners was subtly altered by the fact that television became an often-controlling feature of family life. The once clearly defined boundary between clergy and laity was becoming blurred. The previous reality where priests dominated liturgy was giving way to a new situation where lay people were more and more involved in the shape and celebration of Mass and sacraments. Where only a few years earlier, the only lay people on the sanctuary were altar boys, lay people were now involved as readers, in the distribution of Communion, in the direction of music, as occasional commentators – as directors and facilitators of the worshipping community.

More formal liturgical occasions seemed to continue as before. Children were still baptised, First Communion and Confession were occasions of special celebration, Catholic weddings and funerals were still the norm... but even there, things were changing, perhaps most noticeably in the area of Confession.

What happened to sin?

It's difficult to pinpoint a time when most Catholics stopped going to Confession – or even stopped thinking about how such a significant, regular event simply disappeared from their consciences. Catholics of a certain age recall how churches were often packed with penitents seeking Confession at Christmas and Easter. Funeral vigils always involved people going to Confession; school children were regularly brought in classes to church for regular Confession.

It could be, of course, that as a result of the Vatican Council, priests themselves recognised that it was time that they, as well as lay people, needed to rethink their understanding of sin, forgiveness and especially the focus on sexual sin that had developed among moral theologians in the recent centuries. (Remember the parish 'missions' with visiting, hell-fired preachers putting the fear of God into us and urging us to go to Confession?)

The eventual option (in the 1970s) of three rites of celebrating the Sacrament offered creative and pastoral solutions but any enthusiasm for those was eventually frustrated by the Vatican's growing reservations about the apparent 'soft option' provided by the third (communal) rite and severely restricted its availability to ordinary Catholics. Sadly, by then the Confession horse had bolted. But perhaps another reason for the decline of the sacrament can be traced to another monumental event in the post Vatican 2 history, the encyclical *Humanae Vitae* of 1968.

Humanae Vitae – blessing in disguise?

Encyclicals are occasional letters written by popes, offering authoritative direction to the Catholic faithful, generally on matters of doctrine or morals. Often, they have had a pastoral or liturgical focus, sometimes about changes in church law and practice. Occasionally, they are monumental in encouraging new understandings of social justice, new directions in approaches to Scripture, innovative changes in liturgy.

In areas of moral theology, they generally reinforced previous teachings – popes are naturally reluctant to suggest that their predecessors were wrong. This was especially true after the First Vatican Council had proclaimed the infallibility of the pope, even if that proclamation itself was surrounded by so many conditions as to make the actual exercise of such infallibility exceptional.

The authority of the pope and his standing within the Catholic community had developed enormously, especially after the French Revolution, and most Catholics – even after the Second Vatican Council – would have considered devotion to the pope as a significant element in their identification as Catholics.

The 1960s saw the development of oral contraception and many bishops – aware of growing pastoral concerns – wanted the issue of birth control raised and debated within the Council. Pope John XXIII, instead, established a commission of non-theologians to consider the issues involved. His successor Pope Paul VI added theologians, bishops and cardinals to the commission, but also greatly expanded its membership to include women. The commission was to report to the Pope with findings and considerations for his decision.

Over the years, various 'reports' were formulated and leaked to the Catholic world and there was a general expectation – from the majority reports – that the church's teaching on birth control would somehow be modified. However, Pope Paul VI seems to have been convinced that it would not be possible for him to change the clear teaching of previous encyclicals – especially *Casti Connubii* of Pope Pius XI in 1930 – and the universal teaching of church authorities and theologians in the decades since then.

Humanae Vitae was issued in 1968. While insisting that sexual activity needed always to be open to procreation, it did acknowledge the practice of 'natural methods' of planned birth control.

It is doubtful if Paul VI could have anticipated the reaction to the encyclical. Modern Catholic history until that time had so assumed the function of the papacy as the final arbiter of faith and morals that there had never before been any discernible degree of dissent from official papal teaching. The encyclicals of Pius XII, for example, condemning certain theological trends, had caused some dismay among some theologians but largely these were considered internal theological issues that hardly affected the lay members of the church. The decrees of the recent Council, resulting in large scale changes in language, liturgy, ecumenism and other areas of church life had – for the most part – been generally accepted by church members as part of a general movement within the church to adapt its structure, worship and social teaching to reflect the modern world – a basic intention of the Council itself. These changes generally affected how Catholics worshipped or related to other Churches but had minimum impact on their day-to-day lives as the faithful People of God.

Humanae Vitae was different. It was not about worship but about sexuality; it was not about broad issues of relating to other Christians but about how people were to live within their marriages; it was not about new ways of being church but old ways of understanding the function of sexuality within marriage and in society more broadly.

Dissent to the encyclical was not slow to show itself. On one level, the dissent grew from the encyclical's basic assertion of what is called 'natural law', a concept that owed it narrowness to a prescientific understanding of society and humanity. And, more specifically, an approach to sexuality that took little account of the growing awareness of its function in creating and sustaining relationships rather than simply as an activity whose purpose was procreation.

Throughout the Catholic world, the encyclical proved divisive; and, for present-day Catholics, it seems extraordinary that artificial birth control could become a major source of controversy. Probably this is because so much has happened in society in the more than fifty years since *Humanae Vitae* – the growing voices of women, the gradual legalisation of laws concerning homosexuality, the acceptance of no-fault bases for divorce, the availability of contraception, the development of sex education, an openness to different expressions of sexuality, an acceptance of people in relationships without the need for marriage. But the official church teaching did not change and in the pontificates of John Paul II and Benedict

XVI, acceptance and promotion of *Humanae Vitae* was accepted as a condition for episcopal appointments – which simply reinforced the growing disregard of Catholics for any kind of papal and episcopal guidance.

So, was *Humanae Vitae* a blessing in disguise or a mixed blessing? A blessing in disguise if it signalled a 'growing up' among Catholics with an almost collective realisation that, at least in areas of sexuality, the opinions of celibate males lacked a degree of credibility. Sadly, however, it meant that in other areas of morality, the opinions of popes and bishops and clergy generally became less respected, even when their instruction was soundly based on the clear teaching of the gospel. On the other hand, the growing number of theologically educated lay people, graduates of Catholic universities and institutions, more than complemented the marginalisation of bishops and clergy as the only authoritative interpreters of the tradition.

In the recent and current situations of legislation surrounding issues of abortion, same sex marriage, voluntary assisted dying, etc., Catholics no longer automatically look to the bishops for guidance on how to vote or make up their minds – such episcopal authority is no longer considered binding; for some, it almost has the opposite effect.

Clericalism revisited

But perhaps, on reflection, the most noted result of the encyclical was that it seems to have hastened the rapidly growing disenchantment within the church as more and more Catholics simply grew away from the faith of their ancestors as something that they could easily live without. There had always been a certain anti-clericalism in some parts of Europe but the even in traditionally Catholic strongholds – Ireland is a good example – the collapse of the church's role as moral, social and political guide was as rapid as it was unforeseen. And shows not many signs of being reversed in the near future. The rapid decline in vocations to priesthood and religious life is another sign of the growing marginalisation of what traditionally were features of a healthy and confident Catholic society.

Of course, it is not simply a Catholic phenomenon. Most of the traditional Christian churches are in decline. And even within the more successful denominations, there is little evidence of a sustained, long term life growth – which seems to suggest that we are confronted by a longer-term issue of how to make sense of our lives without the traditional reliance on religious teaching, symbols or tradition.

So why religion?

At its heart, I suspect, all religion is an attempt to help us respond to the most basic philosophical question of all: how am I to live? More precisely, how does the Catholic and Christian tradition continue to make sense as a guide to living in the context of our awareness of the vastness of the universe, the reality of evolution, the existence of other faith traditions and the acceptance of their validity as ways of teaching us how to live?

Yet if we reflect on our particular Christian history, we find, in fact, that the pressing emphasis of the tradition is not how am I to live but what am I to believe. And perhaps therein lies a source of the current dissonance among Catholics. The Second Vatican Council was surely a morning star event – a time of renewal, of enthusiasm, of hope, of newfound vigour, of fresh opportunities. As far as those who opposed its emphasis on reform – like Archbishop Lefevre – were concerned, they simply retreated and bided their time. If they waited long enough, the voices of disquiet among those who longed for the certainties and structures of the past would surely find expression in new authorities: church leaders who would stem the enthusiasms and reverse the movements that had brought changes in authority, imbalances in attitudes towards bishops and clergy, and the growing secularisation of Catholics in society.

Their desire for a return to former certainties was not slow to be achieved. Paul VI's *Credo of the People of God*, John Paul II's *Catechism of the Catholic Church*, Benedict XVI's various encyclicals were all aimed at re-establishing sound and clear teaching of the faith of Catholics – or at least reinforcing what they were to believe, as if that alone was the mark of the disciple of Jesus. The underlying attitude seems to have been that if we can reinforce clear and authoritative doctrinal teaching, the recovery of the old ways will follow; peace and order will be restored.

What is the church?

Perhaps, that is why some would suggest that the Council was a false dawn. To be sure, in the years immediately following the Council, vocations were strong, parishes were vibrant, religious education was invigorated. But I suspect there was a latent but powerful disquiet among church leaders and especially members of the Roman Curia about what was happening. And while it is true that the documents of the Council were passed with impressive majorities among the bishops of the Council, I suspect that many of them simply did not understand the thrust of what was being endorsed in the decrees and – on return to their dioceses – became increasingly uneasy about developments that seriously challenged traditional ways of being Catholic. The response of many bishops to the dissent among priests following *Humanae Vitae* is one sign of their preparedness to act with a theological and pastoral insensitivity that seemed contrary to the renewal that was the focus of the Council.

I suggest too that probably the majority of the bishops at the Council – and certainly the priests in their dioceses – had been trained to understand the church in a certain way that had been unchanged for centuries. A detailed expression of this understanding is reflected in what happened in Nazi Germany in the 1930s and 1940s. The 2004 book *Catholic Theologians in Nazi Germany* by Robert A. Krieg, provides a good summary of how Catholics generally understood the church, an understanding that helps explain why the German church (and the Vatican) is perceived as being so ineffective during the tyranny of the Nazi state. It recalls that the German bishops and their clergy generally understood the church as a perfect society, sufficient in itself for the salvation of its people, and unprepared and even unwilling to confront the dictatorship of Hitler and his anti-Semitic and other immoral programs.

The 1925 encyclical of Pius XI, establishing the Feast of Christ the King, asserted that the Catholic church was the Kingdom of God on earth; and the various Concordats negotiated between the Vatican and some European dictators in Germany, Spain and Portugal were meant solely to ensure the freedom of the Church to continue its liturgical and educational ministries, allowing the states to act without overt criticism from church leaders. Thus the separation of church and state was the reality so that even the small but growing number of German bishops and theologians found it difficult to express their comments openly in the context of a church assumed to have no real concern with issues beyond the church buildings.

And even if there were voices of dissent, encouraged by Pope Pius XI's 1937 encyclical *Mit brennender sorge*, the idea that the church might be a voice to society was largely overshadowed by the idea of the church as a perfect society, utterly self-sufficient and comfortable within its own structures.

Naturally, this was a church of power, obedience and clericalism, whose members were teachers (clerics) and learners (laity). The adage 'pray, pay and obey' as the role of the laity is not far from the truth in such an understanding of the church's nature and function.

Fewer than thirty years separates the times of those German bishops of the 1930s and 1940s from the Second Vatican Council and it is likely that most of the bishops at the Council (and their clergy) still understood the church in those ways. The textbooks being used in seminaries in the 1960s were those that had been used for centuries. The basic thesis in *De Ecclesia* (concerning the church), for example, was simple. The church was founded by the Son of God, its dogmas and structures endorsed by him, its infallibility guaranteed by the Holy Spirit. Not much room there for development along the lines of democracy, individual freedom, lay involvement. No wonder the concept of church as the People of God was so revolutionary. Perhaps above all, sadly, not much room for humility! All this was clearly understood by Archbishop Lefevre and his followers; and perhaps explains why when the *Humanae Vitae* crisis arose, there was such a spirited response from bishops in many countries.

Being or believing

Amy-Jill Levine is an unusual Jewish academic because she teaches New Testament at Vanderbilt University in the USA. In her latest book *Reading the Bible with and without Jesus*, she asserts that the Jewish tradition is about orthopraxy (how are we to live) while Christianity is about orthodoxy (what do we believe), a phenomenon – she claims – that makes it possible to be a Jewish atheist but not a Christian atheist. But if we look at the New Testament, we discover – especially in the earliest Gospels – that they record the teaching of Jesus of Nazareth in a context that is basically Jewish, concerned about orthopraxy – how are we to live. It is only in the writings of Paul that – probably reflecting a growing rift between traditional Judaism and the emerging Christian interpretation of that tradition – we find a drift towards orthodoxy, with an emerging concern about the identity of Jesus as the Christ, as opposed to his teaching – in the earlier gospels – about how we are to live as children of the kingdom of God.

Sadly, too, much of the rest of the Christian tradition increasingly focuses on orthodoxy – Creeds, Councils, Synods, Catechisms – all telling us what we are to believe rather than focusing on how we are to live. More emphasis on the divinity of Jesus, the nature of the Trinity, the definition of sacraments, the meaning of transubstantiation, preoccupation with the Last Things rather than an emphasis on the gospel teaching about compassion, mercy, love, forgiveness, hope.

Of course, this summary must also allow for the history of mystics and reformers who throughout the church's history have reminded us of the centrality of the Jesus story; but sadly, for example, most of us recall that we tended to emphasise what separated us doctrinally from other Christians rather than the common gospel teachings that we shared together;

and our history recalls that we presented images of division and hatred rather than a common commitment to making the kingdom of God a present and common goal of our shared Christianity.

Restored orthodoxy

If the intentions of church leaders in those post Conciliar years was to recover and impose orthodoxy, with a view to strengthening faith and promoting growth, it would seem to have failed. Even in overtly Christian countries like the USA, the decline in church attendance and membership is a statistical reality. In Australia, the research from Government and Church-focused censuses reveals that here too the numbers of people identifying as Catholic and Christian shows little sign of recovery. The vitality of the Catholic school system is an exceptional sign of life but even there, the numbers of families actually committed to regular church attendance shows little sign of a hoped-for, long-term recovery of identity and belonging.

The Tablet of 7 August 2021 reported that the Catholic parish of St Mary's in Gosport in England has the following statement on the parish website: 'All non-Catholic religions are false and only the Catholic Church contains the entire deposit of faith given to the Apostles by Christ... (this) is fully in accord with common sense and the constant teaching of the Church that there is "No Salvation outside the Catholic Church"'. This statement reflects an understanding of church unmoved by the Second Vatican Council and perhaps welcomed by many seeking old certainties and securities.

Elsewhere, for example, the apparent reluctance of many US Bishops to accept the guidance of Pope Francis on issues of climate change or same sex relationships would seem to indicate a moving back towards an understanding of church as a perfect society, indifferent to broader issues happening, apparently, outside the church's concern; or even a retreat to moral principles based on outdated understandings of 'natural law'.

And the desire of some US bishops – with the approval of many influential lay people – to refuse Communion to Catholic politicians who support legislation that decriminalises abortion or encourages programs of sex education in schools could be another sign of disquiet among bishops that perhaps the Vatican Two legacy of Catholics thinking for themselves needs drastic revisiting to recover clerical authority and ethical certainty.

But, as noted earlier, if adherence to *Humanae Vitae* was a condition of episcopal appointment by John Paul II and Benedict XVI, it is hardly surprising that many bishops all over the world are conservative in their understanding of the church, its function, its structure and its mission.

Other voices

And yet, the witness of other Catholic bishops – including many US bishops – suggests a more positive, open, humble understanding of their ministry. The martyred Oscar Romero, Archbishop of San Salvador, was among those who clearly understood that the church is not an inward-looking 'perfect' society, preoccupied solely by its own status but a church that must speak the truth to the wider society, proclaim the gospel of Jesus Christ to the increasingly indifferent and powerful in our world. Only someone like Romero could remind us that 'A Church that does not provoke any crisis, preach a Gospel that does not unsettle, proclaim a word of God that does not get under anyone's skin, or the word of God that does not touch the real sin of the society in which it is being proclaimed: what kind of Gospel is that?'

So what's next?

Perhaps all of the above reflection on our lives as Catholic Christians since Vatican 2 has been too focused on change within the church and resistance to that change. Throughout, unaddressed, is the assumption that people in the pews will continue to lead their lives directed by faith in Jesus Christ as an authentic interpretation of the purposes of God for humanity and the universe. As already suggested, religious faith informs our response to the perennial question: How am I to live? The gospel tradition's response can be summed up in the more ancient teaching of Micah; do justice, love kindness, walk humbly.

Humility implies a degree of uncertainty. A wise person once pointed out that the opposite of faith is not doubt; the opposite of faith is certainty. That seems to contradict much of what we were taught in the past – that faith implies certainly, assurance, absolute conviction about the truths we received and celebrated. But to walk humbly means, I think, living with a certain openness to what God reveals, not exclusively in the Jesus/Jewish tradition but in every ancient and contemporary effort to make sense of our world and the purposes of life itself.

An aside: our parish priest in England told us one Sunday that he had been taking Communion to a sick parishioner. As he drove along, he was listening to a Brains Trust radio program that was discussing the existence of God. He told us solemnly that he realised, at that moment, that he had God in his pocket. If we are to walk humbly, perhaps it means we need to walk even with our fellow Catholics who have God in their pockets.

Accepting difference, walking humbly

At Mass each week, I really don't know how everyone else in the congregation responds to the readings, the preaching, the prayers, the liturgy. I have little idea of how they understand Eucharist although I expect they would be surprised by my personal experience of being in communion at that moment with my Catholic ancestors and those to come after me; that my Amen to the sacrament is more than an act of faith but a renewed acceptance of trying to be formed by the gospel as an authentic way of making sense of my life, with values and truths that form the community called church.

The reality for us in Australia and other parts of the western world is that the church is in decline if measured by numbers at Mass or traditional celebrations of marriage and funerals. Shortage of clergy, the affirmation of women's ministry, lay involvement in local decision-making have all been raised, especially in the context of the Plenary Council, but change will be slow and expectations varied. Some will continue to be disillusioned by the ongoing clericalism of the structures; others will continue to have low expectations of the quality of preaching and presidency; some will continue to belong, convinced that change will come and in any case being Catholic is integral to their identity and on-going formation as disciples; others will look for new ways of belonging and worshipping together, perhaps outside the traditional structures, but in ways that reflect the first Christians, in small, informal gatherings to pray together, to reflect on Scripture, to break bread, to care for the poor.

I have no idea what the church will look like in a hundred years. At the end of his book *A History of Christianity*, having explored how the church has changed and developed over two thousand years, the author Diarmaid MacCulloch says: 'It would be very surprising if this religion, so youthful, yet so varied in its historical experience, had now revealed all its secrets'.

Amen!

Words for Life: Wisdom Distilled at Julian's Window

Janette Bredenoord Elliott

The title of this publication represents a reaching out, a stretching out, an *ekstasis* toward the Divine Other who calls us beyond the boundaries of faith, of freedom, and to embrace our identity borne of that faith and freedom. At least this is what we witness in Julian of Norwich, the 14th century anchoress who set down in writing her Vision of the crucified Lord of glory, and, later, her theological reflections on that same Vision.[1] In this chapter, I present Julian of Norwich and shine a light on her ministry of 'wise counsel' with a view to the Australian Context – post Pandemic and post Royal Commission into Institutional Responses to Child Sexual Abuse. As anchoress, Julian shared her 'distilled wisdom'

---

[1] In this chapter, I am using Mirabai Starr's translation of Julian's Revelations of Divine Love because of its 'accessibility' to today's reader. See: Mirabai Starr. *The Showings of Julian of Norwich: A New Translation* (Charlottesville, VA: Hampton Roads Publishing Company, Inc., 2013) Please note that unless specified I will use Starr's translation. Regarding any text references I will adopt the abbreviated form of LT for Long Text and ST for Short Text.

giving spiritual counsel and words of comfort to pilgrims at her 'window of welcome'.[2]

In the earlier work *We Too: The Laity Speaks*, I presented Julian as a Mystic for 'today',[3] where I adopted the Deuteronomist understanding of 'today' in the broader exhortation to 'Choose Life' (Deuteronomy 30:19-20). This remains relevant as I ask what more can Julian offer us for our today right now, at this time in the Australian context, in the Australian Church? During the still current health pandemic, Julian has been drawn on greatly by various scholars in the academic disciplines of philosophy, theology and spirituality, as also in the fields of pastoral and spiritual care. Julian also lived through a pandemic with three waves spread out over a few decades. The worst of these – writes Jane Maynard – was that of 1348 when Julian was six years of age. Maynard notes 'This epidemic constituted one of the greatest disasters the Western world has ever experienced'.[4]

In noting the connection made by these scholars between our experience of living through (and now with) COVID-19 and Julian's experience of the Black Death, I have asked the question 'Why?' What is the actual connection scholars and practitioners are actually wanting to make? Is the connection simply on the level of living through a traumatic time in history? We need to be aware of the situation facing Julian

---

[2] The term 'window of welcome' is taken from: Elizabeth Obbard, *Through Julian's Windows: Growing into Wholeness with Julian of Norwich*. (London: Canterbury Press Norwich, 2008), 57.

[3] Janette Elliott, 'Julian: A Mystic for Today' in *We Too: The Laity Speaks!* Edited by Berise Heasly and John D'Arcy May. (Bayswater, Victoria: Coventry Press, 2020), 128-154.

[4] Jane F. Maynard. *Transfiguring Loss: Julian of Norwich as a Guide for Survivors of Traumatic Grief.* (Cleveland, Ohio: The Pilgrim Press, 2006), 45.

during the 14th Century because her experience – unlike ours – included observing significant numbers of dead and decaying bodies. Certainly in Australia, we were not exposed to such graphic devastation. As a chronicle of the cathedral priory of Rochester in England reads:

> Alas, this mortality devoured such a multitude of both sexes that no one could be found to carry the bodies of the dead to burial, but men and women carried the bodies of their own little ones to church on their shoulders and threw them into mass graves, from which arose such a stink that it was barely possible for anyone to go past a churchyard.[5]

An account such as this provides some perspective on what Julian would have lived through, and our experience some six hundred years later. We have the benefits of modern hospitals, technology, vaccines and real-time knowledge of events across the world. That does not mean our experience is any less real, valid or traumatic. It's just different, and so my question remains: what was the actual connection scholars and practitioners were making in linking our experience to Julian's in Norwich, as both child and adult, of what came to be known as 'the Great Mortality?' I would like to suggest that this shared traumatic experience in terms of loss, grief, isolation and separation from communal support structures are the shared experiences between Julian and ourselves. This pertains not only to the Pandemic, but to the ongoing effects of the Royal Commission noted above in the Australia context. Thus, I believe that Julian does offer us more today, and that she can share her wisdom with us in negotiating the boundaries of faith, freedom and identity.

---

[5] Maynard, *Transfiguring Loss*, 63.

Building on the earlier work: *We Too: The Laity Speaks!*, I introduce Julian, a mature woman, well equipped to share her words of life, that is, her distilled wisdom at her 'window of welcome'. Before explaining what this term 'window of welcome' refers to both vocationally and architecturally, I would first like to introduce Julian to those less familiar with her. I will also round out this introduction for those who have read Julian, or even visited her 'cell' with a brief treatment of Julian as 'communicator'.[6] This will then situate us well to consider how the title of this book found expression in Julian's life and ministry. How did Julian live beyond the boundaries of faith, freedom and identity? Does her response find resonance with the Australian context today; and if so, how might Julian encourage or challenge us in our individual or collective response? Finally, and by way of conclusion, I will focus on Julian's wisdom for living with awareness that we are kept whole and safe in Christ – even in the midst of the challenges to our faith, freedom and identity today. This is key to an understanding of Christ, Deep Wisdom as the Lord of our faith, our freedom and our Identity. It is the Easter Christ, the Risen Lord who calls forth our trust in this understanding, enabling us to move forward together in hope.

Julian as Creature, Interpreter and Communicator

Julian of Norwich lived c.1342 to 1416 and is credited with being the first woman to write a book in English. This distinction is currently being challenged by scholars such as

---

6 The term 'cell' is used in reference to Julian's 'anchorhold' which is a small dwelling attached or anchored to the Church. The term 'cell' is the more popular term at the Julian Centre in Norwich, U.K for visitors. The same term is used to refer to rooms occupied by monks in monasteries.

Mary Wellesley in her fascinating publication *Hidden Hands: The Lives of Manuscripts and Their Makers*.[7] However, the important point here in relation to Julian is that she wrote a book in the vernacular sharing her 'words of comfort' with everyday Christians who simply longed to know God's love, and live more aware of God's loving presence in their daily lives.

Julian lived in an age where vernacular theology emerged strongly in spiritual writings in England, and on the Continent, enabling the nourishment of faith beyond Latin-centred Church teaching and practices. Her early devotional response sharing her Vision was directed to those who, like her, would be God's lovers. As the Vision opened out and she received greater insight into the Lord's teaching in the Vision, she desired to share this profound experience with her fellow Christians, and for those, like her, who struggled. This struggle reflects those who sought to embrace the hope that God's absolute, unconditional love went way beyond the limitations put up by sin, by judgment and especially the human condition.

The woman who wrote *The Revelations of Divine Love*, and who is popularly known for the statement of deep faith 'All shall be well' was not about making a name for herself. Julian sought only to share the graces she had received that we might know with her that Love is God's meaning. This became the crowning 'lesson of love' for the whole Vision of Sixteen showings as Julian records:

Would you like to know our Lord's meaning in all this? Know it well: love was his meaning. Who revealed this to

---

[7] Mary, Wellesley. *Hidden Hands: The Lives of Manuscripts and Their Makers*. (London, U.K: Quercus Editions Ltd, 2021).

you? Love. What did he reveal to you? Love. Why did he reveal it to you? For love. Stay with this and you will know more of the same. You will never know anything but love, without end (LT 86).[8]

The graces she prayed for as a youth are reflected in a Vision she received at the age of thirty and a half as she recovered from a near fatal sickness. These graces may also be described as the deepest desires of her heart. The three graces read as follows:

The first was to have mind of the Passion of Christ. The second was a bodily sickness. The third, to have, of God's gifts, three wounds... the wound of contrition, the wound of compassion, and the wound of wilful longing for God (ST I).[9]

As reflected in the earlier work, Julian's understanding of desire liberates us from the reductionist concept of desire, and reflects the broader medieval understanding in which desire, longing, yearning and the thirst for justice are shared between God and the soul. Julian's understanding of desire reveals that God is the ground of our prayer and that God is the ground of our whole being in love.

Julian has been referred to by some scholars as both 'creature' and as 'interpreter' but less often as 'communicator'.[10] By *creature*, Julian is simply the person who received Sixteen Showings of Love in a Vision. These Sixteen Showings are

---

[8] Starr, *The Showings of Julian of Norwich*, 224-225.

[9] In this instance, I have used the Short Text taken from the edition by: Anna-Maria Reynolds, *A Shewing of God's Love: The Shorter Version of Sixteen Revelations of Divine Love.* (London: Longmans, Green and Co. 1958).

[10] Margaret A. Palliser, *Christ, Our Mother of Mercy: Divine Mercy and Compassion in the Theology of the Shewings of Julian of Norwich.* (Berlin: Walter de Gruyter & Co. 1992, 11).

provided in an Appendix at the conclusion of this chapter. This Vision was in many ways an answer to the prayer of desire as a youth for three graces. Julian's prayer is deeply grounded in her deep desire to be united with God – whether in life or in death. For someone who had lived through three waves of the Black Death, her desire to be united with God – whether alive or dead – made total sense. Julian's survival is of immense significance as Maynard has shown in her powerful study which I quoted from earlier. Julian's desire to be 'substantially oned' (LT 5) to God even as she recovered from her illness indicates that her whole reason for living was this desire for union with God.[11]

Consistent with the key characteristics of English Spirituality of her time with its focus on affective spirituality centred in and around Christ's humanity, Julian was devoted to the broken body of Christ. Thus her prayer to experience a bodily illness is really about her desire to know suffering in order to come closer to Christ. Her prayer to have mind of Christ's passion is about her desire to grow in deeper compassion, and also sorrow for sin. Her prayer for the three wounds of contrition, compassion and longing toward God is really a double backing

---

[11] The term 'oned' or 'oneing' or 'ones' or 'at-one-ment' are all related to a term reflecting a union with God that expresses the deep understanding that we knew this union in the moment of our creation 'substantially', that is of God's own substance. The desire even in our sensual nature encompassing our senses, our psyche, our intelligence and memory, to be 'substantially oned' to God reflects our origin and end. Through Christ, knit to our sensual nature through the Incarnation, this 'oneing' may take place even in this life. Mirabai Starr's language may assist in illuminating the phrase 'substantially oned' as she writes: 'And I recognised that until I am completely one with him I shall never have deep rest nor full joy. No, not until I am so thoroughly joined to him that no created thing can come between my God and myself.' See: Starr, *The Showings of Julian of Norwich*, 13-14.

over the first two desires that keep her entire focus – with all her heart, soul and strength on Christ. Julian as Creature is entirely focused on Christ with her prayer of the desire to desire, to the extent that it becomes a wound of passion, and com-passion. Julian's 'Short Text' is the earlier record of her Vision and attests the 'devotional' creature whose spirituality is reflected in the images that pervade her Vision and the more biographical account of the moment in her recovery when she encountered Christ speaking to her from the image of the Cross on which she had fixed her gaze.

Julian as *Interpreter* comes to the fore in the later writing of the Longer Version of her 'Showings'. Some fifteen to twenty years after the Vision – as Julian herself notes in the Long Text – we encounter this woman, the mature Julian most likely now an anchoress. It is Julian the Interpreter who has gained the attention of great scholars like Thomas Merton, Rowan Williams and so many others. It is Julian the Interpreter who has been the subject of theological studies adding to earlier decades of studies in Middle English Literature, Medieval Mystics, Visionary Women's writings and academic studies in spirituality. The reason for this is the recognition of the quality of Julian's own reflection in her context of a life of prayer and her determination to understand the Lord's meaning in the 'Showings'.

Julian is noted as not looking for easy answers, and nor for 'hasty solutions' to problems. Her own wrestle with the problem of sin in the face of God's unconditional love and Church teaching in her time on punishment for sin is very real. It also puts paid to those who have viewed Julian as representative of a 'Pollyanna Christian' in relation to her phrase 'All shall be well.' Julian's wrestle is finally addressed through what is referred to as 'The Example of the Lord that has a servant.' This Example addressed in my earlier chapter is reflected in Julian's journey toward understanding of the 'true knowing of love' vs the 'unknowing of love' – both in relation to our experience of well-being and woe.

The mature Julian highlights that, beyond our vacillating experiences of joy and pain, of light and dark, of well-being and woe, there is a choice to be made. Julian's choice, beyond all these varying experiences that sin, judgment and the human condition, is for Christ. Her creaturely ascent to fix her gaze on the Image of her Saviour, becomes a choice through interpretation to embrace Christ as her source of joy, of light and of well-being, regardless of what experience is encouraging or challenging her at any given time. Julian reminds us that our capacity for God is innate, and our desire for God is the expression of this innate capacity. Created in God's love that is without beginning, this love is the life-source of this innate capacity and keeps the remembrance of God's endless love aflame in each one of us.

We come now to a brief but no less important consideration of Julian as 'Communicator'. This term used by Margaret Palliser reflects Julian's ministry of both writing and counselling at her 'window of welcome'. Julian shares all that she received in the Vision, and the understandings that came to her through the years of prayer and of wrestling, of writing and of living attentive to the Spirit in whatever way it was communicated to her. Julian's expertise is noted by a contemporary Margery Kempe who visited Julian at her window in 1413.[12] This account is one of a few historical facts attesting Julian's existence and vocation at the Church of St Julian's Conisford,

---

[12] Margery Kempe, *The Book of Margery Kempe* translated by John Skinner. (New York: Doubleday, 1988), 3-5.

Norwich, and adds to the knowledge that she was still alive in 1413.

. The practice of providing a word of comfort to visitors at the window is noted in The *Rule for Anchoresses*.[13] With it comes the warning against setting themselves up as teachers, which most likely was to counter the heresies of Lollardy at the time, and certainly women endowing themselves with any kind of authority to teach. Considering the location of Julian's anchorhold attached to a Church on a busy trade route in and out of Norwich both by road and by river, in a city second in size only to London, the visitors to Julian's window could comprise not only pilgrims and simple folk, but foreigners and noble women among so many others. In terms of Julian's ministry at her window, Julian – as indeed other anchoresses in England – would not have had a choice about who might present themselves, nor any preference for whom they would minister to. There is a vulnerability and raw honesty in this, necessitating real authenticity, empathy, accountability and the courage to simply 'be there' or to 'show up' – literally – for Christ's sake.

Julian's Life as an Anchoress

Julian's life as an anchoress was not as unusual in her time as it is in ours. The phenomenon of men and women 'anchoring' themselves to their local churches happened through screening to ensure maturity, and soundness of mind for such a rigorous and seemingly isolating vocation. After the experience of COVID lockdowns, the thought of

---

[13] Refer to: *Anchoritic Spirituality: Ancrene Wisse and Associated Works*, translated by Anne Savage and Nicholas Watson (New York: Paulist Press, 1991).

someone choosing self-isolation is difficult to comprehend. Often anchoresses required a patron to support their living, and certainly a maid was engaged to attend to the practical needs of an anchoress in relation to provision of food, clothing, washing needs, and also removal of waste and rubbish. The rhythm of the anchoritic life was regulated by the *Rule for Anchoresses*, which governed not only the daily routine, but spiritual practices and engagement with the church, the world, and, conversely, spiritual counsel for the anchoress. Obbard describes this aspect of Julian's vocation, writing:

> In Julian's time the hermit or solitary was usually a lay person who had no vested interest in the hierarchical Church or any particular religious Order. Julian is very clear that her focus is on her 'even Christians', others like herself who are 'ordinary' and whose path to God is in the lay state, even though their way of living may differ from hers. The vocation of hermit-counsellor means having an openness regarding the outcome of another's spiritual journey. It is to enable the other to find and walk his or her own personal path.[14]

The architecture of the anchorhold attached to the local church appears to be of a standard type. The rite of interment of the anchoress into the anchorhold was that of the rite of burial and always performed by the local bishop.

While anchorholds might have an enclosed garden to walk in, or in fact to tend, the most symbolic and evocative aspect of the anchorhold was that of the three windows. The window from the anchorhold, sometimes called a 'cell' to the Sanctuary of the Church made possible participation in the Liturgy, access to Holy Communion, and inclusion in the communal

---

[14] Obbard, *Through Julian's Windows*, 65.

life of the congregation through prayer. This window on to the Sanctuary is linked by Obbard to Julian's prayer for the wound of longing. This is because the Sanctuary symbolised the holy place shared by Julian and the Lord enflamed with mutual desire and longing.[15] The window on to 'everyday life' – again borrowing from Obbard[16] – is the window that symbolises our common humanity in our 'fleshliness' or 'bodily existence', which the Lord loves and was 'knit' to through the Incarnation.

The basic needs of life to eat, to sleep, to excrete waste are all part of our bodily existence and to be well, care of the body for love of the soul that it houses, is important to God. As Julian wrote: 'For love of our souls, which he made in his own likeness, he lovingly serves us in our most basic bodily functions' (LT 6). As Julian learned of God's care of all that God had made, she also learned that God is closer to us than our own skin. Julian expresses is thus: 'The body is held in its clothes, the flesh in the skin, the bones in the flesh, and the heart in the breast. So are we – body and soul – draped and contained in the goodness of God.' (LT 6).

For anchoresses – apparently 'walled up' to live their vocation of prayer and desire for God in this particular way – a maid was engaged to serve the anchoress in these needs and ultimately serve God. The vocation of anchoress was in this sense shared and was part of the local Church community, the responsibility of the local parish under the Bishop's direction. It is also possible that anchoresses were sponsored by a patron whose motives could be both honourable, and also to secure prayer for him or her.

---

15 Obbard, *Through Julian's Windows*, 78.
16 Obbard, *Through Julian's Windows*, 35.

Regarding the final window, that is, 'the window of welcome', *The Showings of Julian of Norwich* states that this reflects the heart of compassion that is Christ's heart. Christ's heart, broken open on the Cross, is open to all to enter to find rest and peace in Christ's love. In this safe space provided by Julian reflecting the compassion of God at her window, she listens to the deeper life of the visitor, is powerless with them, empathetic and open to what God wants to offer the person, that is the Peace of Christ's grace and mercy.

Beyond the boundaries of faith, freedom and identity

The Vision of the Crucified and Risen Lord Julian witnessed as a thirty-year-old exploded her categories of faith, of religion, of life and her place in the church, the world and in God. Julian's encounter with Christ may be seen as a 'heart to heart' conversation, sought and desired intentionally by Julian from her youth. Paradoxically. the greatest source of delight, joy and blessing for her was that she came to understand that Christ was seeking and desiring her engagement with his 'love-longing' (LT 31). This is no insular mystical foray but what Christ desires for all of us. Julian understood this even before she committed her profound encounter with Christ to paper in the Short Text believed to be written soon after the Vision. Her conclusion to this earlier text gives expression to the 'hospitality of God' Julian came to understand as the fabric of living well in and through Christ. She wrote:

> For God wills that we be secure in love and peaceful and restful, as he is to us. Just as he is to us, so wills he that we be to ourselves, and to our fellow-Christians. Amen. Explicit Juliane de Norwych. (ST XXV)

What does this mean? How are we to remain secure in love and peaceful and restful? How is God secure in love, peaceful and restful with us? What does it mean to be 'as he is to us' to ourselves, and 'as he is to us' to our fellow Christians? Julian's life as an anchoress as well as her writings in the Long Text help us explore this 'as God is to us' way of hospitality. How God is to us, or the way God is lovingly and constantly present to us is communicated through the Sixteen Showings'. (See Appendix.) This list of the Sixteen Showings is only found in the first chapter of the Long Text. As a kind of summary of Julian's *Revelations*, there is both a sense of Christ who, with the Trinity, is our Maker, Protector and Lover; and a sense of Christ as servant who did not disdain to knit himself to our sensuality to be one with us in our experience of dailiness, fleshliness and vulnerability.

In the descriptions of Christ's Passion it is easy to recognise our own experience of Passion and suffering in our life. In this, the accompanying teaching is that God does not blame us for our falls or our failings, our sin or our suffering. Our own sense of shame and tendency to blame result from our pain, which Julian says punishes us, not God. God only wishes to reward us for the sufferings we encounter in this life. As the Seventh Showing attests, God uplifts us in joy and protects us in sorrow (LT 15).

Through and beyond all this, however, is the encouragement to fix our gaze on Christ and God's love through everything we experience. To focus purely on our pain and sufferings draws us into the murkiness of our own limitations often leading us to despair. Embracing the reality of God's loving perspective borne of wisdom and goodness, keeps us in peace – that is, the knowledge of Christ dwelling in our soul. The point of connection from the First to the Sixteenth Showing is signalled from the outset when Julian writes of the essential unity or 'oneing' between the human soul and the Divine.

Julian's life may be described in a number of phases just as our life may be viewed in this way. In all these phases, Julian's life is consistently 'shot through' with the reciprocity of desire between Julian and Christ. There is Christ with his love-longing in the spiritual thirst accompanying his physical thirst on the Cross, and Julian with her prayer of longing to desire ever more of Christ's love. These key phases may be summed up as prayer and pandemic, sickness and vision, encounter with the Crucified and Divine Love, Divine Love and the tensions of sin, Church teaching and the limitations of the human condition.

Finally, through Julian's Vision of Sixteen Showings, there is the Divine Response to the human condition, to sin and to judgment. In the context of Julian's life and ministry reflected in those phases, I will briefly explore what faith, freedom and identity looked like for her. Here I simply note their expression in Julian's life of faith as an anchoress; the freedom she sought as a survivor of traumatic loss in reference to her experience of the Black Death; and the emergence of her deeper identity through her 'survivor mission' in her writing and ministry of spiritual counsel at the window of welcome.

a) Julian as Anchoress as an expression of Faith

As anchoress, Julian's life of faith is expressed intentionally now, giving credence to her words that she has chosen Jesus for her heaven in well-being and in woe. Julian is no longer swept by the alternating waves of joy and sadness, of delight and sorrow, of well-being and woe. This conscious choice has led her to embrace the conviction that God keeps us secure whether we are in weal or in woe. The life of an anchoress with its rhythm of prayer, both liturgical and personal, fasting and keeping her hands busy as guided by her 'Rule' now comprises her daily life. The Sarum rite most likely guides the liturgy of the Day, and Julian will be aware of the days and seasons when she may receive Communion. Julian will be careful about her outside window, neither teaching nor gossiping, but placing herself between Christ in her cell and the Sanctuary – and the pilgrim at her window.

The spirit animating all this is, of course, the Christ of the Revelations whom Julian has always desired, but has come to know, to serve and to love. Julian knows that Christ sitting in her soul in rest and peace has made his home in her, as she now seeks to make hers in him, symbolised in the anchorhold. The well-established metaphor of enclosure pertains not only to Christ within Julian, but also to her life within the anchorhold connected to Christ through the Church and Christ at the heart of the world. Julian's faith expressed in her life as anchoress leads her to be enclosed in Christ as Christ is in her. Julian welcomes the Divine Feminine, that is Christ Deep Wisdom our Mother who was born of Mary, and of whom we are born through the Incarnation, through his Passion and Resurrection, and through his indwelling in our soul.

b) Julian as Survivor of Traumatic Loss and a New Freedom

At the time of Julian's youthful prayer, she would have experienced at least one wave of the Black Death and potentially witnessed the death of a family member among others in the bustling city of Norwich. At the time of her own illness, Julian's approach to death was coloured by this youthful prayer and is filled with desire to have mind of Christ's Passion, and in her own sickness to have empathy with

Christ. Yet her desire for a wound to long earnestly toward God is a wound of passion that embraces the quest for union, or what Julian calls 'oneing'. Julian expresses a freedom in her acceptance that she can be united to Christ whether she lives or dies. As a result, she does not know what she prefers, because the subject of her desire is the same – Christ. Through her recovery from illness, and having witnessed death all about her, Julian becomes a Survivor of traumatic loss. The inner freedom Julian sought through union with Christ is the inner freedom that Julian seeks in living beyond the Black Death. Frances Maynard writes:

> Life following traumatic loss poses a tremendous challenge to survivors. Perhaps the greatest struggle they face is attempting to integrate the new understandings of life and God wrested from their traumatic experience into their everyday human experience.[17]

As a survivor of traumatic loss and grief, Julian embraces the wound of desire as a desire for the freedom to live through love in God's presence. This God is represented by the Christ of the Revelations who opened his wounded heart and side to Julian, declaring both his love for Julian, and his heart as a place to come and to rest in order to find freedom in peace and love. Julian discovers freedom of heart and of mind in seeking God unto the beholding of God. Julian embraces the lesson of the Example of the servant that beholding ourselves only, especially in our time of pain and despair, achieves nothing that is life-giving.

---

[17] Maynard, *Transfiguring Loss*, 142.

c) Julian's 'Survivor Mission' and her Recovered Identity

As a result of Julian's experience – as a child – of the Black Death with the traumatic losses and grief encountered, Julian's prayer is clearly fervent and yet the objective is consistent to seek her rest in God. Her own illness and recovery – although not necessarily related to the Plague – are absorbed into her Vision of the Crucified. This becomes a paradigm for the ministry she will exercise through her writing and her practice of spiritual are at her outside window. Frances Maynard has called this Julian's 'Survivor mission'.[18] The relevance of this is in Julian's identity as expressed through this 'survivor mission'. Maynard astutely observes that 'A critical spiritual need of survivors of trauma is to achieve an empathetic connection with human community.'

Julian's concern for her fellow Christians, and her desire to share God's love as revealed in the *Revelations* comes early in both her Short and Long Texts. Julian's identity is enclosed now in the heart of Christ, and her mission is to reveal, through her experience, that our human identity finds its meaning and purpose in this same Christ – who has made his home within humanity. The symbol of the hazelnut encapsulates that our existence is the gift of God's love, and that, however small, it lasts because of Divine love (LT 4). As the shell encloses the nut, we are kept safe and whole in Christ whom Julian came to understand as 'Mother' of all (our) life (LT 62).

The above three sections explore aspects of Julian's faith, freedom and identity as we recognise them in her life and ministry. I believe it is possible to identify a significant resonance with the Australian context which is not confined

---

[18] Maynard, *Transfiguring Loss*, 105.

to the Church, but the whole of society. Julian can speak to us in the aftermath of the global pandemic, which, in the post Royal Commission era of the Church in Australia, has left each of us traumatised in ways that we would never have imagined previously. In the isolation of pandemic lockdowns, what has been the focus of our reflection and to whom have we directed the deeper questions that have surfaced? For victims and survivors of child sexual abuse, what has the pandemic meant for the isolation already experienced through their original traumatisation? Returning to the opening lines of this chapter, what now of that *ekstasis*, the reaching out beyond the boundaries of our traumatisation for faith, freedom and identity? Julian shows us a way to move beyond the boundaries of traumatisation, to strengthen us in faith, foster inner freedom and ground our identity in Christ who, as 'Deep Wisdom', dwells within our soul at home in our 'fleshiness'.

The Australian context

In brief, Julian's own life and ministry speaks to our own context made both fragile and in more obvious ways, hardened by the aftermath of the pandemic and the Royal Commission into Institutional Responses to Child Sexual Abuse, the ongoing plight of the refugees in our country, and a Plenary Council that holds in balance the tension of hope and despair of many for living what it means to be Catholic in Australia today. Julian speaks to the people in the pews whether by literal 'bums on seats' – as the saying goes – or those who are in the pews virtually. By 'virtual', I am addressing a reality much broader than the impact of COVID-19 on church attendance. For as the Royal Commission identified, those impacted by the trauma and devastation of child sexual abuse in the Church have been wounded spiritually as much as sexually, emotionally, socially and psychologically as much as physically. This traumatised cohort represent the ghosts of the pews, souls who long for spiritual and healing of their sexuality, for connection and recognition, for forgiveness – mostly of sins not of their making, and for true at-one-ment with God who – in Julian's words – is Maker, Protector and Lover.

When we talk about abuse in the Australian context, we must acknowledge also, and especially, our indigenous sisters and brothers who were the first to experience abuse in this Great Southern Land, and all too often in the church context. The courageous work of Katharine Massam attests to this tragic historic reality, and the courage of those who survived along with the generations that have succeeded them.[19] The abused have become the traumatised and the traumatised sit beside us in the pews whether in the flesh or virtually totally unrelated to COVID. Regarding the plight of the refugees, the deeper questions around acceptance of difference – whether of ethnicity or culture, gender or sexual orientation, with disabilities, or of whatever – that seems to single people out as 'not one of us' come rushing to the surface. What the health pandemic has highlighted through the various forms of social, physical, spiritual and emotional isolation is that we are all in fact traumatised. By virtue of the pandemic and those of us who have experienced the dark night of harsh, protracted lockdowns, each one of us has known the pain and trauma of isolation. If ever there was an equaliser related to personal suffering, then the health pandemic of

---

[19] Katharine Massam, *A Bridge Between: Spanish Benedictine Missionary Women in Australia.* (Action, ACT: ANU Press, 2020).

the past two years and more has to be it. This is not to take anything away from those who have suffered abuse whether sexually, or by discrimination, rejection or other cruel means. Nor is the brief of this chapter to address issues of child sexual abuse, nor abuse of our first nation peoples, or even our pandemic traumatisation. What I am identifying in our Australian context is that we have less and less reasons by which to believe that the person standing beside us, or hidden from us due to abuse is not our sister, or brother whom with us is unconditionally loved, accepted and cherished by God.

On a personal note, I am identifying our Australian context which cannot ignore the reality of the various forms of abuse in church contexts, and the traumatisation that pervades the sensibilities of Australian society and churches. For myself as an Australian Catholic, the sense of traumatisation of all of us as a result of child sexual abuse in the Church, in whatever 'pews' we claim, I am convinced that Julian of Norwich really can and does offer us more today. Julian's lived experience infused with the knowledge, love and wisdom of Christ reaches out to each one of us.

I would like now to address the ways in which Julian was called and challenged to live beyond the boundaries of her faith, freedom and identity. They may look like simple ways but they speak into our context and thus provide both encouragement and challenge to us for living together, aware of the God in whom we are enclosed, and who is enclosed within us both individually and collectively. We are in fact together, the body of Christ.

a) Wisdom Distilled at Julian's Window – Beyond the boundaries of faith

At her window, Julian would not have known who might present themselves, nor what their motive was, and if they brought humility or violence. Yet she was available to speak with pilgrims on the road in and out of Norwich, on the road in and out of the corridors of their heart. There is an honesty in Julian's vulnerability and openness to hear pilgrims, an integrity in the non-judgment, absence of assumptions about them, and readiness to share what she had learned. Moving beyond the boundaries of faith asks for a trust and openness to listen at the level of the heart. Here the tenets of faith are left at the window, while the deeper search of the soul rises up and finds a voice from within to speak to Christ through Julian. Julian's window allows room to explore faith in the liminal space between window and sanctuary. As Julian lives on the margins of society, of religious and secular life, of liturgical and canonical life, so the pilgrim at her window comes to pour out their soul at the margins. There is an implicit trust in this encounter since it is often at the margins where the soul can express its innermost fears, anxieties, concerns and deepest desires.

b) The Post Royal Commission Church Today – Beyond the boundaries of freedom

Julian at her window represents an accountability that pilgrims of today crave, an authenticity of life and of the expression of values that say: 'I am here, I am present and I am here and present to you and for you'. The accountability that today's Church is challenged to is the commitment to show up and be counted in the open, but also in solidarity with the poor, the traumatised and the marginalised. Julian was no 'performer' of her faith, of her vocation as anchoress, or of spiritual guidance. Julian lived the theology she taught in her writings and embodied its meaning in her care for pilgrims at her window. The practice of professional supervision today is a necessary measure of accountability that assists in this 'showing up'. The Christ whom Julian engaged with is the Christ who lives in us and from which we minister to others. None of us has all the answers, nor do we have to. At Julian's window, there is no power structure to operate from. Julian simply facilitates a heart to heart with Christ. She becomes invisible.

c) The Window of Welcome – Beyond the boundaries of identity

At her window, Julian simply offers welcome. One would think that the pandemic facilitated a moment in time, a favourable time in the Church to offer a new kind of welcome to all. In the post Royal commission era, especially when so many in the Church feel isolated, dis-enchanted, unheard or irrelevant, a simple voice of welcome – sincerely invitational, open, non-judgmental, inclusive and transparent – presents a great opportunity for inclusivity. How does the Church convey such a welcome to all people, but especially those who have been most hurt in the context of the Church? Where are the real welcoming spaces? Where are the communications to make sense of so many layers of isolation among God's people and society in general? Why was the focus almost entirely on simply being unable to gather in churches? Where were the real meeting points for those on the Church's margins? In the context of Julian's understanding of our creation as already whole in God, what of the opportunity to embrace the needs of body and soul together? The threat to our physical health became a threat to our spiritual and emotional health. For those who remain isolated whether due to COVID, or to historical abuse, or to being seen as different, this threat remains. We are not just bodily realities, nor are we only spiritual creatures. We are embodied spirits who need to be nourished as whole persons.

Can we only be Church by gathering in consecrated place of worship, sharing the sacrament of Eucharist? What does it mean to gather? What does it mean to be a eucharistic people when, through the pandemic, our lives were broken down, compartmentalised? What happens to our desires for community and communion, for wholeness and for justice? Have we missed an opportunity for a new theology of the body, and a re-claimed understanding of the beauty of eros? Our identity as Church, our identity as individual is as beloved of God. Yet as Church, in the collective space through our isolation, our identity as beloved of God is somehow distanced. What can Julian say to us?

Kept ever whole and safe in Christ

Even as Julian moved through the different phases of her life, she grew in her conviction that we are kept whole and safe in Christ. When she wrote of the 'Godly will' in us which desires only good and never evil, she wrote that this Godly will is kept whole and safe in Christ. This teaching, this 'lesson of love' out of all so many profound teachings explored through each of the Showings, is the one we as Church most need to communicate to our fragile and fractured society in the post pandemic context. This teaching which reinforces the stunning reality of our innate capacity for God is the one we as Church most need to act upon in our broken and frayed post Royal Commission context. To impart a generosity of spirit toward those most fractured by society and broken in the Church by communicating the 'lessons of love' can lead past the barriers to our faith, freedom and identity as God's beloved. This is the prophetic task we are each called to.[20]

Julian of Norwich lived through a time in the Church when the boundaries of faith, freedom and identity could be described as both prescriptive and profoundly challenged. The boundaries – which may well have seemed more like barriers – were prescriptive in the efforts to quash the threat of heresy and uprisings, with laws both sacred and secular laid down regarding the practice of confession and punishments for transgressions. The boundaries were profoundly challenged by rising nationalism in England, and on the Continent where use of the vernacular symbolised the freedom sought to express both faith and identity in sync with national interests. Living in the pre-Reformation context, Julian – a woman, English and a survivor of three waves of the Black Death – was challenged herself to re-negotiate these boundaries. The Vision Julian received at the age of thirty and a half seemed at first an answer to Julian's prayer as a youth for three graces. However, her reflection on the content of this Vision through her engagement with Christ, Crucified and Risen, provided a frame of reference to re-negotiate the boundaries of faith, freedom and identity.

---

[20] All references to prophetic action in this chapter are inspired by the presentation of Joan Chittister at the Melbourne Town Hall (12 May 2022). Well-grounded in her Benedictine charism that identities even the care of the young and aged in the Benedictine Rule in the context of wise governance and care of the whole community, Joan's prophetic voice cuts across a multitude of blind spots we are all prone to as we aspire to follow Christ in the vocations we have embraced whether married or single, religious, lay or ordained.

Call to wisdom: living beyond the boundaries of faith, freedom and identity

It is well documented that the central motif at work in the *Revelations* is the Passion. The Christ that Julian engages with is the crucified Lord of Glory. Julian's encounter with Christ in her Vision is not unlike that of the Resurrection account of Thomas and Christ (John 20). Christ's wounds are still visible on the Risen Christ. Thomas is invited to see the holes made by the nails in his hands and feet, to touch the wounded side of Christ. Julian is exhorted by her Curate to find comfort on her death bed by gazing at the image of her Saviour, the Crucified Lord (LT 3) . Yet, in her Vision, the Risen Christ, the wounded Healer, invites Julian to sweetly behold and enter Christ's wounded side. She is invited to sweetly enjoy the heart – broken open – for love of humanity (LT 24). Christ desires to bring peace to Thomas as he declares 'Peace be with you'. Christ desires Julian to find not only peace, but rest in the great love of Christ symbolised in the outpouring of blood and water from his side. The graphic depictions of Christ's Passion in the *Revelations* open up as great acts of God's might, wisdom and love. Wisdom is the attribute best aligned with Christ in Julian's understanding of Christ as the Second Person of the Trinity.

Yet, Julian welcomes in the Divine Feminine by bringing together Christ as Deep Wisdom and Christ as Mother in one unified understanding. Thus even the scene described above where both Thomas and Julian are invited to touch into Christ's wounds, Julian discovers in Christ's wounded side and broken heart – a place for the re-birth of our souls in the rest, peace and love of Christ.

In her own way, Julian calls us to wisdom for living beyond the boundaries of faith, freedom and identity. However, the way in which we are to embrace this call is to follow her into the deep heart of Christ to first rest our wounds and find healing in the peace of Christ's love. In bringing our wounds to rest in Christ's wounds, there is healing, and the re-birthing of the desires that we carry with longing in our hearts. This longing is itself the expression of the Godly will within us. Christ Deep Wisdom who is also our Mother – in Julian's theological understanding – draws us to trust Christ's presence within us. For our innate capacity for God holds this treasure in us where Christ dwells in rest and peace. In embracing this call by first seeking Christ Deep Wisdom within our soul, we can then move to the prophetic task of facilitating the opening up of new windows of faith, freedom and restored identity.

- Regarding faith: let us embrace those at the margins, listen to them and to the Spirit in the liminal spaces where the deeper spirit has a wound of longing.

- Regarding Freedom: let us be genuine in our search for God and our care of others. Let us embrace vulnerability... it's something precious we share with each other.

- Regarding identity: we belong to God first and ourselves next... if we wish to minister to others, treat them as we would ourselves... then we will truly be God's beloved.

Julian's words of life, her 'wisdom distilled' at her window and through her writings enfolds us in God's hospitality which in us becomes an authentic way of being with ourselves in God, and in God and ourselves – with others. Julian's distilled wisdom is ultimately the Wisdom Christ she shares with her readers and visitors to her window. The Wisdom Christ is Lord of our faith, our freedom and our identity.

Appendix.
Julian's writings: Revelations of Divine Love (LT 1)[21]

The **first showing** revealed his crown of thorns. This showing described the Trinity in detail, as well as the Incarnation, and the essential unity between the human soul and the Divine. I received many beautiful revelations of love and teachings of boundless wisdom here. All the showings that followed are rooted and connected in this first one.

The **second showing** revealed the darkening of his lovely face, which symbolised his supreme passion.

The **third showing** revealed that our God – who is almighty and all-loving and the embodiment of wisdom – created all that exists and is the cause of everything that happens.

The **fourth showing** revealed the lashing of his tender body and the copious blood he shed.

The **fifth showing** revealed that the precious passion of Christ overcomes the spirit of evil.

The **sixth showing** revealed that our God rewards all his blessed servant with profound gratitude in the world to come.

The **seventh showing** revealed that both joy and suffering are bound up with the human experience. When we are illumined by grace and touched with well-being, we believe that our joy will never end. When the sadness and weariness of life descends on us, we are tempted to believe that this, too, is endless. But we take refuge in a deep inner knowing that just as God's love uplifts us in joy, it protects us in sorrow.

The **eighth showing** revealed the final sufferings of Christ and his cruel death.

---

[21] Starr, *The Showings of Julian of Norwich*, 3-5.

The **ninth showing** revealed the outcome of Christ's terrible passion and heartrending death is the pure delight that infuses the blessed Trinity. He wants us to take comfort in this and be happy with him, until the time comes when all things are made clear to us in heaven.

The **tenth showing** revealed that the heart of our Lord Jesus has been broken in two for love.

The **eleventh showing** was an exalted revelation of his blessed Mother.

The **twelfth showing** revealed that our Lord is the supreme source of all life.

The **thirteenth showing** revealed that our God wants us to deeply appreciate the magnificence of what he has done and truly cherish all that he has made, especially the excellence of human life – since he placed human beings in charge of all creation-and acknowledges the precious amends he made for our shortcomings. He transformed all our blame into everlasting honour. In this showing he said, 'Behold! By the same power, wisdom and goodness that I have done all this, I shall make well all that is not well. You will see this for yourself'. He also revealed that he wants us to have faith in his holy community and not demand that he disclose all his secrets now, but trust that we will know whatever we need to know in this life.

The **fourteenth showing** revealed that God is the ground of all our seeking. Two great things are contained in this single truth: one is the perfection of our prayer; the other is the importance of faith. In this way, our prayer becomes his joy, and the emptiness of our longing is filled with his goodness.

The **fifteenth showing** revealed that one day all our pain and sorrow will be lifted and his goodness will deliver us to a place where he will offer himself as our reward and we shall live with him in everlasting bliss.

The **sixteenth showing** revealed the Creator, in the form of the blessed Trinity and contained within our redeemer, Christ Jesus, eternally dwells in our souls. From this place, he righteously rules over all things, rescuing and protecting us with his wisdom and power. For the sake of love, he prevents us from succumbing to the spirit of evil.

Promises and Pitfalls

Gideon Goosen

Introduction

As can be seen in the previous volume in this series, *We too: The Laity Speaks!*,[1] the Catholic Church is in turmoil. The two main contributing factors to this turmoil seem to me to be the decline in membership numbers (down from 27% in 2001 to 23% in 2016) and in church attendance over a number of decades (now down to just over 10%), and secondly, more recently, the calamitous revelations of sexual abuse of minors by members of the clergy not only in Australia but throughout the world.

In Australia, this has given the ACBC[2] ample reason to call a Plenary Council to address 'the specific needs of the time' as it has done in previous years.[3] Canon Law (#439) allows for Bishops Conferences to call for a plenary council with the Pope's approval, and to determine 'the matters to

---

[1] *We too: the Laity Speaks!* ed. Berise Heasly & John D'Arcy May, Melbourne: Coventry Press, 2020.

[2] The Australian Catholic Bishops Conference.

[3] Cf. 'The Plenary Council and Canon Law', Ian Waters, *The Australasian Catholic Record*, Vol. 95 Issue 4, Oct. 2018, 399-411.

be considered'. One would think and hope the matters to be discussed in 2021 are obvious to all.

The turmoil in the Catholic Church has given rise to demands for reform. The reform goes beyond the Catholic Church in Australia and hence concerns global leadership. After the conservative reign of Pope John Paul II and then Pope Benedict XVI, some serious issues are finally getting the attention they need by the leadership of Pope Francis. Not that he is going to be able to achieve everything in his papacy. All this is taking place in a global context where change (social, technical, political, religious and moral) is comprehensive[4] and forever accelerating ('rapidification'[5]), while humanity is being threatened by a pandemic, climate change (better 'climate emergency') and some outbreaks of political madness.

The aim of this chapter is to reflect on the efforts to renew, reform, revitalise, and, better, 're-generate' the church so that it can once again be seen to be what it is called to be, a sign of hope. I will do this by identifying the promising signs of re-generation before tackling the dangers or pitfalls. The nature of these promises and pitfalls includes plain and obvious facts such as 'the Australian Catholic Church is multicultural', as well as procedural and attitudinal factors which can sometimes overlap. My focus is mainly on the Catholic Church in Australia in the context of the Plenary Council, but it will be obvious that much applies globally.

---

[4] Pope Francis, *Laudato Si'*, Encyclical Letter, (London: The Incorporated Catholic Truth Society, 2015), #102.

[5] Pope Francis, *Laudato Si'*, #16.

Open discussion

The first sign I see that is promising is that of the possibility of frank and open discussions. I mean this at all levels of church life from the Roman Curia to the parish council. We have reason to be hopeful about open and frank discussions in the church because of the leadership of Pope Francis. We can trace our hope back to the Synod of Bishops in Rome in 2001, according to Christopher White.[6] At that time, Francis was simply Archbishop Bergoglio from Buenos Aires. He was adjunct relator (organiser) to the main relator to the Synod, Cardinal Egan of New York. When Cardinal Egan was eventually allowed to go back to New York after 9/11, Bergoglio became the relator of the Synod. This was the turning point for the rise of Bergoglio. The job enabled all the participants (bishops and cardinals) to get to know Bergoglio better. What they saw they liked. If we fast forward in history to the 2013 conclave after the resignation of Pope Benedict, the voting cardinals were convinced Bergoglio was their man.

When Bergoglio took over as relator, his manner contrasted sharply with what had gone before. The manner in which the centralist governance of the Roman Curia handled meetings and synods was to control everything. Control the agenda, control the speakers, do not allow any topics other than those on the agenda.

I can recall an example of this control which relates to Australia. An Australian theologian, who had been nominated

---

[6] This insight comes from an article by Christopher White, 'How Sept.11 inadvertently paved the way for the future election of Pope Francis', NCR 9 September 2021, http: https://www.ncronline.org/news/people/how-sept -11-inadvertently-paved-way-future-election-pope-francis, accessed on 16 September 2021.

to be a member of the International Theological Commission, told participants at an ACTA[7] conference that he had resigned from the Commission because, whenever he went to Rome for a meeting, the agenda had already been fixed, the speakers chosen and all that he was asked to do was sit and listen. At no stage did anyone ask for his experience or what were the issues in the Australian church.

Thus all meetings and synods were pre-fabricated events with no real consultation. Many bishops throughout the world had had enough of this control including the Archbishop from Buenos Aires. Regarding the 2001 Synod, Bergoglio is quoted as saying:

> I was rapporteur of the 2001 synod and there was a cardinal who told us what should be discussed and what should not. That will not happen now.[8]

Now as leader, Pope Francis is showing great leadership in spite of traditionalists resisting change and even working actively against him.

Synodality

Another important aspect of this new approach is synodality about which much has been written. It was an attempt to bring the church together as a group and listen to each other so that they could act together. This is in contradistinction to a secular parliament where the atmosphere is adversarial and each party tries to force its opinions on others or simply outvote them. Much has been written about the meaning of synodality,

---

[7] Australian Catholic Theological Association.
[8] C. White, op.cit.

'walking the road' with someone, so I will not pursue the matter here. The opposite would be a dictatorial, highhanded, or authoritarian style. A classic example of this latter style was the issue of artificial birth control in 1968 when Pope Paul VI, having received the results of the consultation of experts, decided to go the other way and ban artificial birth control. This is the antithesis of synodality and makes a mockery of consultation. Pope Francis has also warned us to avoid the 'three risks' in synodality: 'formalism', 'intellectualism' and 'complacency'.[9]

In the lead up to the Australian Plenary Council which opened in 2021, there were some who wanted to stick to the exact parameters for the Plenary and avoid difficult topics such as women pastors, celibacy and ordination, and divorced and remarried persons, to cite just a few issues. The process of consultation from individuals and groups which numbered over 17,500 led to the next step which was reducing the feedback to six themes. Many did not see the connection between the two steps, and this disconnect cast doubt on the consultation. The fact that the 17500 plus submissions were not made available to the public undermines trust in the process.

Young people will not be tied to old structures

By this I mean that young people are a lot freer in their approach to religion and its structures than the older generations. They do not feel obliged to attend a boring Mass where there is zero involvement for them. They are free from sectarianism, so

---

[9] 'Pope urges Church to leave behind "outworn pastoral models"', Read more at: https://international.la-croix.com/news/religion/pope-urges-church -to-leave-behind-outworn-pastoral-models/15028 , accessed on 12 October 2021.

they can appreciate a lively worship in another denomination. They are open to other world religions if they are genuine and have something to offer; they are accepting of different sexual orientations without the hang-ups of some Christians. They see that climate change is threatening their futures and accept women's equality in society. These are all positives and promise much for the future.

Young people will latch onto a new spirituality that is meaningful to them like that focused on creation rather than on pious practices. I think this is one of the most promising features of the spiritual landscape at the moment. It seems to dovetail with the general interest in society in the environment and climate change. At the same time, some younger people do get fixated on Latin Masses and the 'bells and whistles' devotionalism of the past.

Desire for change

Another promising aspect of our turmoil is the desire for change. The fact that some in the church want change is an indication that the organism, known as the church, is still alive; it is not dead. A worst-case scenario would be if no one wanted anything and just walked away. We have seen some do this. They have simply given up on the possibility of the Catholic Church reforming itself. There is also the phenomenon of Catholics who refuse to change and adhere to the past and old formulas of devotion. This suggests that the church (or part thereof) is dead in the same way that dry branches on a plant indicate that at least some of the plant is dead. Overall though, we can take courage and inspiration from the fact that in Australia and New Zealand we have twenty reform groups (composed of the ordained and laity) who espouse the challenge of reforming the church. They (ACCCR) have come together to form a coalition of reforming groups.[10]

The rise of feminism in society

The rise of feminism, not only in Australia but in much of the world, is another promising factor. It has given a great impetus to shaking up the misogynist attitudes found in the Christian church (as well as in society in general). In fact, the secular world is in some aspects moving on this issue with greater alacrity than the churches. The feminist movement is not going to go away; the issues will remain there until they are addressed. A proof of this came to the fore in the preparatory parish meetings where the issue of the role of women in the church and their ordination came up repeatedly. In spite of Pope John Paul II forbidding the very discussion of the issue (an impossible order if you think of it) and in spite of Pope Francis also saying it will not happen, women keep raising it. In passing, I note that the same Francis has moved to open up the role of acolyte to women as well as men. He has also appointed women to roles which are new to them in the church, like vice-chancellor of a university and secretary to bishops' synods.

The following little story encourages me regarding the role of women in the church. At a theological conference I attended in Europe some years ago, a Cardinal who had given the main talk, was asked by someone in the audience, if women would ever be ordained. He replied in a very diplomatic way. He said

---

10 ACCCR (Australasian Catholic Coalition for Church Reform). The role of ACCCR, established in 2012, is to foster collaboration and support among its member groups and to disseminate messages of hope and opportunity.

that we all knew the teaching of the pope at the time and he respected that. He also pointed out the evolution in the roles of women in the church over the last fifty years. He said the trajectory was only going in one direction – up. And he left it at that.

The sex abuse scandals

The sex abuse scandals have ironically given us hope that something will finally be done. Again a story that illustrates the problem. It relates to when the sex abuse stories first came to my attention. It was at a conference in Ottawa, Canada, towards the end of the last century. A group of us had gathered for a meal and to socialise. A pastor[11] from Canada was present and he told of one of the first sex abuse cases in Newfoundland. The parents of the child who was abused were beside themselves with anger and desperation at what had happened to their child. In desperation, they went to see their bishop who has pastoral care over all in the diocese, they assumed. To their dismay, the bishop said he could not talk to them about the 'case', and they should immediately get a good lawyer. They could not believe their ears! Here was their bishop who should show pastoral care, giving them a legal response!!

Other than highlighting the precedence of legalism over pastoral care in the church, it galvanised many lay people to take action. Had the bishop or other pastors had their own children, their response might have been different. Today,

---

[11] I use 'pastor' rather than 'priest'. Priest suggests a cultic role whereas pastor emphasises the pastoral role. Using 'pastor' will also help in the elimination of clericalism. It is not a question of rejecting the cultic role but in changing the emphasis which promoted a certain clericalism.

there are still bishops who appear not to have realised the seriousness of what happened. Let me give one example. When the report of the commission came out in Australia, I would have expected the Australian Catholic Bishops' Conference to call a meeting to focus on the report. Instead they did nothing and waited for their next regular conference. This was like being told your house is on fire and replying: I'll wait and come around later to have a look!

Had there been no sexual abuse scandal, I think reform would have been even harder. It has certainly motivated many people to call for a pastoral orientation in the church and to reject clericalism, misogyny, arrogance, authoritarianism and demand better governance[12] in the church.

Cultural Catholicism

Cultural Catholicism is also a factor to be considered. It does have a promising aspect which we will come to shortly. By the term 'cultural Catholicism', I mean the way religion has been passed on as a cultural phenomenon. Individuals are born into a family and born into the religion of that family. In Catholicism, it means being baptised, going to a Catholic school, being introduced into certain sacraments, attending Sunday Mass and above all learning all the correct answers in the Catholic Catechism - which latter seems to make religion a cognitive exercise. This is what you do if you are a Catholic. One can do all this without necessarily being convinced of any religious truths or values. In Australia, it also meant

---

[12] Such as suggested in the thorough report called, *The Light from the Southern Cross: Promoting Co-responsible Governance in the Catholic Church In Australia* (2020). It was published by The Australian Catholic Bishops Conference and Catholic Religious Australia.

voting Labor but this aspect no longer applies. Catholicism as a cultural value has faded. Just think of how today many children are prepared for first communion while their parents do not attend church and know little about their faith. The parents have little or no Catholic culture to pass on to their children.

Today many have felt that they are not getting the spiritual nourishment from their Catholicism and are looking for some deeper spirituality. Attending a pastor-centred Mass has become boring and some parishes no longer provide the spiritual nourishment they long for. The devotions of the past (rosary, novenas, adoration of the Blessed Sacrament, Holy Hours) in many cases, do no satisfy the spiritual hunger of today.

Karl Rahner is often quoted on this issue of looking for a deeper spirituality when he said that future Catholics will be mystics or they will be nothing. So it is not surprising that many today explore a mystical spirituality. Some people (perhaps not many) are taking to meditation, spiritual book clubs, reflection groups, biblical studies. They are reading and meditating on the writings of authors like Rahner, Bodo, Rohr, Chittister, Steindle-Rast and others. They are also learning from Aboriginal spirituality. It is interesting to note that having once seen Aboriginal culture as barbarian and backward, western society is turning to first Nations to learn from them how to relate to the natural environment. There are many authors in Australia who probe into this area of study and learning from a post-colonial viewpoint, such as Ungunmerr,

Rainbow Spirit Elders, Fletcher, Stockton, Pascoe, Sutton, Walshe.[13]

The movement away from a cultural Catholicism to a genuine living out of what it means to be a Catholic Christian in Australia today is the promising aspect of this movement. It could mark the coming of age of Australian Catholics. It will perhaps mean a decrease in numbers but a new and deeper level of religious commitment.

Environment consciousness

One final comment can be made which brings with it a promise of better things to come. The rise of environment conscientiousness and ecological conversion to save our planet from disastrous climate change is on the increase. There is a greater appreciation and an increased awareness of the interconnectedness of all creation. This awareness overlaps national, religious, racial, gender and continental boundaries. The new perspective on humanity and the road ahead is clearly described in the inspiring encyclical of Pope Francis, *Laudato Si'*! This promises to be a solid and inclusive platform on which to build the future. This document ought to be studied and reflected upon in every parish as it ushers in a new plan for living and will inspire the younger generation as they think about their future. The threat of extinction through climate change and now the covid-19 pandemic, has thrown humanity

---

[13] Peter Sutton and Keryn Walshe, Farmers or Hunter-Gatherers? The Date Emu Debate, Melbourne: MUP, 2021). Bruce Pascoe, Dark Emu, Broome: Magabala Books 2014. Eugene Stockton, The Aboriginal Gift: Spirituality for a Nation, Alexandria: Millennium Books, 1995. Frank Fletcher, Jesus and the Dreaming, Strathfield: St Pauls, 2013.

on its heels as it is forced to stop and think. This pause brings with it a potential promise for a new way of living.

This awareness of all things being connected is often referred to as creation spirituality. This awareness prompts Christians to look for a more satisfying spirituality that links up with our present understanding of science, the environment, and cosmology.

Cover-up

Now we move on to some of the pitfalls of the reform movement as I see them. Let us look at the dangers or pitfalls that lie on the pathway to reform. There is always the possibility that the clergy will seek to pretend the situation is not as bad as some make it out to be and try another cover-up job. They might become defensive and refuse to face what is a huge challenge. We have seen the cover-up approach regarding sexual abuse in the church which many bishops tried. This did not work because many in the church – ordained and lay – have learnt to speak out. The clergy might well claim that the changes that are suggested are beyond their authority to realise, and therefore they will do nothing. Slowness to grasp the seriousness of the situation is another stalling process. The pitfall is to accept these excuses instead of continuing to speak out. A speaker like the prophetic Benedictine nun, Joan Chittister is insistent on continuing to speak out.

We can also understand why there is a lack of leadership. The criteria for appointing bishops have been loyalty to Rome (meaning the Pope and Curia) and a good background in Canon Law. Bishops were never appointed because they had the gift of challenging the institution, or because they sought the truth (*parrhesia*). Without stating it in so many words, it looked very much as if the reputation of the church was more important that the gospel. I can recall a certain bishop saying, after being installed as bishop, that his number one commitment was to the church. At the time I thought to myself: surely it should be to Jesus Christ and the gospel. The priority of loyalty to the church was transparent in the way church officials responded to the sexual abuse cases.

Power points

Cover-ups happen when people are aware they have the power to cover-up.[14] There must be the chance of being successful in a cover-up otherwise it would not be attempted. This brings me to the key question of power in the church. It is a topic few in the church wish to discuss. It is either not a problem or it is too mundane a topic to associate with the holy church. Although the use and abuse of power is relevant to pope and parishioner, I see two main power points requiring immediate attention: bishops and pastors.

Some cardinals and bishops in recent years have mentioned the need to restrict the power of bishops and pastors. It is clear to me that if bishops were accountable to a group of people as well as to the pope, things might be different. At the moment, a bishop needs to keep in the Pope's good books otherwise he could be dismissed. He is not responsible to the national bishops' conference or to any other body. This

---

[14] The abuse of power leads to a lack of trust in the people as the renowned psychologist Dacher Keltner asserts in his book, *The Power Paradox: How we Gain and Lose Influence* (Penguin Books, 2016), 99-136. The cover-ups and lies regarding the sexual abuse scandal has led to further erosion in the laity's trust of the hierarchy.

is a mistake. It is not good governance. If a bishop were accountable to a group of elders (lay and ordained), he would have to report accusations of sexual abuse. He would not be able to procrastinate. If all in the diocese knew about this body of elders and its role, it would put a check on the powers of a bishop.

Likewise, a parish pastor ought to be responsible to a group of local elders as well as to the bishop. Currently pastors seem to be unrestricted as to what they do, as long as they keep in the bishop's good books. The choice of elders and their exact powers would have to be carefully worked out but they would introduce a system of checks and balances to a medieval system that needs upgrading.

This suggestion of a system of checks and balances would be hotly contested because in human affairs no person in a position of power willingly gives up some power.

The different global context

The different global context in which we live today is something to consider carefully. It would be a big pitfall if it was not taken into consideration when thinking of the church of the future. There can be no returning to business as usual.

Compared to the recent past as in Vatican II and the 1960s, many things have changed, not only in the Catholic Church but in society as a whole. Within the Catholic Church, patterns of church attendance in the Catholic Church have declined, biblical studies has progressed and caught up with Protestant scholars, theology does not accept Thomism as the main, or only, theological framework for theologising; rote learning the catechism is rejected as the best way to teach children about their faith; Pentecostalism has grown in size and the charismatic approach has been accepted formally in the Catholic Church at Vatican II.

The Catholic Church in many countries is no longer the dominant religion and has lost much of the societal authority it enjoyed in the past. Whereas in the past the majority of Catholics were white and found in Europe, today the majority is people of colour and found in Africa and South America. Whereas the Catholic Church in ages past was looked up to for moral guidance, its moral standing in the world after the sexual abuse scandals and cover-ups has, understandably, plummeted.

In society in general, institutions are viewed with suspicion, the gap between rich and poor countries has widened, refugees are a major concern in many parts of the world, and the events of 9/11 still haunt countries. Climate change is a global threat as humanity contemplates its extinction if global warming goes unchecked. United Nations seems at times to be inadequate to maintain global peace. Social media has positive and negative aspects, like spreading false news and promoting popularism. Democracy is under threat in many countries; issues arising from colonialism persist in some places. Peace is constantly at risk in many parts of the world.

The Catholic Church has got to find a way of being realistic when addressing problems in this global context. It is no good to apply solutions that have worked in the past to an environment that is very different. The church cannot conduct business as usual. Spiritualities of the past may not be what will inspire people today. This is where one needs to remind oneself that what is needed is a 're-generation' of the church, not a band-aid application. Actually, words like 'renewal', and 'reform' may suggest the latter, but 're-generation' suggests new shoots coming out that were perhaps unthinkable in former eras.

Myopic attacks on the clergy

There are many groups of people involved in trying to change the church. The laity are obviously the largest group. However, I note that there is a real danger that some sections of the laity are turning this revival movement into an attack on the clergy and especially bishops as they are the persons in authoritative positions. (The bishops do have to change and we will come back to this shortly) These attacks can be very myopic. The point is that we all have to change our ways. We are all called to conversion. There seems to me to be the unspoken assumption by some reformers that if some teachings were changed tomorrow, all our problems would be solved. Thus, for example, if the bishops decided divorced and remarried persons could go to the sacraments, all would be well in the church, or, if *Humanae Vitae* was repealed, all would be fine. This is a mistaken notion of church 'regeneration'.

There can be no renewal unless everyone is prepared to start with themselves. No one is denying that the bishops need to change, but so do we all. One example I can give is this. Good parishioners have become accustomed to relying on the parish pastor for everything regarding their faith. They are happy to be told what to read, what prayers to say, what devotional customs to follow, what to do. Can they now become more independent and creative in their faith? Can they be creative in re-generating their faith and communities?

Regarding the tendency to attack one section of the church is demonstrated by the careless use of the word 'church', as in the sentence: *the 'church' has done nothing,* or: *the 'church' has covered things up.* What is meant is that the hierarchy has done nothing, or bishops have covered-up, or the Curia in Rome has covered–up. Often it seems to me when the laity say 'the church must change', they mean the hierarchy must change, and exclude themselves. There is the danger that in calling for reform, the laity are not including themselves. It would help discussion if the word 'church' is not used when what is meant might be *bishops, the pope, laity, clergy, the hierarchy or the Curia*.

Above, we said the bishops do have to change. Let me refer back to the opening section in this article on 'Open Discussion' where Archbishop Bergoglio, as relator, said he did not intend telling the bishops at the synod in Rome what topics they could, and could not, discuss. The Australian bishops need to convert to this open-minded approach. The fear is that with the restrictions around a canonical Plenary Council, they could use it to restrict and control the agenda of the Plenary Council and then, as only they have deliberative votes, they can make their decisions. A restricted agenda already seems likely with the diminution of the 17,500 odd submissions nation-wide to six themes which are written in a document in language very different to the submissions.

Repeating old model

Another possible pitfall is that reform groups will mirror the old model of operating. The older generation grew up with a very authoritarian church where one had to conform or be ostracised. This was the case with parish pastor, the bishop and the pope. In Rome, the Curial department ('dicastery' in Roman language) known as the CDF (Congregation for the Doctrine of the Faith[15]) was the most feared of all the Roman congregations. In reality, they were the heresy hunters.

---

[15] Established in 1542, it was formerly called 'Supreme Sacred Congregation of the Roman and Universal Inquisition' or 'The Holy Office'. It was founded to protect the church from heresy.

The way they exercised their task was a model sometimes reflected by bishops who were looking for promotion. So if a bishop showed he was strong and confronted theologians who wrote ambiguous sentences, they could denounce him in an authoritarian way. I recall one archbishop who said the accused pastor could get as many canon lawyers as he wished, but he (the archbishop) would decide if he were a heretic or not.

So, the danger is that reform groups consciously or unconsciously might mimic this adversarial approach. They might be too keen to ostracise anyone who does not agree with their approach to reform. There must be room for inclusiveness and patience and a desire to listen to others; otherwise, we are simply swapping one set of authoritarianism for another. At some point, though, the church needs to lead groups into a post Vatican II church. If people want to be part of the church community there must be broad parameters that define it.

Let me add an additional note. It has been very noticeable how Pope Francis from his instalment as Pope has played down the importance of the CDF and is not interested in heresy hunting. Evangelization is his passion. The church should be about preaching the gospel and doing the gospel, not heresy hunting.

Expectations of reform can be too high

That the expectations of reform can be too high is a possibility because the need for change has become so obvious, and the damage so serious, that people are demanding and expecting change. The sexual abuse cases are an example. People will not accept anything less than strong action. We have still to see that. It has taken the Vatican a long time to take strong action. Some bishops still do not seem to understand the seriousness of the issue nor have any empathy for the victims. However, there are other aspects to reform where expectations are strongly felt: liturgy, church governance and role of women in the church, clericalism, and others. Here is where history can be a guide. We can recall that historical reforms are seldom complete. In fact we need only to go back to Vatican II in 1962-5 and remind ourselves that not all the changes brought in by Vatican II have been fully implemented. Liturgy in some cases is still lacking in reform; ecumenical efforts are non-existing in some dioceses who might have a commission on ecumenism but do little or nothing to promote it. Some pastors and bishops seem anti-ecumenism; the same applies to interfaith dialogue. In my experience, there has been a striking absence of educating the parishioners in the teachings of Vatican II over the last fifty years or more.

If we go back further in history, one thinks of attempts to reform the clergy regarding celibacy. The First Lateran Council (1123–1153) brought in the law forbidding pastors in the Latin rite to marry. Has this worked? Obviously not, and it continues to be on the agenda for reform. Then there is the reform of monastic life. Bernard of Clairvaux thought the Benedictine life at Cluny was not strict enough, so he reformed them by founding the Cistercians. Later on a group of monks thought Bernard's order needed reform so they founded a group known as the Trappists.

The conclusion is that reform is never perfect and complete. So we can expect this wave of reform in the Catholic Church to be human and imperfect. That does not imply that reformers should not keep trying.

Listening can be superficial

Another pitfall is that what is referred to as 'listening' can be superficial. This obviously applies to all in the church leaders and followers. Listening implies a genuine effort to hear what the other is saying and thinking it over. It might mean no resolution and further listening required. As the Uniting Church in Australia has discovered, listening and consensus can be painfully long-winded. Authoritarian decision-making is a temptation. An enlightened despot has historically had its attractions.

This also means that voting should not be seen in the secular sense of putting down the opposition or winning a contest. It will be a big ask to change from the secular adversarial approach which is taken in parliament. The new approach of synodality is a new skill which church members will have to learn.

Consumerism

With this goes the idea that the laity also has the problem of being tainted with consumerism. We live in a society that is secular and consumerist. It is not surprising if the consumerist attitude becomes part of the attitudes we bring into the faith community. By that I mean we can easily begin to demand certain services from the church as religious consumers. Let me give a real-life example. A certain bishop wanted to cut down the number of Masses in a particular parish because of a lack of numbers. One old parishioner objected very strongly saying he had always had a vigil Mass on a Saturday, and he felt entitled to it and wanted it to continue.

Another example would be the attitude that the parish must supply all kinds of ministries which individuals see as services to which they are entitled because they put money in the plate. What is missing here is the vision that we all are part of a faith community and bring our gifts to share with others. The focus is on community not on the individual. The question is what can I offer? Not what am I entitled to receive? The consumerist society and western individualism is all about me and my needs and desires. The parish is about a community of equals who bring different gifts to share.

Multiculturalism

One pitfall that is often overlooked is that the church in Australia is very multicultural. I do not want to go into all aspects of multiculturalism, the meaning of the words such as assimilation, integration, diversity, racism, ethnicity, acculturation, inculturation... All I want to say is that the fact is that parishes are multicultural.[16] Not all, but many. In the diocese of Parramatta in Sydney, the second most-used language after English is Spanish. These are people from the Philippines, South America and Central America. The implications are that they practise their religion is a somewhat different way to Anglo-Celtics. Most of what I have read about renewal, reform in Australia regarding the Plenary Council is from the Anglo-Celtic perspective.

As the document *Social Profile of the Catholic Community in Australia Based on the 2016 Census* points out:

---

[16] Around half (51%) of all Australian Catholic parishes are multicultural according to a report in Catholic Outlook. 12 April 2018. Accessed on 27/9/2021. https://catholicoutlook.org/catholic-parishes-lead-the-way-as-multicultural-communities/

Catholics born overseas, especially those born in non-English-speaking countries, are likely to have different approaches to faith and spirituality, and different experiences and expectations of Church life, from those of Catholics born in Australia.[17]

The Australian Catholic Church of the present and future must allow for a great diversity of religious practices and spiritualities and reject the idea that the Irish-Catholic tradition is the only, or best, tradition in Catholicism.[18] Uniformity must not be imposed and confused with unity. The Eastern rites, such as the Ukrainian, Melkite, Maronite and Chaldean rites, have been with us for some decades and show us that there can be diversity in unity.

According to Dr Powell, a researcher for this NCL study, this has implications for leadership:

While cultural diversity in churches is a strength, it is critical that both church leaders and scholars continue to engage with underlying systemic issues, including the importance of diverse leadership.[19]

One can ask how many bishops in Australia are from non-Anglo-Celtic background? The answer would be very, very few. Perhaps the answer lies in the laity having a say in the selection of bishops.

---

[17] Australian Catholic Council for Pastoral Research *Social Profile of the Catholic Community in Australia based on the 2016 Census*, 2016, 17.

[18] J.J.Smolicz writing about the assimilationist attitudes of the Australian Church, cites the opinion that many locally educated clergy and religious were convinced of the inherent superiority of Catholicism in the Irish-Australian style. *Ethnicity and Multiculturalism in the Australian Catholic Church*, CMS Occasional Papers: Pastoral Series 8. Centre for Migrant Studies, New York 1988.

[19] *Catholic Outlook*, op.cit.

In conclusion, we can note that there are positives and negatives to be borne in mind when thinking about the Plenary Council and regeneration in general. The ideal is always to listen to the Spirit, but being humans, and noting historical attempts at reform, we need to bear in mind that the church is human and divine, and that often the all too human prevails. Let us hope and pray that on this occasion we have reached a *kairos*, a turning point, in church history.

A question of authority

Ian Hamilton

The reader may wish to skip or skim sections one and two and simply read the interpretive conclusions. These early sections are intended to lay the academic foundations for the more editorial style of the conclusions.

Some definitions

So as to aid clear exploration of some aspects of authority and power within the Catholic tradition, some definitional work is useful. First, a foundational distinction is between religion and spirituality: the former is expressed within some form of human organisation, while the latter is more personalised and, perhaps, idiosyncratic. That is not to say that people cannot share aspects of their spirituality, nor that every expression of spiritual belief needs to be unique. Oftentimes spirituality builds on the experience and wisdom of others. Furthermore, it is true that spirituality can be nurtured within a religious tradition, or conversely, exist independently of any explicit membership of a tradition.

For the purpose of this chapter, the relevant distinction is that genuine spiritual beliefs are rarely an evangelical phenomenon: rarely are they proclaimed in a bid to convince others of them. Consequently, they are not concerned with matters of power or authority. By contrast, religion is a human expression of some aspect of supernatural (numinous) faith. Because it is characterised by some form of organisation (one belongs to a religion in a way one does not belong to a spirituality), it involves aspects of group identity and individual identity within that group.

In Christian history, these matters of the identity of the group and individual identity within the group date back as far as the apostolic church. Acts 15 recounts the disagreement between some Judean Pharisaic converts and Paul (Acts 15:1,3) about whether only those circumcised could be disciples of Jesus. Issues of authority (and therefore of power) are as old as the church itself. Paul and Barnabas press the case for gentile membership (which, as we know, is the argument that won the day) but this was a challenge to the apostolic authority of the Jerusalem leadership.

The Acts of the Apostles tends to portray Peter as the leader of the early church but James, as 'a brother of the Lord', clearly had a strong claim too. He was stoned to death in 62CE but, before that event, Eusebius (c265-339CE), in our earliest church history text, describes him as the leader of the Jerusalem Church, and that he was replaced by Symeon, son of Clopas, whose mother was at the crucifixion (John 19:25). The least we can conclude was that authority was not solely Peter's. The tradition of tracing authority back to the apostles, and especially to Peter, may be said to be historically problematic, as discussed in more detail below.

One thing which a diverse range of Christian denominations have in common is that they wish to demonstrate that their form of governance has its roots in the canons of scripture. This is especially true of those evangelical Protestant churches who regard the sole source of revelation as the Bible (*sola scriptura*), but it is also true of the Catholic tradition which places great emphasis on the Petrine texts in Matthew 16:18ff.

Broadly speaking, there are two distinct forms of church polity. The first of these traces itself back to the leadership role of the bishop (*episkopos*). The second places greater emphasis on the elder (*presbyteros*). Whether or not these were always seen as separate roles is open to some debate,[1] but most scholars think that some combination of these roles, and that of practical ministers (*diakonoi*), were evident by the second century CE.

Both Catholic and Protestant apologists for episcopal or presbyterian polity like to justify their tradition with scriptural evidence. The former propose that the authority of bishops can be traced back to Christ and his 'investiture' of Peter as the rock (upon which a church will be built). By this reasoning Peter was the first among apostles. The text in question (Matthew 16:18) is seen as commencing an unbroken line of apostolic, indeed, Papal succession.

This reasoning is not without its problems and a brief discussion is appropriate.[2] The Petrine texts are normally cited as: 'And I tell you, you are Peter, and on this rock, I will build my church, and the gates of Hades will not prevail against it' (Matthew 16:18) and 'He said to him the third time, "Simon,

---

[1] David Edwards notes that: 'The letter to Titus envisaged *presbyteroi* in every congregation in Crete and also mentioned an *episkopos*. It seems that there was as yet no formal distinction between *episkopoi* and *presbyteroi* (in English, between bishops and presbyters). But neither was there complete equality: *presbyteroi* who worked hard as leaders, preachers and teachers could be paid double the normal stipend.' (Edwards, p. 31)

[2] The following five paragraphs were first written by me for 'Jesus rediscovered: Church reimagined' in *We too: The Laity Speaks!* (Coventry Press, 2020)

son of John, do you love me?" Peter felt hurt because he said to him the third time, "Do you love me?" And he said to him, "Lord, you know everything; you know that I love you". Jesus said to him, "Feed my sheep"'. (John 21:17). Although neither text has, strictly speaking, multiple attestations, they have been used as proof-texts for the role of the priesthood and the hierarchical clerical structures that have been built from interpretation of these pericopes.

As B. A. Johnson notes, early Christian writers were at variance about who exactly is 'the rock'. While Cyprian follows Tertullian in seeing Peter as the rock, later thinkers varied this interpretation. Augustine saw the rock as Jesus Christ, not Peter, while Chrysostom stressed the expression of faith ('You are the Christ') (Matthew 19:17)) as the rock. Johnson further notes: 'Origen believed that all who professed the same belief as Peter also could be called "rock". Indeed, he even held that those gifts which were conferred on Peter were no less conferred to any other believer!' J. C Fenton neatly aids us to understand the further words ('my church' – *'mou tēn ekklēsian'*). Bearing in mind that our English rendering comes from Aramaic via Greek,[3] Fenton reminds us that *ecclesia* may be translated as 'the people', 'the assembly', 'the congregation'. (Fenton, p. 269) Even a brief dip into exegetical scholarship,

---

[3] In *Confronting Power and Sex in the Catholic Church: Reclaiming the Spirit of Jesus*, Bishop Robinson spends time discussing the question of Jesus' 'perfect knowledge'. This is a difficult area of Christology, as he notes, and has implications for our insights into Jesus' understanding of himself and his mission. In general, it is true to say, that the synoptics do not present Jesus as having perfect foresight or even necessarily having a plan for the future of his work. It may be helpful, that is more accurate, to see him as a charismatic, prophetic reformer of Judaism, rather than as a founder of a meta-Jewish religion complete with institutional structures and a priestly caste. See Robinson, *Confronting Power and Sex in the Catholic Church: Reclaiming the Spirit of Jesus*.

and without any survey of views about the historicity of the pericope, seems to indicate strongly that Matthew 16:18 is a very poor proof-text for supreme Petrine authority and the ecclesiology the Catholic tradition has built on it.

It is also quite common to view John 21:17 as a commissioning of Peter and it is clearly so. But what is the context of the commission and the nature of the commission? First, this is not an historical encounter, in any normal sense of the word, as it is a post-Easter narrative about a post-Easter event, written for a post-Easter faith community. In it, Peter has an experience of the Risen Christ. The resurrection narratives present a rather enigmatic portrait of Christ who does not appear to dwell in time and space in exactly the same way as the historical Jesus did (consider Luke 24:36ff; John 20:19ff); whose disappearance from the tomb is seen as suspicious (consider Matthew 28:11ff) and is not readily recognised (consider Luke 24:13ff; John 21:4). This alerts the reader to be attentive to context and literary inferences.

The second important note is that this exchange may be read as much an admonishment of Peter as a praising of him. The Risen Christ seeks assurance three times (twice to love as *agapē* and once as the less demanding *philia*) which both recalls Peter's triple denial (Mark 14:66ff; Matthew 26:69ff; Luke 22:56ff; John 18:17ff) and seems to have the literary purpose of presenting Peter as a figure of vacillation, simplistic incomprehension and unreliability. A possibly divergent interpretation is given in catechetical style by the 'free Catholic online resource' Agapē bible study site.

Thirdly, what are we to make of 'feed my sheep'? We may take it as a familiar reference to pastoral care. It does imply attentiveness to the needs of the many and willingness to work for their welfare. It does not, intrinsically, denote authority over others. Interesting also that the Marcan commissioning has the Risen Christ showing himself to the Eleven and saying to *all* of them: 'Go into all the world and proclaim the good news to the whole creation.' (Mark 16:15). Both the commissioning and the commission are open-hearted and expansive. It is not by a caste for an elect (although the next verse does require that those who receive the Good News believe and be baptised).

The structure of Episcopal polity is obviously one in which a single leader (bishop) has pastoral, doctrinal and administrative leadership of a certain area (a diocese). He (or she, in some Protestant churches) exercises this role in a theoretically monarchical way, although most will take advice from senior priests and/or from a synod. Catholic Bishops are also answerable to Rome, if the Vatican curia becomes aware of an issue about which the Bishop has made a decision. The question of accountability, and synodic accountability in particular, is discussed in my conclusions.

Protestant apologists wish to present the view that it is presbyterian polity which is dictated by the scriptures. Writers such as L. Roy Taylor[4] typify this style of reasoning. Reference to Jerusalem elders (rather than the apostles) is found in Acts 11:30. Clearly, these were a group of believers who were trusted to act authoritatively (in this case to receive food contributions from the Antioch church, in the face of a prophesised famine). Other references to the pre-eminent role of elders include Acts 14:23; 15:2; 16:4; 21:18, Ephesians 5:17, Titus 1:5 and 1 Timothy 5:19. Some Protestant writers even cite practices within the Twelve tribes of Israel as Old Testament evidence to support the definitive role of

---

[4] In Cowan, Steven B., *Who Runs the Church?*

elders. L. Roy Taylor notes: 'Lay leaders who had gifts for leadership (Romans 12:8) and administration (1 Corinthians 12:28) served together with the pastors' (Taylor, p. 81). This fits with the evangelical practice of allowing non-ordained persons to lead worship and shape practices and policies. It also fits with the belief in the inerrancy of scripture, which is fundamental to much of Protestant thought. It also gives rise to Biblical literalism in some Protestant denominations, with its concomitant disregard of the context, form and complex authorship of many Biblical texts.

There are various forms of elder-based polity. In some Protestant churches a single person (usually a man) will be elected (or 'called') by the church to which he belongs, to be its chief teacher and preacher. This role may be extended to financial control and discipline of members, especially if the single elder is also the founder of that church. This model has been subject to abuse and scandal on occasions and, without strong accountability to the congregation (or other elders) can slide into a form of sect.

To guard against cultic devotion to the single elder, many churches devolve equal responsibility and authority to a group of elders. This may involve some form of election or discernment by the adults of the congregation. If the lines of polity lie within a single, discrete and local congregation, then these churches are accurately described as congregational.

If the local group of elders contributes to a presbytery of elders responsible for multiple congregations, then the structure may be described as presbyterian. The likely way in which this operates is that each local church has elected or 'called' its leadership and has a representative on the group of overseers who have responsibility for the good governance of several churches. These layers of polity could, and do, grow to cover a whole region or country.

While it is rare for Christian leadership to be a theocracy in the strict sense of the word (where there is no meaningful difference between the religious and secular realms of government), some church governance does overlap with secular authority. National churches, such as the Church of England, are a clear example, as the appointment of bishops lies with the duties of the monarch of the United Kingdom, although this is normally delegated to the government. The Pope has the status of a Head of State and until the abolition of the papal states (1870) had many functions of a secular governor.

A further refinement of church governance concerns the use of a synod. A synod may be defined as a council of church members (clergy and sometimes laity) whose role is to discuss and/or debate matters which require some manner of policy or decision. In episcopal polity, it is usual for the bishop to have a weighted vote but in theory, at least, it is a chamber in which views beyond those of the bishop may be aired and considered. The exact authority of the synod varies from denomination to denomination.

While a synod may be seen to have some parallels with a parliament, it is rare for Church governance to use the principles of secular democracy, for instance one member one vote. Some congregational churches may exercise this model but, definitionally, they only operate as discrete local churches. In most churches, decision-making is in some way centralised. This is probably the wisely workable way but can become problematic if an organisation is entirely self-referential (that is, the decision-makers are accountable to no one but themselves). Case studies from recent Catholic history illustrate some of the ways in which matters of governance and authority are central to our future authenticity as a Christian organisation. The four authors discussed below provide insights into some case studies.

Four authors

The late Emeritus Bishop Geoffrey Robinson begins his 2007 book *Confronting Power and Sex in the Catholic Church: Reclaiming the Spirit of Jesus* with a concise summary of abuse scandals. Sexual abuse of children was certainly not limited to the Catholic Church or, indeed, the Christian churches. It occurred in many other institutions and in private domestic settings. However, the Catholic Church has been seen as particularly culpable. Perhaps this is because it has presented itself as a forthright guide to morality, especially in bioethics and sexual conduct. Thus, the failure to protect vulnerable children seems a form of gross hypocrisy and profound betrayal of trust. Furthermore, some of the very pastoral and theological leaders who should have worked to lessen the pain and hurt of victims deliberately and callously preferred protection of what they perceived as the reputation (and prestige) of the institutional church to right action. The Royal Commission into Institutional Responses to Child Abuse was instigated by Julia Gillard in 2013. Its findings continue to be a source of consternation, even horror, for many Australians. Bishop Robinson may well have been even more damning in his criticisms of the church had the book been written after the report.

The abuse scandal and the cover-up scandal are not the only reason why concerned lay people are calling for a season (*kairos*) of reform, but they are a particular and sharp impetus to books like this.

Bishop Robinson makes clear that his purpose is wider than a response to abuse but he also frames it as something symptomatic of the need for charismatic leadership. In his introduction, he specifies that the Pope has the power and duty to lead in such matters and it is clear that he regards the then Pope (Benedict XVI) to have failed in that regard. More positively, he offers the fruits of his own discernment in chapters one to six. In chapter seven, he takes up the theme of authority, which is, obviously, also the primary focus of this chapter.

In his view, there are significant improvements available to the governance of the church within its present structures. I depart somewhat from this view for reasons which will be explained in the final section of the chapter. He places strong emphasis on the unifying role of the Papacy. Although he does not exactly endorse the traditional historical simplicity of Apostolic succession (Jesus commissioned Peter, and by implication the other apostles, to establish and lead an ecclesiastical institution), he does refer to the role of the Pope as the rock upon which much depends and through whom much can be achieved. He names three levels of governance: the whole people (the Body of Christ); a synodic or parliamentary level and a leader. He believes that there is too great a gap between these levels and suggests something like national presidents (traditionally called Patriarchs) who would be a conduit between, for example, a national church and its global leader.

This is a universal (catholic) perspective and has the merits and limitations of 'big thinking'. Its obvious merit is that it seeks to stress our unified and catholic identity. Its chief limitation is that the church is such a large institution that global synodic structures would probably soon transmogrify into another layer of complex, and dubiously effective, bureaucracy. In an attempt to lessen that tendency, he notes that one synod (which could have a diverse membership) could be charged with practical and pastoral matters, while another (probably with bishops and perhaps academic theologians) could deal with issues of moral teachings and faith. The difficulty is obvious: should matters such as annulment and divorce be discussed within a pastoral synod or a morals synod? The other difficulty with this model is that final authority rests with the Pope. Recent history has demonstrated that Popes often see themselves primarily as defenders of orthodoxy, rather than primarily as chief pastors.

One of the strengths of the late Bishop Robinson's reasoning is that he cites historical precedent (in 1215 the Fourth Lateran Council had participants other than bishops) to defend re-thinking the constitution of synods. He is also very clear on the process of good decision-making: it has two essential elements. The first is that announcements (or edicts) should always be based on the quality of the arguments presented, rather than a raw expression of power. The second is that the church should always be a place where decisions are reached prayerfully. Intelligent discernment, informed reading of Scripture and humility are foundational. We know that Jesus stressed sincerity over ritual, forgiveness over judgment and integrity over hypocrisy.

Many Australian Catholics will be familiar with the circumstances that led to Bishop William Morris' 2011 resignation from his role as the Bishop of Toowoomba. His book about the events (*Benedict, Me and the Cardinals Three*) was written in 2014 and though it has a different purpose to Bishop Robinson's book, it has some important light to throw upon any discussion of authority (and power) within the Catholic church. The essentials of the story are these: soon after Bishop Morris took up his appointment in 1993, he commenced a detailed process of assessment of the pastoral needs of the diocese (which covers 488,000 square kilometres). The Cathedral city of Toowoomba is at its far eastern edge. Like many other dioceses of the church, fewer priests were available to meet the needs of the faithful. By careful planning and implementation of a Pastoral Vision the bishop and his collaborators proposed to face reality and make alterations as needed.

The most obvious way to do this was to license existing lay talent to exercise leadership. These leaders would have focused training and work in collegial groups (normally including ordained members). The name given to such people was Pastoral Leaders and because they remained lay, they could be men or women of suitable charisms. The work asked of them sounds very like the work of the elders (*presbyteroi*) described earlier.

Some ultra-conservative Catholics within the diocese (self-nominated 'Temple Police') did not approve of this perceived blurring of leadership and authority (that is, ordained and lay people working in collegial equality) and wrote directly to Rome about any departure from what they interpreted as liturgical (rubrical) purity and zealous compliance with Church Law. Other particular practices – which caused dismay amongst some – included the use of General Absolution (Third Rite of Reconciliation). For reasons which I have never understood, this rite was removed soon after its creation. It was a communal prayer involving individual examination of conscience and sincere contrition. A single priest could then absolve the congregation *en masse*. It was often a beautiful spiritual experience and very suitable in many contexts, including school retreats. It could be argued that banning it destroyed the relevance of Reconciliation for almost all Australian Catholics. (A classic 'own goal' by the Magisterium.)

Under Bishop Morris' leadership, the practice was still sometimes permitted, according to the particular circumstances of his people. He was instructed to severely restrict (that is, abolish) the rite and he sought to do so gradually. His explanation and apologia (in reference to Canon law and Vatican II documents) fell on deaf ears. His two other 'grave errors' were to send a Pastoral Letter to his diocese in which he explicitly named options which could helpfully be considered for the future of the church. These are quoted below. He also chose to defend himself when investigated by a Visitator (discussed below) and it seems that this was seen by Rome as a failure of obedience on his part.

The Pastoral letter noted:

> Given our deeply held belief in the primacy of Eucharist for the identity, continuity and life of each parish community, we may well need to be much more open towards other options for ensuring that Eucharist may be celebrated; as has been discussed internationally, nationally and locally, the ideas of:
>
> - ordained married, single or widowed men who are chosen and endorsed by their local community;
> - welcoming former priests, married or single, back to active ministry;
> - ordaining women, single or married;
> - recognising Anglican, Lutheran and United Church orders.' (Morris, pp. 56-7)

It is clear that all that is suggested is a rational discernment of options. It is also notable that these ideas are examples of the 'reading the signs of the times' which was intended to follow from the deliberations of Vatican II. The bishop used his authority to 'think the unthinkable' and this was clearly seen as a profound threat to the 'right order of things' within the Church because it set in motion a series of events that led to his retirement (an outcome negotiated with the Pope as a substitute for enforced resignation).

In his detailed writings about the events, Bishop Morris relates the consequences of his openness. In short, he was assumed to be guilty of a lack of silent compliance. The Pope appointed an Apostolic Visitator (Archbishop Charles Chaput OFM Cap) to investigate the charges communicated by the 'Temple Police'. Although the visit was amicable at first, it was too brief for the Visitator to gain any real insight into the distinctive nature of the diocese or the sacramental needs of its people. Bishop Morris draws the conclusion: 'Unfortunately, Chaput was only interested in whether or not I was obeying the canonical and liturgical norms of the Church, and not how effectively the rite [of reconciliation] was pastorally.' (Morris, p. 77)

The bishop was also required in Rome to account for himself before three Cardinals. Several chapters of the book relate to the exact order of events and the documents that were prepared but not made available to the people of Toowoomba, or even the Bishop himself. As the famous theologian Hans Küng notes in his preface to this book: 'I note my personal impressions of these events from the personal trajectory of a similar Roman process. This looks all too familiar: It stands in contradiction to the most fundamental rules of 'due process' and Human Rights as laid down in the

General Declaration of Human Rights from 1948.' (Morris, p. xii). Bishop Morris himself notes that his unavailability to go to Rome on the dates nominated by the Curia, and his general demeanour of collegial equality, were probably the things that most irritated the Roman authorities, who expected their directives to be obeyed, rather than met with reasoned arguments (such reasoned responses are sometimes referred to as 'loyal dissent'). In any case, the story outlined in the book reveals a church still deeply entrenched in a model of hierarchical, feudal-like, masculine power structures, lacking in the safeguards provided by all members of an organisation being accountable for their decisions, at least by public disclosure of their deliberations and assumptions.

In *Between the Rock and a Hard Place*, Paul Collins notes the difference between authority and authoritarianism. He personally experienced a dispute with the Vatican's Congregation of the Doctrine of the Faith because of the views he expressed, while still a priest, in his book *Papal Power*. As happened to Bishop Morris, authorities wanted him to align his views with that of Roman clericalism. It seems fair to say that during the Pontificates of John Paul II and Benedict XVI, conservatives' voices were favoured and reformists' were not. The well-spring of open-minded engagement with the possibility of wise change that had, rather surprisingly, emerged from Vatican II clearly fell into disfavour. Such a situation emboldens the ultra-conservative to see themselves as guardians of what is right and true. Paul Collins expresses it in this way:

> They (fundamentalists) take an absolutist approach to faith and tend to see themselves as involved in a titanic struggle with the forces of evil represented by secular

modernity. They are people who feel cornered and are determined to fight back. Anyone who opposes them is demonised. They often see moderates who belong to their own faith as the worst traitors. Christian fundamentalism is a deeply patriarchal approach to religion, with women usually excluded from all leadership roles. (Collins, p. 181).

All this stands in disturbing contrast to the actions and words of Jesus and to the core message of the early preachers of the word. An overview of Paul's writing reveals his deep commitment to belief in the freedom of heart which comes from faith in Christ (for instance in 2 Corinthians 3:17). Repressive and oppressive behaviours, hypocritical actions, excessive pre-occupation with the prestige of the Church are all antithetical to such freedom of heart. Mary Ward (1585–1645)[5] had sage advice for her Sisters and, indeed all the faithful, about freedom and integrity. Her sayings have both pleasing cadences and succinct verity: 'Be such as you appear and appear such as you are'.

Paul Collins discusses various cultic expressions of Catholic fundamentalism and the common threat exposed is that such groups see themselves as superior to the ordinary faithful because of their purity of doctrine and gnostic-like insights into the mind of God. Some of these groups have in fact been condemned by Rome but the tendency to favour ultra-orthodox (an orthodoxy often extending to what may be argued to be the least important aspects of Christian tradition) over reformist voices is part of the frustration experienced by many of the 'people in the pews'.

---

[5] Her religious sisters are known by various names. In Australia and elsewhere, they are the Institute of the Blessed Virgin Mary (IBVM) or Loreto Sisters. In Germany and England they are now called the Companions of Jesus (CJ).

Gerard Windsor takes up these ideas in his book *The Tempest-Tossed Church* when he divides contemporary Catholics into two broad groups: the Laws and the Spirits. He notes: 'The primary battleground since the 1960s has been that of authority – how far does the hierarchy's right to compel obedience go?' (Windsor, p. 203). It is often noted that conservative reactions to the 'movement of the spirit' evident in Vatican II were largely successful in shutting down impetus for reform of the church. The decision to continue the ban on artificial contraception (*Humanae Vitae* 1968) caused some Catholics, especially women, to re-assess their loyal compliance. While Gerard Windsor's two groupings – and their disparate views of Christian authority – are helpful, I believe one could offer greater detail. For instance, the Laws include at least the following sub-groups: first, the benign conservatives who dislike change in general but are not especially confrontational or antagonistic; secondly, those who miss the elaborate Latin liturgy, piety and tribal identity of pre-Vatican II Catholicism and thirdly, Catholic fundamentalists. Interestingly, Catholic fundamentalism expresses itself as a zealous devotion to the magisterium, whereas Protestant fundamentalism expresses itself as a zealous devotion to the authority (inerrancy) of Scripture (*sola scriptura*).

Similarly, Windsor's 'spirits' have nuances of expression. I consider that there are at least three types of 'spirits'. First, there are those trained in modern theology, scripture studies and Historical Jesus scholarship who hope to separate the authentic Jesus tradition from later cultural and political accretions. Within this broad sub-group are feminist thinkers, especially those who see no reason why a woman may not be ordained a priest. Secondly, there are those who want to see a church in which change is discussed, rather than feared. It has been joked that Vatican II was the Church's opportunity to drag itself into the 16th century! (Admittedly some Protestant insights were finally acknowledged as relevant and worthy, and Galileo was forgiven in 1992). The third group are charismatics, who favour animated prayer, a personal style of emotionally candid faith and the key place of healing rites. Each of these groups within the Catholic laity are likely to have different understandings of the source and scope of clerical authority. In the final section of this chapter, I will draw together some ideas of where we are and what reforms could shape our future. Obviously, I will be writing from my own experience of church and my own intellectual and spiritual preferences. I readily acknowledge that these preferences are not held by all Catholics.

Some interpretive conclusions

The historical evidence about abuse, especially sexual abuse by clergy and religious, and the evidently deliberate 'cover up' of these crimes, makes it very clear that there are aspects of Catholic governance that require radical reform. Unfortunately, diverse allegations against very high-ranking church officials continue, so it is unwise to believe that the errors are all in the past and the solutions to failures of responsibility all in place.[6]

---

[6] Cardinal Giovanni Angelo Becciu is accused of crimes of embezzlement and misuse of office. 'Compulsive viewing as Vatican loses the plot': *Weekend Australian* 10/11 July 2021. Former (defrocked) cardinal Theodore McCarrick is charged with historical sexual assault. 'Former cardinal McCarrick charged with sexual assault': *Weekend Australian* 31 July/1 August 2021.

We know from the gospels that Jesus was deeply upset by religious hypocrisy: indeed, he tells a daring story in which a godless foreigner acts with greater integrity and compassion that a senior representative of Judaism (Luke 10:29ff). How is it then that men in great positions of responsibility within the Catholic church have, in small but significant numbers, failed to understand the scriptures? I believe the answer lies in the self-referential structures of our church. I mean by this that the senior clerics (and sometimes senior leaders of religious orders and institutes) surround themselves with people trained in the same way of thinking. It is the clerical caste who select who may train for the priesthood (usually in institutions deliberately disconnected from the wider world). It is the clerical caste who devise and administer canon law. It is the clerical caste who decide who is worthy of promotion (and demotion). It is the clerical caste who decide what legal advice to adopt in times of dispute and it is the clerical caste who decide what will be made public and what will be held in secret. It was rare (is rare?) for any of these important matters to be informed by outsiders' advice (except for legal advice – which is shaped according to the stated or implied perceived best interests of the client, and a legalistic mind-set).

It would be grossly wrong to suggest that all clerics – of high rank or low – are guilty of wrongdoing. In fact, quite the opposite is the case, I believe. Most priests and bishops are good men who work hard to promote the reign of God. The vast majority of religious men and women are figures of integrity, wisdom and prayerfulness. We live in a time when church leadership is a fraught undertaking; however, it continues to be a serious failure of leadership not to learn from the terrible harm done by a minority. It will be a serious failure of leadership not to see this time as a season of reformation.

Some episcopal voices do see it as this season. Bishop Vincent Long OFM Conv. delivered the 2021 Helder Camara lecture. He entitled it 'My hope for the Plenary Council' and his words are, indeed, a bright light of hope. He does not mince words: 'Nothing less than a root-to-branch reform that will align our minds and hearts to the Gospel will do.' He strongly critiques 'clerical hegemony' and notes pathways which the Australian church could, and should, follow. Notable among these is instigation of a body like the lay Central Committee which has, in his assessment, a 'key role' in the German Synodal Assembly. As noted below, I strongly believe that is a direction which the Australian Catholic church should take.[7]

Unfortunately, as I have suggested above, it is my observation that those whose view of faithfulness is dominated by adherence to doctrinal purity have placed the church in an unbalanced position. I suspect that such people have disproportionate influence on the way the Church acts (as evidenced by their influence in Toowoomba diocese). Saint Paul reminds us that if we are not open-hearted and open-minded then doctrinal purity counts for little (1 Corinthians 13ff). Many, if not most, of the promotions approved during the pontificates of John Paul II and Benedict XVI appear to have favoured loyalty to a 'perfected' church (with its concomitant prestige and implied inerrancy) rather than men whose highest purpose is compassionate and loving pastoral engagement with the world.

It is appropriate to note that much has already been achieved, although not necessarily as part of intentional

---

[7] Professor Gabrielle McMullen's response to Bishop Long's lectures is also elucidating. https://vox.divinity.edu.au/opinion/professor-gabrielle-mcmullens-response-to-bishop-vincents-2021-helder-camara-lecture/

reform. Many of the works of the church are carried out mainly, or entirely, by its lay members (especially if one includes religious sisters and brothers as members of the laity which, technically, they are). Most of the Church's work in education, health, welfare and social justice is undertaken by the unordained. There are also lay appointments to positions of authority and leadership (for example, as custodians of the continuing work of religious orders and institutes – in the role of Public Juridic Persons). It is a shame that rarely are those reforms announced and celebrated; perhaps too rarely are positions open to the normal application and interview processes common in the secular world. It would be a great day when the ordained leaders of the church were publicly happy to share their responsibilities and power. Such a day would betoken awareness that the *status quo* is problematic, as we have painfully learnt.

Having noticed that some changes are occurring, it is also obvious to me – and I'm confident that it is also obvious to other Catholics (lay and non-lay) – that the church is still an organisation dominated by an hierarchical ecclesiology.

What do we need to learn and how do we need to change?

First, we need to face the limitations, and indeed dangers, inherent in any self-referential institution. Such institutions are either unwilling, or incapable, of seeking wise counsel beyond their immediate peers. They are like a group of people all facing inwards; all concerned with their own perceptions and status. Too many in authority 'solved' the problem of priestly (or brotherly) sexual abuse by simply moving the perpetrator to another site. It is sadly clear that they placed the public prestige of the church above the needs of the known and future victims. They were not accountable to wise and honourable representatives of the wider church and so made harmful decisions.

Such hubris was aided by the implicit view that ordination was a conduit of special and exclusive grace: the priestly state automatically bestowed holiness. Clearly this was not so. A person's holiness depends on their graceful response to God as revealed by their commitment to Jesus' mission, a mission typified by faithfulness to God and loving compassion for others (Matthew 22:34-40; see also Luke 6:36-49; John 13:33ff). Any religious organisation where the worldly survival of the institution is more important that the integrity of its mission has lost its way. Secondly, I believe we can learn from the governance structures of other churches. This is not to say that there is nothing of value in the Catholic way of doing things, but that re-imaging the roles of *presbyteroi* and the *episkopoi* as practised in some Protestant traditions may be of value. At the very least, greater lay involvement in synodic decision-making should broaden the range of voices heard, so as to begin to include the wider church (the *sensus fidei*). As discussed earlier in this chapter, the work of Bishop Morris and his co-workers in Toowoomba is a good template from which to re-think collegiality and accountability. Wherever possible, decisions and the processes of decision-making should be a matter of public record.

Thirdly, one obvious way in which the softening of hierarchical dominance could occur is greater influence of qualified lay people in the selection of priestly candidates, parish staff and even bishops. Again, the work done in Toowoomba provides a starting point for discussion and implementation. I believe that the majority of Catholics look to leadership which is pastoral, compassionate and charismatic. That is not to say that faithfulness to tradition has no place in the selection of candidates, but it should not be allowed to be the dominant criterion. In any case, many lay Catholics would know that 'tradition' (e.g., priestly celibacy) is not actually ancient. Many would know that Church history is a complex set of ideas and events that are best understood within their particular contexts. Literalism, in its various forms, is not an aid to wise insights.

Fourthly, I suspect that many Catholics look upon the selection criteria for priesthood as unnecessarily rigid. To be a candidate one needs to undertake many years of full-time study in an exclusive institutional setting; one needs to embrace one's priestly state as a life-long commitment; one needs to accept life-long celibacy and to be male. It is possible to examine each of these criteria. Could we have more flexible methods of priestly formation? Could we have priests who have some form of secular employment to complement their priestly work? Could we seriously reconsider the rules of celibacy? Could we wonder out loud about the gender requirement upon which we currently insist? In these matters, we have much to learn from those churches who have already had these discernments. We know that the issues can be complex, divisive and heated. But if a two-thousand-year-old institution is not adult enough to engage in colloquia about them, it is a rather sad situation. Modern Catholics from liberal democracies are, I believe, unimpressed with the parental edict: these matters are not to be discussed! What is it of which we are afraid?

Fifthly, the reforms to priestly training instigated by the Council of Trent marked one intelligent and pastoral response to the Protestant reformation. If we agree that we are in another age of reformation, as we need to be, then reconsideration of how priests are trained, where priests are trained and the range of people involved in that training is eminently appropriate. A more detailed discussion of this is Chapter Five of Dr Heasly's book.[8]

Sixthly, of-course, the leaders of the church do have a duty to teach on matters of social justice and morality. However, the credibility of such voices has taken, sometimes unfairly, a battering. It is worthwhile, I think, to acknowledge that some of our moral traditions are different from many current mores and it is important to adopt a tone that shows awareness of that reality. Jesus is our clear guide in all of this (consider Mark 2:15-17). A church that allows itself to sound unforgiving and morally superior, especially about difficult bio-ethical matters, is unlikely to influence informed debate in the way it deserves to.

I have been somewhat reluctant to express these ideas for fear of sounding exactly as I criticise: intractable and oblivious to contrary voices. I have been privileged to have known many, many inspirational Catholics, many wise priests and to have been taught by great theological thinkers such as the late Denis Edwards. It has also been an honour to teach Religion and Ethics to hundreds of teenagers – not always an easy undertaking. These are the reasons I readily accepted the invitation to write this chapter and why I continue to embrace the Catholic tradition as my spiritual home.

---

[8] *Call No One Father*, Coventry Press, 2019.

Bibliography

Adams Jay E., *The Place of Authority in Christ's Church* (Hackettstown: Timeless Texts, 1994).

Brand, C. and Norman, R. (eds) *Perspectives on Church Government: Five Views on Polity* (Nashville: Broadman and Holman, 2004)

Collins, Paul, *Between The Rock and a Hard Place: Being Catholic Today* (Sydney: ABC Books, 2004).

Cowan, Steven B., *Who runs the Church?* (Grand Rapids: Zondervan, 2004).

Edwards, David L., *Christianity: The First Two Thousand Years* (London: Cassell, 1997).

Fenton, J. C., *Saint Matthew* (London: Pelican New Testament Commentaries, Penguin, 1963).

Ferguson E. (ed), *Church, Ministry and Organisation in the Early Church* (NY: Garland, 1993).

Heasly, Berise, *Call No One Father* (Bayswater, Vic.: Coventry Press, 2019).

Johnson, B. A.,*Is Peter the Rock? Early Interpretations of Matthew 16:18-19* https://owlcation.com/humanities/Who -Was-The-Rock-Interpretations-of-Matthew-1618 -and19-in-the-Early-Church (accessed 30 October 2019).

Long, Bishop Vincent, *My Hopes for the Plenary Council*. Helder Camara Lecture, June 2021. https://holytrinityqueenscliff.org.au/bishop-vincent-long-dom-helder-camara-lecture/ (Accessed 6 August 2021).

Morris, William, *Benedict, Me and the Cardinals Three* (Hindmarsh: ATF Press, 2014).

Osiek C, Macdonald Margaret Y, 'Women Leaders in Households' in *A Woman's Place: House Churches in Earliest Christianity* (Minneapolis: Fortress, 2004).

Robinson, Geoffrey, *Confronting Power and Sex in the Catholic Church: Reclaiming the Spirit of Jesus* (Mulgrave, Vic. Garratt Publishing, 2007).

Todd, John M., *Problems of Authority* (London: Darton, Longman and Todd, 1962)

Windsor, Gerard, *The Tempest-Tossed Church: Being a Catholic Today* (Sydney: Newsouth Press, 2017).

Yarnold, G. D, *By What Authority?* (London: Mowbray, 1964).

Tensegrity – the basis of created life today

Adrian Hubbard

In her earlier works, Dr Berise Heasly has proposed the concept of 'Edu Tensegrity' as a model to conceptualise her theory of education to counter the scourge of what she describes as 'binary thinking'.[1] The model proposes incorporating twelve 'Categories of Influence' into an overarching structural model based on the geodesic dome structures popularised by R. Buckminster Fuller in the late 1940s.[2] These spherical domes were built using a triangular lattice arrangement to distribute large stresses over a wide area.[3][4][5][6]

---

[1] Heasly B. *Towards an Architecture for the Teaching of Virtues, Values and Ethics.* Peter Lang International Academic Publishers, Bern, p. 179.

[2] Snelson K., 'Snelson on the Tensegrity Invention', *International Journal of Space Structures*, Volume 22, Number 1 & 2, p. 43.

[3] Snelson K. (2012) The Art of Tensegrity, *International Journal of Space Structures*, Volume27, Numbers 2&3, 71.

[4] The Geodesic Dome is the tensegrity model cited by Berise Heasly in her previous editions. This follows the same principles, but is not the same strut and cable model as the exoskeletal form often modelled in Biotensegrity.

[5] Snelson K. (2012) The Art of Tensegrity, *International Journal of Space Structures*, Volume27. Number 2&3, 71.

[6] https://www.bfi.org/about-fuller/big-ideas/geodesic-domes

Each aspect influences and supports one another and is equal in significance and importance.[7]

The concept of Tensegrity can be so simple that a small child can understand it. The strut and cable models that you are probably most familiar with are based on the work of the artist Kenneth Snelson who is acknowledged for designing a system of floating-compression structures (usually rigid beams bearing compression loads and wires/cables withstanding tension).[8][9] From 1959 he explored ways of extending the conventional kite frame, 'a sturdy, pre-stressed, triangulated, endoskeletal structure whose parallelogram shape is endlessly adjustable'. It is also a space-filling structure that can be repeated indefinitely by adding kite-frames module after module in all directions'.[10]

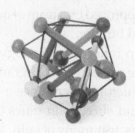

[7] Heasly B. (2015) *Towards an Architecture for the Teaching of Virtues, Values and Ethics*.

[8] Bordoni B, Varacallo M, Morabito B, et al. (2019) Biotensegrity or Fascintegrity? Cureus 11(6): e4819. DOI 10.7759/cureus.4819.

[9] Snelson K. (1996) The Art of Tensegrity, *International Journal of Space Structures* Volume22, Number 1&2. p.43

[10] Snelson K. (2012) The Art of Tensegrity, *International Journal of Space Structures* Volume27, Number 2&3, 72.

This is a picture of a toy I keep on my desk at work. Called a Skwish,[11] (designed by Tom Flemons.) it encourages infants to explore the interplay between tension and compression elements and marvel at its capacity to spring back after being squashed. Technically, it is a 20 faced Icosahedron. I can attest to the fascination it receives from young babies and their grandparents alike. I tell them that it is simultaneously a model of the bones and muscles as well as the connective tissue, right down to the skeleton of the individual cell and even its constituent parts.

In construction, the concept of 'framework' gives the sense of something strong and reliable, structurally sound, that will stand the test of time, be there for the next generation. It sounds like something that has been purposefully designed by a talented architect, engineered, looks beautiful, been thoroughly tested, approved by a team of qualified professionals, and built by a skilled builder.

Places of worship reflect the theology of their time. From austere Romanesque architecture to grand audacious Gothic cathedrals, these structures were once a sign of permanence and surety, safety and succour in times of peril. Once grand statements, witnesses, testimony of faith, strong, filled with the faithful, occupying prime locations overlooking or central to an emerging city, how awesome they must have been to the population when they were built? They now stand dwarfed by skyscrapers. Once bustling, the focal point, centre of people's lives, whether by fear or awe, many now stand empty...

Whilst some early adopters were enthusiastic about the potential of Tensegrity principles to be applied to architecture,

---

[11] https://www.manhattantoy.com/collections/skwish - Skwish model designed by Tom Flemons

you will probably note that you have not seen many examples of this type of tensegrity in modern building design. The reason is best articulated by the founder of tensegrity, sculptor Kenneth Snelson in 1990 – 'It is my belief based on long experience and making endless numbers of tensegrity structures of all shapes and sizes that the principle in itself is impractical for building buildings. As you know, many architects and engineers have worked toward that end and still do. Fifty years of it now. None have shown there is the slightest structural advantage'.[12] And he later continues 'As the engineer Mario Salvadori put it to me many years ago, "The moment you tell me that the compression members reside interior of the tension system, I can tell you I can build a better beam than you can"'.[13]

We are very used to looking at and building structures that rely primarily on compression for support. The brick wall is the classic example: one brick is piled on top of the other. This is a 'continuous compression' structure – where the compression created by gravity is carried from one brick to another, all the way to the ground. The bottom brick must be compressively strong enough to carry all the bricks above it.[14] Tensegrity structures are composed of localised compression struts held together by a series of continuous tension cables that hold the struts up and stabilise them against gravity.[15]

---

[12] Jáuregui V. G. (2004) Tensegrity Structures and their Application to Architecture. Thesis for MSc in Architecture, School of Architecture, Queen's University, Belfast. P. 72 also Appendix A. pp. 108-111.

[13] http://www.grunch.net/snelson/rmoto.html

[14] Myers T. (2011). *Anatomy Trains*. London: Urban & Fischer.

[15] Chen & Ingber (1999) Tensegrity and Mechanoregulation: from Skeleton to Cytoskeleton. *Osteoarthritis and Cartilage* (1999) 7, pp. 81–94.

Look to nature

Buckminster Fuller contended that 'all structures, properly understood, from the solar system to the atom, are tensegrity structures'.[16] supported by a balance between tension and compression, between 'push' and 'pull'. As such, tensegrity principles can be applied in many diverse fields such as architecture, sculpture, bridges, towers/masts, art, furniture, toys[17] as well as modelling body parts, organs, cell structure, even chemical and biological processes.[18] Used to conceptualise the mechanics of dinosaur and giraffe necks[19][20] down to demonstrating the structure of viruses, pollen and crystals.[21] Even the weave of the clothes you are wearing is a tensegrity of sorts.[22]

Living systems must be lightweight, strong and efficient. Able to easily change shape and spring back to their original form in a constant state of balance, all the while maintaining

[16] Buckminster Fuller R. (1975) *Synergetics: Explorations in the Geometry of Thinking* (700.04) Macmillan Publishing Co. Inc. p. 641.

[17] Jáuregui V. G. (2004) *Tensegrity Structures and their Application to Architecture.* Thesis for MSc in Architecture, School of Architecture, Queen's University, Belfast.

[18] Pflüger C. (2008) *The Meaning of Tensegrity Principles for Osteopathic Medicine.* Thesis for Master of Science in Osteopathy submitted at the Donau University Krems, and the Vienna School of Osteopathy.

[19] Levin S. (2002) *The Tensegrity-Truss as a Model for Spine Mechanics: Biotensegrity.* Presented at 12th International Conference on Mechanics in Medicine and Biology, Lemnos, Greece, September 2002. Later published in *Journal of Mechanics in Medicine and Biology*, vol. 2, Number 3&4, pp. 375-388.

[20] Ingber D. (1998) The Architecture of Life, *Scientific American*, pp .48-57.

[21] Scarr G. (2014) *Biotensegrity: The Architecture of Life*, Handspring Publishing, Scotland.

[22] Snelson K. *Tensegrity, Weaving and the Binary World.* http://kennethsnelson. net/tensegrity/

their function. Models of living systems (Biotensegrity), like the Skwish, convey a living structure in a simplistic form. Each cable is under tension and every strut under compression. These forces act in straight lines over the shortest possible distance. Body workers recognise the utility of these models and use them to demonstrate the similar properties they recognise in biological structures such as muscles and joints.[23] It is tempting to simplify joint movements as a series of levers, acting around a fulcrum, pulled by muscles acting like wires, a concept first introduced by an Italian mathematician Pirelli in 1680[24] that persists relatively unchallenged (even in modern computer models). It sounds absurd to think that these models have not been adequately revised, given their obvious flaws. According to existing rod & lever models, the forces generated would tear muscles and crush bone.[25][26]

Orthopaedic surgeon Steven Levin describes characteristics of human movement from a tensegrity standpoint: The spine is not a stack of blocks bearing up against gravity. Each vertebra, including the sacrum, is suspended by triangulating fibres of connective tissue. The sacrum can be compared to a bicycle wheel hub, with the ligaments acting like the spokes. The pelvis serves as the outer rim of the wheel. Muscles create a tone in the system operating fluid filled compartments in

[23] Scarr G. (2014) *Biotensegrity: The Architecture of Life*, Handspring Publishing, Scotland.

[24] Levin S. *Biotensegrity & Dynamic Anatomy* https://www.youtube.com/watch?v=jnpshtyvWr0

[25] Levin S. (2002) *The tensegrity-truss as a model for spine mechanics: Biotensegrity*. Presented at 12th International Conference on Mechanics in Medicine and Biology, Lemnos, Greece, September 2002. Later published in *Journal of Mechanics in Medicine and Biology*, vol. 2, Number 3&4, pp. 375-388.

[26] Oschman J. (2000) *Energy Medicine the scientific basis*. Churchill Livingstone. Elsevier Health Sciences. p.62-

the body that end in joints. The joint is a frictionless plane which cannot be compressed when synovial fluid is in place and ligaments are intact. Joints, in general, are in tension, not compression. Changing the tension across a joint makes the joint move. This phenomenon does not follow Newtonian laws of physics.[27]

Structures do not have to be composed of struts and wires to be recognised as tensegrity structures.[28] It is the way they distribute their forces to balance and self-stabilise that defines tensegrity. The tension and compression elements are also physical representations of the invisible forces acting on them, for example tension (attraction) and compression (repulsion). Imagine an elastic skin like a balloon. Substitute 'air' in place of the compression rods pushing out, and elastic balloon 'skin' pulling in and you have a classic tensegrity structure. The skin pulls in until it balances the air pushing out (determining the size of the balloon). Every child has explored the tensile limits of a balloon, either by overinflating or puncturing it!

Water

Water is the most plentiful molecule in the human body. It is proposed that the body is made up of 70% water by volume but 99% water by sheer number of particles (due to its relatively

---

[27] Levin S. (2002) *The tensegrity-truss as a model for spine mechanics: Biotensegrity*. Presented at 12th International Conference on Mechanics in Medicine and Biology, Lemnos, Greece, September 2002. Later published in *Journal of Mechanics in Medicine and Biology*, vol. 2, Number 3&4, pp. 375-388.

[28] Chen & Ingber (1999) Tensegrity and Mechanoregulation: from skeleton to cytoskeleton. *Osteoarthritis and Cartilage* (1999) 7, pp. 81–94.

tiny physical size).[29][30] Water is essential for life. It is the only compound that exists in its 3 forms (solid, liquid, gas) within the temperature range of life, and life can utilise all three forms simultaneously. It is the only substance where the solid form floats upon the liquid.

Despite its abundance, water has historically been viewed as an inert ground substance, to be ignored while studies are made of the interesting components/elements. Albert Szent-Gyorgyi, who won the Nobel Prize for discovering vitamin C and is commonly regarded as the father of modern biochemistry, suggested 'it is possible that modern biochemistry and cell biology have missed the point, by ignoring the centrality of life's most abundant constituent: water'.[31]

Rather than being the inert substance that you discard to study the real properties of a compound, there is credible research that is investigating the structural lattice of water, which gives it properties that are able to hold information.[32][33] The Pollack Lab at the University of Washington investigates a structured form of water that you've probably never heard of. It has a gel-like plasma consistency that exists in a state between that of a liquid and a solid. If you've ever observed clear fluid oozing from a wound, you've witnessed this 4th phase. It has properties that are able to separate charge, meaning that it can act like a battery – charged by sunlight, it

29 Emoto M. (2004) *The Healing Power of Water*. Hay House Sydney, p. 121.
30 Pollack G. (2013) *The fourth phase of water: Beyond solid, liquid, and vapor*. Ebner & Sons Publishers. Seattle.
31 https://www.pollacklab.org/research
32 https://www.pollacklab.org/research
33 Meyer S. (2021) *Return of the God Hypothesis: Three Scientific Discoveries That Reveal the Mind Behind the Universe*. HarperOne.

can filter and purify water, as well as account for the movement properties central to an updated understanding of muscle movement.[34] If water can hold information, and the body is predominately water, then it adds a new dimension to the claim of Jesus to be the living water and more depth to the symbolism of the sacraments for which water is so central: such as Baptism.

Given these extraordinary claims, you'd expect that water research would be a major scientific priority, given much funding. You'd be mistaken. Despite its abundance and importance, there is a paucity of research on the qualities that water exhibits. Water research is fraught with problems and contradictions and intense scientific discord, in fact it is seen as a topic that is a graveyard for scientists.[35]

Proteins

Proteins are the building blocks of life and life is animated by the movement of proteins.[36][37][38] Proteins come in all shapes and sizes. They perform many different roles. Antibodies are specialised immune proteins. Proteins can facilitate biochemical reactions, acting as catalysts to speed up chemical reactions. Examples of enzymes include lactase which breaks down

---

[34] Pollack, G. (2001) *Cells, Gels and the Engines of Life*. Ebner and Sons, Publishers, Seattle USA. Chapter 14, p. 225.

[35] Pollack G. (2013) *The Fourth Phase of Water*. Ebner and Sons, Publishers, Seattle USA. p. 22.

[36] Lipton B. (2005) *The Biology Of Belief: Unleashing The Power Of Consciousness, Matter And Miracles*, Hay House. Authors Pub Corp.

[37] Handol N. (2000) *Anatomy of Potency*. Osteopathic Supplies Ltd. Hereford UK.

[38] Goswami A. (2004) *The Quantum Doctor*. Hampton Roads Publishing Company. Charlottesville USA.

the sugar lactose in milk while pepsin aids the stomach to break down protein in the stomach. Hormones are messenger proteins. Insulin, for example, regulates glucose metabolism by controlling the blood-sugar concentration. Oxytocin stimulates contractions in childbirth. Somatotropin is a growth hormone that stimulates protein production in muscle cells. Proteins provide structure. Actin and Myosin have very tight spiral shapes, ideal for muscle contraction and movement. Keratin to strengthen and protect the hair. Collagen and elastin provide support for connective tissue, tendons and ligaments.

Proteins don't remain in the nice long straight lines they're coded in.[39] To be able to perform any function, the protein needs to be able to move. Life could be said to be defined by the quality of the movement of proteins. It's the folding of proteins into a variety of three-dimensional (tensegrity) shapes that is the key to their unique functions. As an example, consider a humble tea towel. Folded into a specific shape, it is ideal for drying dishes, in a different configuration, it can be good for wiping benches, and in yet another form, it can be used to flick your brother on the back of the legs! All made of the same substance, or the same DNA. It is the way that it is folded that determines its suitability for each purpose.

The arrangement of a compound is important. Keep in mind that long-term mechanical pressure changes carbon into graphite and, with further time and stress, into diamond. Magnetised steel differs from non-magnetised steel, only in the alignment of its molecules. Perhaps a more dramatic example from nature is to remind you that the butterfly has the same DNA as its caterpillar.

---

[39] Meyer S. (2021) *Return of the God Hypothesis: Three Scientific Discoveries That Reveal the Mind Behind the Universe.* HarperOne.

DNA is perhaps the ultimate example of a precisely folded protein structure. It has been modelled as a tensegrity double helix structure. In his ground-breaking 2005 book, *Biology of Belief*, Dr Bruce Lipton categorically identifies DNA as the reproductive mechanism of the cell and refutes the Central Dogma of biology, known as the Primacy of DNA that declares the DNA as the controlling brain of the cell, and, instead, he likens the DNA to the ingredient list, responsible for reproduction, making the DNA the gonad of the cell![40] It has been compared to computer software code.[41] DNA stores the assembly instructions for building proteins. Oschman[42] says that the DNA changes its structure 3 million times per second.

What regulates the movement of this protein folding mechanism? The Ingber laboratory at Harvard researches how cells in growing blood vessels are influenced by physical mechanical forces applied to them and how these mechanical stressors regulate their chemical pathways (mechanotransduction). 'We introduced the concept that living cells stabilise their internal skeleton (made of protein microtubules),[43] and control their shape and mechanics, using an architectural system first described by Buckminster Fuller, known as 'Tensegrity'.[44]

---

[40] Lipton B. (2005) *The Biology of Belief: Unleashing The Power Of Consciousness, Matter And Miracles*, Hay House. Authors Pub Corp. p. 66.

[41] Meyer S. (2021) *Return of the God Hypothesis: Three Scientific Discoveries That Reveal the Mind Behind the Universe.* HarperOne.

[42] Oschman J. (2000) *Energy Medicine the scientific basis.* Churchill Livingstone. Elsevier Health Sciences.

[43] Levin S. (2002) *The Tensegrity-Truss as a Model for Spine Mechanics: Biotensegrity.* Presented at 12th International Conference on Mechanics in Medicine and Biology, Lemnos, Greece, September 2002. Later published in *Journal of Mechanics in Medicine and Biology*, vol. 2, Number 3&4, pp. 375-388.

[44] Ingber D. (1997) Cellular Tensegrity and Mechanotransduction: from *Gravitational and Space Biology Bulletin* 10(2), pp. 49-55.

At a fundamental level, it's a changing electric charge, positive & negative, that directs the folding and unfolding of proteins.[45] Tissue structures of living systems are formed in highly organised arrangements. They also have piezoelectric (pressure sensitive) properties, meaning electricity is generated by the movement of the tissues themselves. Add to this the consideration that circulating blood contains haemoglobin, rich in iron, the most abundant magnetic element. This circulation of a magnetic rich fluid around a highly organised network of tissues makes the body into a very powerful electromagnet (evidenced by the diagnostic capabilities of MRI that can detect subtle variations in the composition of body tissues using this phenomenon).

Connective tissue is important for both the shape of the structure but also of its flexibility and adaptability and even its ability to repair. A change of tension anywhere within the connective tissue system is instantly conveyed to everywhere else in the body. There is a total body response, right down to the cell interior.[46][47] Every part of your body including the visceral organs[48] is encased within the body's largest organ (connective tissue) which itself functions as a liquid

---

[45] Lipton B. (2005) *The Biology of Belief: Unleashing the Power of Consciousness, Matter And Miracles*, Hay House. Authors Pub Corp. p. 56.

[46] Levin S. (2002) *The Tensegrity-Truss as a Model for Spine Mechanics: Biotensegrity*. Presented at 12th International Conference on Mechanics in Medicine and Biology, Lemnos, Greece, September 2002. Later published in *Journal of Mechanics in Medicine and Biology*, vol. 2, Number 3&4, pp. 375-388.

[47] Oschman J. (2000) *Energy Medicine the scientific basis*. Elsevier Health Sciences.

[48] Levin S. (2002) *The Tensegrity-Truss as a Model For Spine Mechanics: Biotensegrity*. Presented at 12th International Conference on Mechanics in Medicine and Biology, Lemnos, Greece, September 2002. Later published in *Journal of Mechanics in Medicine and Biology*, vol. 2, Number 3&4, pp. 375-388.

crystal semiconductor.[49][50] Andrew Taylor Still, the founder of Osteopathy was the first physician to direct people to the connective tissue as the place to look for the cause of disease, and the place to look for all cures.[51]

It turns out that the genetic sequences required to make complex three-dimensional protein 'folds' are extremely specific.[52] Without opening a can of worms and launching an evolution/ Darwinism/Theistic argument, suffice to say that origin of life is a contentious subject that hinges on the environmental conditions required to initiate and sustain the universe as we know it as well as the nature of the origins of life itself.[53]

Since proteins are crucial to almost all biological functions and structures, the unique properties of their protein folds 'represent the smallest unit of structural innovation in living systems'.[54] Protein folds can be seen as the fundamental unit of biological innovation. Meaning that to infer that an organism has evolved in any way, you would have to first be able to prove that this smallest condition was met. If you are unable to prove the ability to effectively move or fold a protein, then it's impossible that you can repair your body or build a new cell, let alone a new tissue, a new organ or a new species.

[49] Church D. (2007) *The Genie in Your Genes*. Elite Books, Santa Rosa USA, p. 138.

[50] Lipton B. (2005) *The Biology Of Belief: Unleashing The Power Of Consciousness, Matter And Miracles*, Hay House. Authors Pub Corp.

[51] Oschman J. (2016) *Energy Medicine the Scientific Basis* 2nd Edition. Elsevier. USA. p.169 .

[52] Gawdat M. (2017) *Solve for Happy*. North Star Way. New York.

[53] Podcast. SloMo (5/12/2021) Episode 170. Dr. Stephen C. Meyer - How to Disprove the Theory of Evolution and the Scientific Case for God.

[54] Meyer S. (2021) *Return of the God Hypothesis: Three Scientific Discoveries That Reveal the Mind Behind the Universe*. HarperOne.

Mathematically, it has been calculated that 'the probability of producing even a single functional protein of modest length (150 amino acids) by chance alone stands at no better than a 'vanishingly small' 1 chance in 10^{164}, an inconceivably small probability. To put this number in perspective, physicists estimate that there are only 1080 elementary particles in the entire universe.'[55] To deny the notion of 'Intelligent Design' at work in this case would be akin to suggesting that all the letters and words in this book somehow arranged themselves into their current format by a stroke of divine luck. We know that a number of authors have dedicated a lot of time and headspace to creating this book.

Proteins assist in the building of structure. They also facilitate its breaking down. This is one of the specialised roles of enzymes, to break down larger protein structures into smaller ones and into amino acids. This is most obvious in the digestive tract, but the functionality is present in every cell, e.g. in nerve cells, critical for the breakdown of neurotransmitters and hormones, which should only act on their receptors for short times. If, as Candace Pert suggested, God lives in the frontal lobe (presumably in the capacity of our superhuman ability of creative imagination and thought), then perhaps Jesus lives there as an enzyme, with his redemptive capacity to breakdown those thoughts, because, after all if we had to live in perpetuity with the resultant consequence of our cumulative historical thoughts, is this not the very definition of Hell?

Thought

The interplay between tensegrity and thinking is hidden in plain sight, permeating our language and how we understand

---

[55] Meyer S. (2021) *Return of the God Hypothesis: Three Scientific Discoveries That Reveal the Mind Behind the Universe.* HarperOne.

and teach physical principles. Isaac Newton's third law of motion specifically describes the duality of forces: *For every action there is an equal and opposite reaction.*[56] There are many examples of duality in common language; either/or, good/evil, right/wrong, male/female, north/south, past/future, day/night, up/down, push/pull, life/death...[57]

Candace Pert, a neuroscientist and pharmacologist who is credited with being the first scientist to discover the opioid receptor, is famous for a few notable quotes, one is that 'All thoughts are protein molecules', another, that 'God lives in the frontal lobes' in the form of the action of Neuropeptides (proteins). Pert demonstrated that the same neuro chemicals that act in the brain are found on the membranes of different tissue structures throughout the body. In her book *Molecules of Emotion*,[58] she outlined the direct molecular connection between our body and mind. The structure, and the purpose of that structure, namely thought, and, in the case of the frontal lobes in particular, includes imagination and creativity. She demonstrated that mind is not centralised in the head but distributed throughout the body.[59] Why is this important? Because as we learned earlier when discussing proteins, thinking is a biological process and directly influences the form and function of the structural tensegrity mechanism.

Proteins on the surface of the cell membrane selectively allow certain substances in/out, often by changing their shape due to environmental triggers in their own immediate environment. As the brain of the cell, the density, structure

---

[56] http://kennethsnelson.net/Tensegrity_and_Weaving.pdf
[57] http://kennethsnelson.net/Tensegrity_and_Weaving.pdf
[58] Pert C. (1997) *Molecules of Emotion*, Scribner, New York
[59] Lipton B. (2005) *The Biology of Belief: Unleashing the Power Of Consciousness, Matter And Miracles*, Hay House. Authors Pub Corp. p. 132.

and behaviour of the proteins on the cell membrane determine the functionality of the cell. Thus, it can be postulated that all intelligent decisions are made from information signalling through the cell membrane. Bruce Lipton identifies the cell membrane as its true brain. DNA within the nucleus only responds to environmental signals from outside of the cells. Lipton spoke about the critical role of perception in directing cellular function. How we perceive the world is based on our beliefs about it which is largely based on our experience – not only what we've learned, read, seen, heard or experienced, but also the judgments we've made about these. David Bohm[60] agrees that we cannot be separate from our thoughts. Thought participates in reality. What we think is directly affecting our perception, what we see.

It has been said that human intellect can be attributed to the relatively large size of the frontal lobe. This size has emerged, we are told, by the need for maximum cortical surface area, yet bunched tight and folded up into the smallest space that it can sustain. The same tensegrity properties occupy Fuller's geodesic dome[61] – a tensile balance between surface area and size, with form and function paramount.

The ability of the brain, and particularly thought and emotion can and does override the body's reflex response mechanisms. Training this by repetition is important for learning and certainly a highly valued skill in certain circumstances, for example when training for sports. We know this concept as 'muscle memory', where someone has performed the same manoeuvre over and over again until it is ingrained in the

---

[60] Bohm D. (1992) *Thought as a System*. Routledge. pp. 114-116.
[61] Edmonson A. (1987) *A Fuller Explanation: The Synergetic Geometry of R Buckminster Fuller*. Birkhäuser, Boston. USA. p. 235.

whole and they are able to sense and deploy movement with the utmost efficiency. It is important to recognise the limitations of this mechanism if one were keen to maintain flexibility of thought. The more attention we place in a specialised focus, our perceptions, beliefs and experience adapt to support this. Repetitive thoughts reinforce those characteristics; it becomes easy to maintain the same thoughts and harder to even notice an alternative view. We can even become addicted to our thoughts chemically. This is mediated by protein hormones (such as dopamine).

If thoughts, beliefs and perceptions are capable of changing protein structure, an integral part of the wider tensegrity structure, then theoretically even our physical appearance reveals 'our real beliefs' or reflects the default state of mind to which we return after we exercise our conscious thoughts. Can we see the impact of our thoughts and beliefs in the physical structure? You may be able to recognise the 'body language' of your friends and family and be able to identify whether they're happy, excited or bored. As an osteopath, I hear peoples' exhortations daily to explain their tight neck and shoulder muscles – 'I hold my stress there!' I'm not sure whether persistent, chronic and ongoing muscle pain and tension is caused by ergonomics, physical posture/position, stress, thoughts or so-called repressed emotions[62] or a combination of all of them, or something else entirely. At different times, the resolution can come spontaneously in many different ways, many of them not related to treatment provided!

---

[62] Goswami A. (2004) *The Quantum Doctor*. Hampton Roads Publishing Company, Charlottesville USA. p. 196.

We are reminded in the preface to Dr Berise Heasly's doctoral thesis,[63] the accumulation of information rich, yet wisdom poor learning can lead to errant and undisciplined thoughts, the impact of which magnifies as one ages. This is consistent with the tensegrity model. If we want to strengthen a thought framework, agility and flexibility are an asset. There is a need to challenge the adaptability of a thought process. Just like the analogy of a muscle being strengthened in the gym, it is a requirement to actively engage a thought, to find its limits. Ideas need to be tested under rigorous scrutiny.[64] Just like muscle, such deliberate engagement will only strengthen a coherent structure. As it is stressed, micro-breaks appear, and weaknesses are exposed and can be corrected. This is necessary for growth. Just as repetition reinforces the process, left untrained, a muscle weakens. Nature is always renovating.

We do know that biological structures have functional non-tangible characteristics. Living beings think, move, grow, regenerate, love. They exist in the context of their environment and their relationships. They are both formed and influenced by these. Rupert Sheldrake[65] introduces the concept of 'morphogenic fields' wherein he postulates that physical form emerges from a plan (of sorts) and is ordered by it. He contends that these fields influence the patterns not only of individual cells, humans, animals, places but also the social relationships between them and is embedded into significant natural places possibly more strongly than it animates structures like churches and cathedrals due to their usage by peoples over

---

63 Heasly B. (2015) *Towards an Architecture for the Teaching of Virtues, Values and Ethics*. Peter Lang International Academic Publishers. Bern p. xv.
64 Heasly B. (2015) *Towards an Architecture for the Teaching of Virtues, Values and Ethics*. Peter Lang International Academic Publishers. Bern p. 181.
65 Sheldrake R. (2009) *Morphic Resonance*. Park Street Press. p. 63.

such a long time. This potentially explains the tradition of humans to gather in sacred locations to perpetuate rituals and pass on their legacy.[66] It seeks to explain such diverse behaviours as the imperative for animals to migrate, through to its modern, human analogue, that is pilgrimage.[67] It also accounts for the temporal observance of holy days, feasts, remembrance and anniversaries. These concepts have relationships and connections at their core. These relationships themselves are an example of tensegrity at work.

Science

Modern science acolytes present a materialistic view of the world and with it a 'warfare model' of the history of science and its relationship to religious belief. We are led to believe that we do not need a pre-existent mind (God) to shape matter. Matter has always existed and can arrange itself. We are taught an array of materialistic theories outlining the origin and development of life, including human life, back to the origin of the earth and the solar system and taught subjects such as astronomy, geology, and biology as a seamless unfolding of the potentiality of matter and energy. Biology seems forever influenced by Darwin's theory of evolution. Our current materialistic (atheistic?) world view appears to support the idea of life emerging from so called primordial soup by natural selection and random mutations without any divine guidance. 'Living organisms only appeared to be designed.'

---

[66] Sheldrake R. (2017) *Science and Spiritual Practices*. Coronet. UK. Chapter 5. pp. 111-116.

[67] Sheldrake R. (2017) *Science and Spiritual Practices*. Coronet. UK. Chapter 7. p. 168.

There is a long history of academics[68] who would refute each of these arguments as well as reputable historians and philosophers of science who support the claim that it was in fact Western Judeo-Christian scientists in the 16th and 17th centuries who are responsible for the development of modern science. It was precisely their religious belief that inspired them to challenge pre-existing dogmas of their day and advance scientific knowledge. Specifically, it was through their dedicated observation of nature that they were able to liberate science from the dominance of the previous 'Greek thinkers' who only gave superficial explanations of nature based on what they assumed it to be, rather than be guided by actual observation.

Western science is founded on the premise that nature emerges from a single intelligence (monotheism), that we have the capacity to understand for ourselves (and from which we also come), that can also be understood by scientific methods. Early scientists saw their vocation to 'seek out the evidence of God in the physical world' and then to use that evidence to seek to understand God and share his thoughts. Isaac Newton saw evidence of intelligent design in the complex configurations of matter in both the solar system and biological systems. He also used tensegrity metaphors to describe the apparent stability of the universe, e.g. '... the stars would remain forever suspended in a tension of balanced gravitational attraction'.[69]

Even silence can be conceptualised within tensegrity framework. Contemplative silence is a practice that is deeply rooted in Catholic tradition, from the Gnostics, hermits, monastic life, even to modern silent retreats. To be fully present

---

[68] Professor Colin Russell – In: Meyer S. (2021) *Return of the God Hypothesis* (Chapter 1.37).

[69] Newton I. (1728) *De mundi systemate liber. A Treatise of the System of the World.* University of Lausanne. Translated and published by F. Fayram London.

is to be aware of the pressures on you and where tensions are pulling you. Retreat gives us a moment to step away from these pressures. Theoretically, we could have a silent retreat by ourselves whenever we're able to free up some time. But why don't we? Why do we find it easier to go away to a specific place with a group, so that we can be silent together? Do we find there a temporary safe resting place where the pressures are balanced and stable for the moment, where we can reflect and be still?

Each generation of scientists has described the natural world and the human body and its capabilities by comparing them to the wonders of their age. Throughout history, the three most common analogies are to compare the properties of nature to that of the contents of a Book (presumably the Bible), to the workings of a clockwork mechanism and to the laws of nature.[70] At times it has also been compared to the workings of a steam engine or to a waterwheel. Indigenous cultures tell creation stories and describe these phenomena using allegories to nature.[71] Andrew Taylor Still, the founder of Osteopathy, described the body and its operation as the great machinery of life.[72]

Today, we are wowed by computers and make analogies of software programs and computer networks. We talk about the computational power of various devices, computers, mobile phones, how many bits per second, and try to fathom and conceptualise the power of the brain. These can be useful

---

[70] Meyer S. (2021) *Return of the God Hypothesis: Three Scientific Discoveries That Reveal the Mind Behind the Universe.* HarperOne.

[71] Campbell J. (1991) *The Power of Myth*, Anchor Books.

[72] Still AT. (1902) *The Philosophy and Mechanical Principles of Osteopathy*. Donald Siehl. Kansas City. p. 32.

comparisons because they capture the imagination of the reader, but they can also be limiting and age particularly badly.

Our five senses enable us to perceive our immediate environment. We see, hear, touch, taste and smell our environment. Our sensors (eyes, ears, nose) 'point out' from the body. In the same way that localised cell membrane proteins monitor their environment and respond according to their perception, the same can be said for the whole human person. We respond to sensations from our environment whilst influenced by our perceptions and beliefs. In his book *The Brain: The Story of You*,[73] David Eagleman explores (among other things) the history of contradictions between the raw data received from those sensors and how it is interpreted using a tangle of brain connections, memory, relationships between conscious and unconscious, preconceived bias, how we learn, as well as tackling the slippery concept of free will. He presents a series of ethical dilemmas and how we navigate them, both individually and as a society. He introduces us to the concept of *umwelt*, the small subset of the world that any animal is able to detect. The bigger reality, whatever that might mean, is called the *umgebung*. Interestingly, each organism presumably assumes its *umwelt* to be the entire objective reality 'out there'. Does a fish know that it is swimming in water? Or what exists outside of that water?

Humans exist within a continuum between the infinitesimally small milieu of atoms to the impossibly large-scale solar system, part of a larger universe, all of which have been modelled to us in similar fashion, a series of orbs spinning around a central gravitational point attracted and repelled

---

[73] Eagleman D. (2015) *The Brain: The Story of You*. Canongate Books, Edinburgh UK.

in an expansive space of nothingness by a combination of invisible forces. Our awareness of these worlds is outside of our everyday experience, and often outside of our ability to directly participate in that experience.

We require microscopes to see the infinitesimally small, telescopes to see the celestial bodies, x-rays to see through solid objects, photographs and video to record and publish the experience. Expeditions to extreme environments depend on someone travelling there, having an experience on our behalf and reporting back. We have long been fascinated by explorers traveling to faraway places, deep underwater environments or high mountains, into space, each requiring specialised skills and training. Our experience of their adventure then depends on their capacity for recording their adventures and the quality of their storytelling upon their return.

We require technical equipment to perceive things outside of our *Umwelt* and depend on experts to interpret them for us. But who are these experts that we trust to act as intermediaries for our experience? In the past, the church has taken on the responsibility of mediating the unknown to the people. However, an industrialised twentieth century scientific crusade has delivered an overwhelming amount of convincing information. 'It has become the dominant authority by discovering and promulgating indisputable laws that are repeatable, stable, unchanging descriptions of the nature of things and their interactions.'[74] There is no doubt that science has improved our lives, however the vast majority of lived human experience is still not explained by this methodology.

---

[74] Hunt V. (1996) *Infinite Mind: Science of the Human Vibrations of Consciousness.* Malibu Publishing Co. pp.40-41.

Church

The universal church has long recognised that there is something 'more' out there (or in there). She represents herself as an authority on spiritual matters and warns of the shortcomings of a pervasive mechanistic scientific worldview that is dependent on rigorous methodical reproduction of experiments. She has the infrastructure and audience to convey a strong, coherent universal message. But what is that message? Has it been clearly enunciated? One of the temptations has been that in order to magnify and emphasise the glory of God, the material world has tended to be shunned.[75]

The church has a long tradition of saints, martyrs, philosophers and theologians including Doctors of the Church who used every resource available to them to guide their understanding and write their theses and convey their experience. Many would have been overjoyed with the advancement of a methodology of enquiry that they could have used to spread their message. Yet as some areas of life advance, other worldviews choose to retreat into oversimplistic fundamentalist explanations that were good enough for uneducated congregations of the past but now seem not only banal but contemptuous.

All the while, there is an emerging science community populated by spiritually-minded searchers who in earlier times might have been the scientist-priests. These people meditate and practice yoga or tai chi[76] and are methodically proving the existence of God within the context of the material world as well as incorporating the causation of

---

[75] Campbell J. (1991) *The Power of Myth*, Anchor Books, p. 84.
[76] Hunt V. (1996) *Infinite Mind: Science of the Human Vibrations of Consciousness*. Malibu Publishing Co. p. 38.

consciousness/thought at a time when the practical lived experience of the people has rejected the credibility of the very church best placed to facilitate the discourse.

We are at a time in history where the collection and dissemination of knowledge, the understanding of that knowledge, and ability to make meaningful connections between it, heralded by the emergence and processing capabilities of 'Big Data' means that we must reconsider all assumptions. New ideas in theology are likely to emerge from modern thinkers, innovators, disrupters, healers, scientists even software engineers as much as theologians if they are not attentive. The power, so to speak, will be in the hands of the controllers of the infrastructure. In times gone by, it was bricks and mortar, real estate and logistical ability to gather in large congregations; these days it is in such things as I.T., cloud systems and agile infrastructure. The one-time expediencies of such outdated philosophies as Cartesian Dualism are no longer tenable.

Fortunately, new ideas don't need to be dreamed up by a church in crisis. Science itself has come to form the conclusion that God is visible, a real and living entity. There is a growing community of engaged, highly credentialed people who are proving not only the existence of God but effectively showing us his wonder and backing it up with objective evidence. Are secular scientists doing a better job than the universal church at engaging a new generation of enquiry?

New thoughts and ideas necessarily change the substance of the existing framework. Old structures that resist change do not evolve. They will break. There is a possibility that they will be replaced. Do we want this? Change is inevitable. Any new understandings must be understood with respect to the context of the old. If the old remains true, then just like biological structures, the testing will strengthen it. In denying outright the experience of contemporary scientists who are no longer (and have likely not ever been) the purveyors of reductionist atheism, as we may have been led to believe, the Magisterium has chosen a path which appears to be the antithesis of its ideal.

As we have seen, there is an inextricable relationship between structure and function. There is also a wide scope of knowledge about different subjects emerging from a diverse group of disciplines whose crossover of experience and expertise means that the old delineations and borders between specialties are no longer adequate. Nor are the indulgences of self-appointed experts appropriate to lay claim to being the sole arbiter of such knowledge.

In Dr Heasly's quest to find an educational model to propagate and inspire wholistic inductive thinkers,[77] she has repetitively encountered and tirelessly combatted the scourge of Binary Thinking whereby either by expediency, laziness or ignorance, people have oversimplified concepts and explanations and even ignored inconvenient truths. In proposing Tensegrity as the framework model for reimagining the field of education, Dr Heasly has inspired my own inquiry and allowed me to share my understanding of tensegrity principles with you.

Kenneth Snelson began by exploring a simple kite frame, adding more and more layers to the matrix. Paradoxically, as he expressed: 'Everything about tensegrity is binary just as opposing tension and compression forces are binary.[78] Whilst he was unwilling to represent these structures as anything

[77] Heasly B. (2015) *Towards an Architecture for the Teaching of Virtues, Values and Ethics*. Peter Lang International Academic Publishers. Bern p. 14.

[78] Snelson K. (2012) The Art of Tensegrity, *International Journal of Space Structures*. Volume27·Number 2&3, pp.71-80.

but art, like all good art, others have seen in them a way to understand and conceptualise different and often very diverse concepts. Which seems appropriate.

To present one final consideration: The basis on which computers operate is a tensegrity. Binary code, namely Base 2, where all information is processed by an on/off signal represented by either a 1 or a 0. Once revolutionary, by our standards, early computers were limited in their functionality. Contemporary computer processors are still binary, just with infinitely higher magnitudes of complexity. This is comparable to the inductive evolution of thought that Dr Heasly envisions for humanity. As quantum processing is poised to revolutionise computing as we know it, imagine what can and will be conceptualised by embracing Quantum thought models.

Epilogue

In exploring the wide-ranging complexities of divergent concepts and how they fit into a Tensegrity model, it seems that for each aspect included in the chapter, there are many more that have been left out. Wisdom comes from so many places. I am acutely aware that I have not covered these topics from some critically important perspectives. It is beyond my scope and experiences to write on behalf of experts from different ideologies, faith traditions and cultures, including Indigenous cultures, although their wisdom would have augmented this treatise. Nor have I drawn from the rich tradition of texts, passed down throughout the centuries that have already conceptualised and expressed these ideas in a much more eloquent way than I could have. As such, I have only added my own small perspective to the tensegrity matrix in the hope of sharing a small glimpse of how I conceptualise my own Umwelt in the wider Umgebung.

Part 2

Part 2

Liturgical seasons across Australia

(A Vatican II priest speaks from lived experience)

Michael Elligate

In the sixty years or so since Vatican ll, the lived liturgical life of Australian parishes has undergone unprecedented change and adjustment. Even in remote churches across the countryside, strategic furniture has been turned around to enable the congregation to have a more active participation in the celebration of the sacraments.

The position of the altar table indicates an invitation to share in the meal-like motif of the Eucharist.

Many churches now use carafes rather than tiny cruets holding water and wine for the sacramental action. Yet there is resistance to the recommendation to provide more bread-like food in the eucharistic liturgy. The continued practice in using paper-thin, plastic-style wafers persists. It is difficult to move celebrants from viewing the tabernacle as a sacred storage place for the supply of communion particles that are not linked directly to the action of a celebration of the Eucharist.

The presidential chair is well accepted, yet the occupational hazard of establishing a messy place for holy clutter is always a problem.

The lectern is now seen as an important place for the proclamation of Scripture. It is expected that women and men will share the readings, and many take time to prepare them well.

What is sadly missing are preachers making a real effort to prepare the exploration of the text and its link with everyday life.

Time and again, the alienating experience of people not being engaged in the homily is a regrettable experience. The gap between the research within the Biblical academy not reaching the preparation work of the preacher is nothing less than tragic. Our local Scripture scholars have earned an international standing with a gift for linking the ancient texts to everyday life. The quest to improve the art of preaching is a real challenge.

There is a delightful ease amongst young people who are prepared to read at family funerals simply because they have been encouraged to read from an early age at school Masses. So in many ways, there has been a genuine enrichment in our Sunday Masses as the measures outlined in the Liturgical Constitution of Vatican ll has been implemented.

One of the terrible stumbling blocks of our current liturgy is the so-called 'new congregational prayers and responses' imposed upon us during the time of Pope Benedict. The prayers are so contrived that it is often impossible to work out what they mean.

The other associated problem with our liturgical texts is that our prayers are too verbose. Liturgists may be surprised to be told that extended prayers get lost in their own words.

Hopefully, the motion adopted by the recent Plenary Council calling for a review of the current translation of the Missal will be implemented quickly.

Sacramental programs in parish schools have been well resourced, but catechists often remark that the expectation is often too ambitious, and students become bored as programs seem to run for too long.

When travelling overseas, it is exciting to see how provision of good music is part of the parish budget. Parishes that encourage the place of trained choirs and cantors are often recommended as providing helpful liturgy.

Liturgical planning has to be consistent and simply must never stop. It requires creative imagination and ample doses of energy. Yet just a simple arrangement of flowers, palms and banners on any one Sunday helps bring a liturgy to life.

Each year, workshops that are offered before the seasons of Advent, Lent and Easter are encouraging for liturgy groups in our parishes.

Catholic liturgy really reached an all-time low between the centuries that marked the Council of Trent and the renewed season after the Council of Vatican ll.

The vision of the Second Vatican Council has now sown many helpful seeds. Constant efforts to make our Parish Churches shine must continue; otherwise, the predictable pattern of our dull liturgy will be a sad source of alienation for our people.

On a positive note, the growth within Australian parishes in liturgical awareness has developed well. Many parishes try hard to plan and provide engaging liturgy.

In the words of John Keats, amid the mists of a long year, our responsibility to provide an enriched liturgy is given due attention. What is constantly needed is a readiness to be aware that our rituals can be fresh and as stimulating as the changing seasons remind us.

I, Naomi...

Naomi Wolfe

If God is the Alpha, and the Omega, then God has always been in these lands: recognising and making space for Aboriginal, Torres Strait Islander and global Indigenous peoples.

In 1986, in Blatherskite Park, Alice Springs, His holiness Pope John Paul II boldly proclaimed to Indigenous peoples gathered there and around the nation, 'You are part of Australia and Australia is part of you. And the Church herself in Australia will not be fully the Church that Jesus wants her to be until you have made your contribution to her life and until that contribution has been joyfully received by others'. I was 13 years of age and struggling to reconcile the God of the Church with all of its negative interactions to Indigenous peoples, and the God of our People, a God that I knew loved us, and told us we were created in God's image. To hear the leader of the worldwide Catholic Church make such a historic proclamation gave me an increased curiosity in how it might be possible to be both Aboriginal and Christian.

As I grew up, both chronologically and in the faith, I began to realise that others too had this yearning to be fully part of the Church, and to contribute to the undoing of the trappings of colonial Christianity that denied the very humanity and salvation of Indigenous peoples in Australia and across the world. Those powerful words from Blatherskite Park still resonate within my heart, and within my head, as I seek to make my way within the world as an Aboriginal follower of Jesus, as a member of the Catholic and Anglican communities, and as an academic working within theological education.

How might we come together to focus on issues at the heart of continuing colonisation, and delve into matters such as inclusion of Indigenous Christians as full brothers and sisters in Christ? How might we include Indigenous readings of text and tradition to help the wider community make sense of life and calling? One response is through sharing, listening and reflecting. This chapter reflects on these matters as one contribution to a wider discussion happening within Indigenous and non-Indigenous communities. It brings together both the real challenges and very possible opportunities.

When I was nine years of age, my great aunt Eileen, one of my paternal Grandmother's sisters, came home to Tasmania to visit us and our extended family. There was great excitement whenever a relative came from the 'mainland'. It seemed as foreign a place as any biblical location that we heard about in Sunday school, or the places that we glimpsed watching Aunty (the ABC) on our black and white television. Big Eil, as she was known because one of my dad's sisters was her namesake, was a great storyteller, and someone who had a flair for the dramatic. The infrequent visits from Big Eil were magical and colourful. On this visit, Big Eil took me down to where the river meets the sea in my hometown to collect shells. I wasn't old enough to stand long in the waters, or to participate fully in collecting maireener shells, but we gathered some to make some bracelets and necklaces, a mix of the traditions of our old country women, and the fascination for jewellery of a modern age.

As we stood in the water collecting, my aunt spoke of the old times when previous generations would do similar but also talk of both Palawa and Christian traditions. I can remember asking her, 'Big Eil, when did God come to visit us?' I can remember her smiling and saying: 'Naya, God's always been here. God was here with our Ancestors and God is here with us now. These are to tell us what we should do.' I was known as the question girl, so I kept my aunt busy with all sorts of questions. One about creation was incredibly important. I couldn't quite reconcile that Christian idea of how the world, and us, were made. As I sat in the pews of St Stephen's Anglican Church like so many of my family have done, I heard:

In the beginning when God created the heavens and the earth, the earth was a formless void and darkness covered the face of the deep, while a wind from God swept over the face of the waters. Then God said, 'Let there be light'; and there was light. And God saw that the light was good; and God separated the light from the darkness. God called the light Day, and the darkness he called Night. And there was evening and there was morning, the first day. And God said, 'Let there be a dome in the midst of the waters, and let it separate the waters from the waters.' So God made the dome and separated the waters that were under the dome from the waters that were above the dome. And it was so. God called the dome Sky. And there was evening and there was morning, the second day. And God said, 'Let the waters under the sky be gathered together into one place, and let the dry land appear.' And it was so. God called the dry land Earth, and the waters that were gathered together he called Seas. And God saw that it was good. Then God said, 'Let the earth put forth vegetation: plants yielding seed, and fruit trees of every kind on earth that bear fruit with the seed in it.' And it was so. The earth brought forth vegetation: plants yielding seed of every kind, and trees of every kind bearing fruit with the seed in it. And God saw that it was good. And there was evening and there was morning, the third day. And God said, 'Let there be lights in the dome of the sky to separate the day from the night; and let them be for signs and for seasons and for days and years, and let them be lights in the dome of the sky to give light upon the earth.' And it was so. God made the two great lights — the greater light to rule the day and the lesser light to rule the night — and the stars. God set them in the dome of the sky to give light upon the earth, to rule over the day and over the night, and to separate the light from the darkness. And God saw that it was good. And there was evening and there was morning, the fourth day. And God said, 'Let the waters bring forth swarms of living creatures, and let birds fly above the earth across the dome of the sky.' So God created the great sea monsters and every living creature that moves, of every kind, with which the waters swarm, and every winged bird of every kind. And God saw that it was good. God blessed them, saying, 'Be fruitful and multiply and fill the waters in the seas, and let birds multiply on the earth.' And there was evening and there was morning, the fifth day. And God said, 'Let the earth bring forth living creatures of every kind: cattle and creeping things and wild animals of the earth of every kind.' And it was so. God made the wild animals of the earth of every kind, and the cattle of every kind, and everything that creeps upon the ground of every kind. And God saw that it was good. Then God said, 'Let us make humankind in our image, according to our likeness; and let them have dominion over the fish of the sea, and over the birds of the air, and over the cattle, and over all the wild animals of the earth, and over every creeping thing that creeps upon the earth.'

So, God created humankind in his image, in the image of God he created them; male and female he created them. God blessed them, and God said to them, 'Be fruitful and multiply, and fill the earth and subdue it; and have dominion over the fish of the sea and over the birds of the air and over every living thing that moves upon the earth.' God said, 'See, I have given you every plant yielding seed that is upon the face of all the earth, and every tree with seed in its fruit; you shall have them for food. And to every beast of the earth, and to every bird of the air, and to everything that creeps on the earth, everything that has the breath of life, I have given every green plant for food.' And it was so. God saw everything that he had made, and indeed, it was very good. And there was evening and there was morning, the sixth day.[1]

I loved the beauty of the words, the descriptiveness of the text, and the connectedness of all things. I was struck in particular by verse 26: *Then God said, 'Let us make humankind in our image, according to our likeness; and let them have dominion over the fish of the sea, and over the birds of the air, and over the cattle, and over all the wild animals of the earth, and over every creeping thing that creeps upon the earth.'*[2] I wondered, who was the 'us'? I came the conclusion that it could be our Ancestors sitting with God, however there was no church person to ask...[3] It was still 'shame' to be who we were in many ways in those days growing up, and not accepted by the Church, to have different ideas about God and creation. So, I didn't speak of it. I took comfort though that I was connected to all of creation, in its many forms and knew that there was a sense of reciprocity

---

[1] Genesis 1:1-31 *New Revised Standard Version.*

[2] Genesis 1:26 *New Revised Standard Version.*

[3] According to some scholars, "Elohim' (the name for God in Genesis 1) can sometimes be translated 'ancestral spirits.' In any case, the author of this chapter consistently refuses to name the Creator 'Yhwh' – Israel's national name for God. It could well be that this story deliberates /leaves room for other peoples to name the Creator differently. See, e.g. Konrad Schmid, 'Judean Identity and Ecumenicity: The Political Theology of the Priestly Document,' in *Judah and the Judeans in the Achaemenid Period: Negotiating Identity in an International Context,* ed. Oded Lipschits, Gary N. Knoppers and Manfred Oeming (Winona Lake, Ind.: Eisenbrauns, 2011), 3–26.

between creation and us. My aunt's words would ring in my ears, much later, when I tried to reconcile the old way and the Church way. As a child I was confused by the two different worldviews and, even though I trusted my family when they told me that God and the Ancestors were connected – that we were part of all ways of seeing creation, I didn't have the tools to reconcile what my head told me were different ways of seeing the world. For our old people knew this about creation:

'In the beginning, when all things took their shape, Trowenna, the heart-shaped island, was just a very small sandbank in the southern seas. We now call it Tasmania. Throughout countless ages when the ice came and went, throughout darkness and light, so Trowenna remained. As the sea rose, Punywin, the sun, flashed fire as he moved across the sky. At night, his wife, Venna, the moon, cast a silvery glow over the world as she moved across the sky. Throughout time, they travelled across the sky, creating life. They move from horizon to horizon, where they sank into the seas. However, Venna could not travel as fast as Punywin, so he would encourage her, and his light would reflect onto her, to help her move across the sky. These were the days when the sun and the moon were in the sky together. Sometimes, Venna would feel the cold on the short winter days, and Punywin would allow her to rest on one of the icebergs that surrounded Trowenna. On those days, before he slipped over the horizon, Punywin would come and get Venna, and they would slowly slide over the rim of the world together. These were the days when the moon seemed to be permanently on the horizon, as the sun moved across the sky. The day after, their son, Moinee, was born. Because he was a strong and shiny boy, Punywin and Venna placed him high in the sky above Trowenna. He was the great South Star. On the following day, their second son, the gentle Dromerdene, was born. Dromerdene shone just like his brother. Punywin and Venna placed him in the sky halfway between themselves and Moinee, the* *great South Star. He still watched over Trowenna today. We call him Canopus. The day after Dromerdene was born, Punywin and Venna rose from the sea, and passed across the little sandbank, dropping seeds. They dropped seeds for the great gum tree tara monadro, and the plants that grow on Trowenna today. The next day, rina dina fell to help tara monadro grow. Then, on the day after rina dina had made the seeds sprout, shellfish appeared on the waters around Trowenna. These shellfish were plentiful and of every shape. All throughout the Dreamtime, the seeds sprouted and became trees and other plants. The leaves fell down from the trees and the plants of Trowenna and mixed with the sand and became the soil. The shellfish grew and became numerous. As the old ones died, they became the stones and the rocks of the great mountains of Trowenna. All the shells can be seen in the rocks throughout Trowenna today. Slowly, over time, Trowenna rose from the seas, no longer just a sandbank. Through the ages of Dreaming, icebergs from the great southern seas floated around Trowenna, rubbing against the island, and moving it away from the great South Land. Today, you will see shellfish everywhere. You will see tara monadro - the great gum tree - you will see plants and animals. You will see all that is Trowenna.'[4]*

For me, I can see the beauty and the divine in both creation stories and I keep them together in both heart and mind.

As I grew older, I was taught, and I learnt tools to help me understand that both creation stories are true, both give

---

[4] This story has been passed from several generations right across Tasmania but there is western documentation of this oral history as well. Missionary and Conciliator George Augustus Robinson was told this creation story by Manalargenna, Trawlwoolway Elder (and my Ancestor) and Nuenonne Elder Woorraddy. See: N.J.B Plomley, *Friendly mission: the Tasmanian journals and papers of George Augustus Robinson, 1829-1834*, 2nd Edition (Hobart: Quintus Publications, 2008).

us all invaluable sense of connectedness to creation, and both can serve as reminders to care for creation (although the wording for care of creation is perhaps more direct in the second creation story, in Genesis 2:15, 'to serve and protect' the garden). The need to knit these traditions together has become less pressing, giving way to reflection that prompts me to ask how I might respond to life in all its complexities and challenges, as both Aboriginal and Christian.

Many today seek biblical texts about stewardship of creation in response to climate debate, or climate crisis. Dan Story's book *Should Christians Be Environmentalists?* is one of the growing numbers of Christian texts that seek to discuss what biblical approach is possible to environmental issues. As he writes, 'the controversy of climate change should not distract us from our moral obligation to be obedient to God's stewardship mandate.'[5] In *Ecologies of Grace: Environmental Ethics and Christian Theology*, Willis Jenkins attempts to identify some strategies for how Christians might respond to environmental concerns. Jenkins attempts to provide profound insight into understanding the relationship between creation and Christianity, through presenting the ideas that stewardship, eco-spirituality, and eco-justice are ways in which Christianity seeks to define the issues, contextualise them and attempt to solve them.[6] I believe that we need a disruption to our societal thinking. One such disruption is to include other ways of remembering our place within Creation, of including other ways of reading and hearing the biblical texts that call us back into communion with Creation.

---

[5] Story, Dan. *Should Christians Be Environmentalists?* (Grand Rapids: Kregel Publications, 2012), p.168.

[6] Jenkins, Willis. *Ecologies of grace: Environmental ethics and Christian theology* (Oxford: Oxford University Press, 2013).

Aboriginal and Torres Strait Islander stories, theologies and practices can do this, and, if wider society makes space, it can be a gift to all.

As an Aboriginal person, I am concerned about country, about the health of country, because country is intimately connected with my creation, my family, my spirituality, my very being. This may be similar in some ways to the way that Genesis 9:17 says that all creatures share the same spirit of life (so also Psalm 104:29–30, referring to *ruach*, as does Genesis 1:2). I know I'm not alone in this concern; others, Indigenous and non-Indigenous, worry too about the health of creation. I have read, from time to time, through biblical texts, to find solace, and perhaps justification of the importance for Christians to become more aware of their connectedness to the earth – not as a form of worship, but as a form of acknowledgment that we are part of this wider creation.

Proof texting aside, some biblical passages can be useful as 're-membering' devices. For example, some might read Genesis 1:27-29 as a colonial hierarchical idea with humans at the top in charge of the rest of creation that is there for subjugation and human purposes. But if one reads this as an Aboriginal person, then all of creation is humanity and vice versa. That is, the animals, the seas, *tara monadro* and others are our brothers and sisters, equal to us. They are then unable to be subjected to a hierarchy of priorities because to establish such a hierarchy would be to create disharmony, a disruption to community. This is not to suggest that others should culturally appropriate our ways, but rather perhaps provoke them to think about what does it mean for them to be stewards, to have dominion, to love and care for creation?

After all, there are other biblical passages that remind us that God is in his creation, for example the Psalmist tells us in

Psalm 147 that God is actively involved in creation: '*He covers the heavens with clouds, prepares rain for the earth, makes grass grow on the hills.9 He gives to the animals their food, and to the young ravens when they cry.*'[7] For me, the Psalmist's words are echoed within our Dreaming: '*The shellfish grew and became numerous. As the old ones died, they became the stones and the rocks of the great mountains of Trowenna. All the shells can be seen in the rocks throughout Trowenna today. Slowly, over time, Trowenna rose from the seas, no longer just a sandbank*'.

For me, as an Aboriginal Christian, the biblical text together with our Dreaming stories of creation are invaluable tools for contemplating my response to my brother and sister creatures, Father Sun, and Mother Moon and the collective groaning (and jubilation) of their experiences. For these experiences are my shared experiences, so the impetus is on me to play my role within creation in a way that is harmonious, and sacred. As Garry Deverell, Trawlwoolway priest reminds us, the land is our sacred text; we as Aboriginal people have our lands and our seas, and 'by attending to its secrets, the call and address of the divine can be clearly discerned'.[8]

'For most of the history of western civilization the Old Testament creation stories, especially those in Genesis 1, have been viewed with great respect because of the belief that they give an accurate account of how God created the universe' writes John Rogerson,[9] and I think that this has often been to the detriment of Indigenous people around the world. But

---

[7] Psalm 147:8-9 *New Revised Standard Version*.

[8] Deverell, Garry. *Gondwana Theology: A Trawloolway man reflects on Christian faith* (Sydney: Morning Star Publishing 2018) p. 2.

[9] John W. Rogerson, 'The Creation Stories: Their Ecological Potential and Problems', in *Ecological Hermeneutics: Biblical, Historical and Theological Perspectives*, ed. D.G. Horrell et al. (London: T&T Clark, 2010), p. 21.

if Noah's covenant in Genesis 9 belongs to the same 'Priestly' tradition as Genesis 1, then surely the covenant with animals in Genesis 9 needs to be held together with Genesis 1.[10] There has been a history of misreading Genesis 1, and this has meant that the beauty of our ways was overlooked, and so too was the opportunity to learn a different way of understanding to creation. Indigenous communities are relational, and it is through our ideas and cultural frameworks of relationship that we understand that to harm creation is essentially to harm ourselves and bring shame. We should all seek to live in harmony with creation ̱ to live a life that is reflective of our Creator. After all, 'abusive treatment of God's creation is hardly consistent with such a lifestyle'.[11]

I often think how the environmental challenges that we have today might have been different if Indigenous ways of reading Biblical texts had been accepted and were more prevalent. It is a continuing challenge of colonisation that we are generally unable to be seen and heard on such a crucial issue as caring for Creation, caring for Country. The *Uluru Statement of the Heart* reminds the wider society that Indigenous communities have an ongoing obligation to Country, that our connection that 'the ancestral tie between the land, or 'mother nature', and the Aboriginal and Torres Strait Islander peoples who were born therefrom, remain attached thereto, and must one day return thither to be united with our ancestors. This link is the basis of the ownership of the soil, or better, of sovereignty. It has never been ceded or extinguished and co-exists with the sovereignty of the Crown.

---

[10] Cf. Mark G. Brett, *Decolonizing God: The Bible in the Tides of Empire* (Sheffield: Sheffield Phoenix, 2008), 32–43.

[11] Edward Adams, 'Retrieving the Earth from the Conflagration: 2 Peter 3.5-13 and the Environment', in *Ecological Hermeneutics*, p. 118.

How could it be otherwise? That peoples possessed a land for sixty millennia and this sacred link disappears from world history in merely the last two hundred years?'[12] The challenge is how does the Church take up the call to make space for this continuing connection, and thus continuing challenge to colonization, to be heard?

I'm reminded of the work of Paul Tillich in countering the invalidation of the role of culture in theology.[13] What strikes me is that Tillich is talking about this idea during the 1950s and yet the church still is largely unfamiliar and unprepared for engagement around cultural expressions within theology (and theological education!). I was very glad to see that perhaps some small changes are being made, particularly as the framing question of the Plenary Council was so open and so accessible to many cultural communities that have often been on the periphery of the church. "What do you think God is asking of us in Australia at this time?'[14] brings forth so many opportunities for Aboriginal and Torres Strait Islander Catholics to say it's time for the Church to listen to us, to learn with us, to learn from us. It's time for the words of Pope Francis (echoing those earlier prophetic words of Pope John Paull II) to be heard by all: 'For when you share the noble traditions of your community, you also witness to the power of the Gospel to perfect and purify every society, and in this way God's holy will is accomplished'.[15]

[12] https://ulurustatemdev.wpengine.com/wp-content/uploads/2022/01/UluruStatementfromtheHeartPLAINTEXT.pdf

[13] Tillich, Paul. *Theology of culture*. Vol. 124. New York: Oxford University Press, 1959.

[14] https://military.catholic.org.au/framing-the-central-question-for-the-plenary-council/

[15] https://www.natsicc.org.au/assets/papal-letter.pdf

For a long time, I was confused by the two different worldviews and, even though I trusted my family when they told me that God and the Ancestors were linked : that we were part of all ways of seeing creation, I didn't have the ways to resolve what my head told me were different ways of seeing the world. I know many within our community who reject all their cultural traditions because they cannot reconcile them to their Christian beliefs. I know that the pain of the past is not really the past. It is a daily remembrance of physical abuse, spiritual abuse, and cultural abuse. For them, I feel a great sadness.

But the work being done by Elders and community members across the country can heal this sadness. The work that the international Indigenous theological community of NAIITS An Indigenous Learning community[16] is doing within theological education, and community development spaces also brings opportunities and brings hope to wash away the sadness, because my prayer is that the next generation of Indigenous and Christian don't suffer this anxiety. I heartily concur with Cheyenne man James L. West when he states that the theological task is for the whole Christian Church to actively work towards the 'redefinition of Christian mission and the theology which supports this mission.'[17]

---

[16] NAIITS An Indigenous Learning community is an international learning community that is inclusive of numerous Indigenous communities across the globe, and inclusive of many Christian traditions.
'NAIITS exists to provide an Indigenous designed, developed, delivered, and governed tertiary theological educational program with a commitment to Indigenous ideologies, values, and ontologies as the principal interpretive frameworks for its programs as well as its frameworks for delivery and assessment.'
www.naiits.com

[17] Treat, James. *Native and Christian: Indigenous Voices on Religious Identity in the United States and Canada.* pp. 74-75.

From the time of invasion of Australia, the Church and the State would begin a relationship that would bring (and continues to bring) benefits. Yet, this has had traumatic consequences for Aboriginal and Torres Strait Islander peoples across Australia. In Australia, the murder, rape, execution, segregation, and discrimination of peoples was sanctioned by the Church, and brutally enacted by missionaries and individual Christians across our lands.[18]

There is a challenge to our wider Christian church here in Australia. The church holds a lot of historical baggage, but it is rarely unpacked. I believe that until the wider church in Australia understands the significance of key foundational documents and doctrines of the past, for example the 1493 document of Pope Alexander VI *Inter Caetera*, and how it all influenced invasion and colonization in Australia,[19] then reconciliation is hampered. I particularly liked Muscogee Pastor Rosemary McCombs Maxey's proclamation that Christian churches need Indigenous peoples to help the church reclaim their understanding of 'sacred history and live out their sacred duty to humankind and to the cosmos.'[20] The churches speak of a ministry of hospitality, and give examples where Jesus exercised that ministry of hospitality, but from the Australian Aboriginal and Torres Strait Islander experiences, this has not been the usual practice.

---

[18] Ryan, Lyndall. *Tasmanian Aborigines: a history since 1803*. Sydney: Allen & Unwin, 2012.

[19] Miller, Robert J., Jacinta Ruru, Larissa Behrendt, and Tracey Lindberg. *Discovering Indigenous lands: The doctrine of discovery in the English colonies*. Oxford University Press, 2010.

[20] See Treat, James. *Native and Christian: Indigenous Voices on Religious Identity in the United States and Canada*. pp. 84-85.

There was a balanced life between the Creator and the people within the lands we now call Australia. Invasion interrupted this balance and this connectedness. I think one of the challenges for us working in theological education, in our churches, and perhaps more importantly, our personal faith journey and expression, is how do we authentically express this connectedness? How do we find ways of expressing the Christian concepts in ways that are decolonised, and recontextualised? For example, how might we understand the concepts of sin and salvation, in ways that don't privilege Greco-Roman ideas of sin and salvation?[21] How do we interrogate on a personal, and a communal level our core beliefs? Are they cognisant with the Apostles Creed? If not, how not? And what importance or implications are there for those of us who follow tradition and Christ? These are important questions identified by many Indigenous theologians around the globe.

I think one of the powerful points that continues to echo around my head since I was a child is that Indigenous communities listened to the newcomers, were receptive to the story and person of Jesus. There is a sadness that the newcomers didn't show us the same courtesy or respect. There is time for a new Christology, a re-connection to the

---

[21] There's really not the space to unpack this idea but I think a greater understanding of how Greco-Roman ideas of sin, salvation, and redemption are needed especially by Indigenous peoples so we can begin the process of decolonising the text, and importantly, we can begin to recontextualise and syncretise where appropriate, our traditional ideas of alienation, imbalance, and need. Some interesting scholarly works about the context and history within the development of Christianity: Harper, Kyle. *From shame to sin* Boston: Harvard University Press, 2013.; van Henten, Jan Willem, and Joseph Verheyden, eds. *Early Christian ethics in interaction with Jewish and Greco-Roman contexts*. Leiden: Brill, 2012.

person of Jesus as he was culturally and religiously located. Accepting the Christology that Jesus was a white man is problematic for us Indigenous mob. Understanding Jesus as a Galilean Jew living in colonised lands, allows us to enter into a new relationship with Christianity. It also may allow for our communities to understand such theological concepts as justification by faith that are culturally rooted. I understand that some reading this will be a little troubled by my words, that's ok, let's make time to listen and talk further on whatever occasions we can – for our own theological journeys, and for the theological journeys of those who come after us.

If God is the creator of all, then that includes us. We need to work actively towards presenting God as a Creator that has a relationship with us, that God doesn't and didn't prefer one mob over another, simply because of where they were created. It is time to reaffirm our spiritual birthright. It is time for liberation of old ways that have been in error, that have caused damage across many generations, and stop the flourishing of relationships – between us and God, between us and each other, between us and wider Creation. But we need to avoid the temptation to see what is happening in this space around the globe, and attempt to import it into our part of the world. I am not talking about importing ideas, e.g. liberation theology, that were and are born in other places. I am talking about contextualising things to these lands, to our experiences, shared and unshared.

Liberation theology is something I have struggled with as it often invalidates the existence of the relationship between Indigenous communities and the Creator, often focusing on reinterpreting the biblical narratives to included local perspectives. This is important, of course, but what is missing is the pre-existing relationships of Indigenous communities.[22] And it is a combative or a battle against western ideas and Christian colonising. Again, this is important but Indigenous theologies need, and should, exist in its own right, in their own terms, in a powerful and equal position to any dominant form of Christianity. As Vine Deloria Jr writes 'Eventually liberation theology must engage in a massive critique of itself and its historico-theological context and inheritance.'[23]

Uncle David Mowaljarlai, senior lawman of the Ngarinyin peoples, echoes the generosity of spirit that exists across many Aboriginal and Torres Strait Islander communities when he says:

> We are really sorry for you people. We cry for you because you haven't got meaning of culture in this country. We have a gift we want to give you. We keep getting blocked from giving you that gift. We get blocked by politics and politicians. We get blocked by media, by process of law. All we want to do is come out from under all of this and give you this gift.[24]

There is an invitation freely expressed: come learn from our communities, with the hope of forgiveness, and an ongoing commitment to true reconciliation and the glory of all creation whether (as my nan would've said!) black, white or brindle.

As an Aboriginal Christian who is both Roman Catholic and Anglican, I am looking to those traditions to make space

---

[22] Berryman, Phillip. *Liberation theology: essential facts about the revolutionary movement in Latin America–and beyond.* Temple University Press, 1987.

[23] Treat, James. *Native and Christian: Indigenous Voices on Religious Identity in the United States and Canada.* p. 199.

[24] See Grieves, Vicki. *Aboriginal spirituality: Aboriginal philosophy, the basis of Aboriginal social and emotional wellbeing.* Vol. 9. Darwin: Cooperative Research Centre for Aboriginal Health, 2009. p. 7.

for all of us, our Indigeneity, our pain, and our hopes. The words of Sister Marie Therese Archambault, a Hunkpapa Lakota woman and Franciscan Sister, continue to move me. Her quiet but powerful words of acknowledging what has happened to us as Indigenous peoples, but also what we need for healing. She writes:

> if we do not look at both the life and death aspects of our history, we will deprive ourselves of a means for coming to terms with it and of being healed from the psychological wounds it has left within us.[25]

This is important because it might be more comfortable to stay within the known comfort of our discomfort, fearing what healing can bring. It might also be more comfortable to avoid the sorry business, the sad times and focus upon the happier times. Both extremes are unhealthy. Our redemption from our captivity does not require either. The Apostles Creed speaks of forgiveness of sins, and we should interpret this to include both coloniser and Indigenous. Our work in reconciliation and education must involve the concept of forgiveness. There needs to start with a wider awareness within the Church of how the past and the present are intimately, often violently, connected.

There is an associated challenge and that is to ensure that such awareness isn't used as a technique for stalling, or inaction, because of a misguided paralysis of guilt. The increase in theological education of Indigenous peoples, more resourcing from churches for cultural congruency, and the ordination and/or appointment of Indigenous peoples in paid

---

[25] Treat, James. *Native and Christian: Indigenous Voices on Religious Identity in the United States and Canada.* p. 233.

and unpaid employment will assist in allowing this reflection to become the impetus for action and genuine change.

One of the greatest events in church history with regards to Indigenous Australians was the address of Pope John Paul II in Alice Springs. His historic address to Aborigines and to the wider church are things that many Australian Aboriginal Catholics can quote verbatim! I have long been impressed by many a Catholic Aboriginal Elder who reminded local clergy of those powerful words. Even now, I remain in awe of how powerful those words are, but also how the challenge has not been realised yet. I have felt the pain of my community and the weight of expectation. For a long time, I fought. I tried and tried through the church ways of committees and working groups. In the end, I needed to go out into the wilderness and retreat. Uncle Ray Minniecon, Kabi Kabi, Goreng Goreng, and South Sea Islander pastor and theologian, echoes the difficulties in colonial Christianity:

> For Indigenous Australians, Christianity has been a bitter pill to swallow. We still struggle with the words of Jesus in John 10:10: 'The thief comes to steal, kill and destroy, but I have come that you may have life in abundance'. We have experienced first-hand the first part of this verse. The stealing, killing, and destroying of all that is sacred and meaningful to our identity is still an everyday experience for us. We have no idea what abundant life looks like anymore. We thought Christianity and the Church would deliver the promise of Jesus in abundance. Our expectations of the second part of this verse are an unachievable reality, even though we long for its promise every day. Sadly, history has shown us time and time again that abundant life from the Church is not achievable. And it is quite evident that even the multicultural experiment,

both within and outside the Church, has failed to deliver this promise.[26]

For me, there was a lot of sitting under the moon talking with Creator and crying why, why, why! I needed time to pray and to be away from the busy-ness of church structures. I asked the Creator and ancestors to send me where I could be fully me, where I could be used to make a difference rather than a token, or a cog in the wheel of status quo. So as an Aboriginal woman who is Anglican and Roman Catholic, I found myself at a Baptist theological college, working with Elders and others to develop an Indigenous theological program.

The Lord provides in mysterious ways! Mandan-Hidatsa woman Karol Parker writes of the interruptions to the cultural rhythms of community and life, and the effects on her and others in her generation. I can understand that. I grew up not really knowing where I fitted in, culturally. I was raised in the church, knowing I was a part-Aborigine (this was the terminology of the day) and it was only when I was 16 that I found out the traditional name of our mob. I can remember that day so clearly, as if I was there. That day, a journey back to myself began.

Parker writes that 'most 'white' institutions were totally oblivious to any culture other than the Euro-American'.[27] This was the case for me growing up. The government – let alone the church – did not acknowledge our existence until 1981, choosing to perpetuate and support the myth that Tasmanian Aboriginal people had 'died out'. But I choose to take heart, to

---

[26] Minniecon, Ray, 2021. 'To dream the impossible dream.' *Zadok Perspectives*, (153), p. 24.

[27] Treat, James. *Native and Christian: Indigenous Voices on Religious Identity in the United States and Canada*. p. 371.

continue to fight the good fight, and to work out ways in which we might start to listen to each other more fully, more engaged, with the purpose of decolonising, and becoming whole and healed. My hope is that Aboriginal and Torres Strait Islander Christians might feel encouraged by the words of Pope John Paul II all those years ago:

> That Gospel now invites you to become, through and through, Aboriginal Christians. It meets your deepest desires. You do not have to be people divided into two parts, as though an Aboriginal had to borrow the faith and life of Christianity, like a hat or a pair of shoes, from someone else who owns them. Jesus calls you to accept his words and his values into your own culture. To develop in this way will make you more than ever truly Aboriginal.

And for all of us to strive to continuingly mediate and seek to answer the overall question of the recent Plenary Council: "What do you think God is asking of us in Australia at this time?"[28] As the Church – Aboriginal, Torres Strait Islander and non-Indigenous peoples – we can act collectively to make our churches, parishes and denominations into places that can work for restorative justice and celebrate the diversity of the family of God. The time is right; the time is now. It is attainable through small acts and great acts of courage, commitment, and action – together we can achieve authentic relationships that work towards reconciliation. May we all be blessed in our journey to be fully who God made us to be, and may the words of Aunty Betty Pike and her blessing bring comfort and community:

---

28 https://military.catholic.org.au/framing-the-central-question-for-the-plenary -council/

May you always stand as tall as a tree,

Be as strong as the rock Uluru,

Be as gentle as the morning mist,

Hold the warmth of the sacred campfire within you,

And may the spirits of our ancestors

always watch over you. Amen.[29]

Bibliography

Berryman, Phillip. *Liberation theology: essential facts about the revolutionary movement in Latin America–and beyond.* Temple University Press, 1987.

Brett, Mark G. *Decolonizing God: The Bible in the Tides of Empire,* Sheffield: Sheffield Phoenix, 2008.

Deverell, Garry. *Gondwana Theology: A Trawloolway man reflects on Christian faith.* Sydney: Morning Star Publishing, 2018.

Edward Adams, 'Retrieving the Earth from the Conflagration: 2 Peter 3.5-13 and the Environment', in *Ecological Hermeneutics*, p. 118.

Catholic Church Australia, *First Assembly of the Plenary Council* 24 February 2022 https://military.catholic.org.au/framing-the-central-question-for-the-plenary-council/

---

[29] Aunty Elizabeth (Betty) Pike, *An Australian Blessing*

Grieves, Vicki. *Aboriginal spirituality: Aboriginal philosophy, the basis of Aboriginal social and emotional wellbeing*. Vol. 9. Darwin: Cooperative Research Centre for Aboriginal Health, 2009.

Jenkins, Willis. *Ecologies of grace: Environmental ethics and Christian theology*. Oxford: Oxford University Press, 2013.

Miller, Robert J., Jacinta Ruru, Larissa Behrendt, and Tracey Lindberg. *Discovering Indigenous lands: The doctrine of discovery in the English colonies*. Oxford: Oxford University Press, 2010.

Minniecon, Ray. 'To dream the impossible dream.' *Zadok Perspectives* 153 (2021): 24.

Francis, His Holiness Pope Papal *Letter to National Aboriginal and Torres Strait Islander Catholic Council* (NATSICC) 1 March 2022 https://www.natsicc.org.au/assets/papal-letter.pdf

N. J. B Plomley, *Friendly mission: the Tasmanian journals and papers of George Augustus Robinson, 1829-1834*, 2nd Edition (Hobart: Quintus Publications, 2008).

John W. Rogerson, 'The Creation Stories: Their Ecological Potential and Problems', in *Ecological Hermeneutics: Biblical, Historical and Theological Perspectives*, ed. D.G. Horrell et al. London: T&T Clark, 2010.

Ryan, Lyndall. *Tasmanian Aborigines: a history since 1803*. Sydney: Allen & Unwin, 2012.

Schmid, Konrad, Oded Lipschits, Gary N Knoppers, and Manfred Oeming. 'Judean Identity and Ecumenicity: The Political Theology of the Priestly Document'. In *Judah and the Judeans in the Achaemenid Period: Negotiating Identity in an International Context*, 3–26. Winona Lake, Indiana: Eisenbrauns, 2011.

Story, Dan. *Should Christians Be Environmentalists?* Grand Rapids, MI: Kregel Publications, 2012.

The Holy Bible: containing the Old and New Testaments: *New revised standard version*. 1989. Grand Rapids: Zondervan.

The Uluru Dialogue team: *The Uluru Statement of the Heart* 11 December 2021 https://ulurustatemdev. wpengine.com/wp-content/uploads/2022/01/ UluruStatementfromtheHeartPLAINTEXT.pdf

Tillich, Paul. *Theology of culture*. Vol. 124. New York: Oxford University Press, 1959.

Treat, James. *Native and Christian: Indigenous voices on religious identity in the United States and Canada*. Abingdon-on-Thames, Routledge, 2012.

Synodality, Inclusion and Good Governance – beyond Dysfunction

Peter Johnston

Introduction

Cardinal Carlo Maria Martini, strongly *papabile*[1] at the time of Benedict XVI's election (2005), recorded the following trenchant rebukes of the Church's governance just before his death on 29 August 2012:

> *Our culture has become old, our churches and our religious houses are big and empty, the bureaucratic apparatus of the church grows, our rites and our dress are pompous.*
> *The church must recognise its errors and follow a radical path of change, beginning with the pope and the bishops. The paedophilia scandals compel us to take up a path of conversion. The church is 200 years behind the times.*[2]

---

[1] *'Papabile'* – 'an unofficial Italian term first coined by Vaticanologists and now used internationally in many languages to describe a Roman Catholic man, in practice always a cardinal, who is thought a likely or possible candidate to be elected pope.' - Wikipedia accessed 16 January 2022 at https://en.wikipedia.org/wiki/Papabile

[2] John L. Allen Jr. 'Translated final interview with Martini', *National Catholic Reporter*, 4 Sep 2012, accessed 5 Dec. 2021 at: https://www.ncronline.org/blogs/ncr-today/translated-final-interview-martini

This grave indictment of the institutional Church's governance was ignored by the official Church, reflecting the poor governance outed by Martini.

The institutional Catholic Church is dying – an institution that has alienated most of its members, particularly its youth, is in crisis and its leaders are mostly in denial.[3]

In February 2016, Cardinal George Pell[4] was asked by Senior Counsel for the Australian Royal Commission into Institutional Responses to Child Sexual Abuse whether failures of Catholic bishops across the world to act on clerical child sexual abuse suggested any problems in the way in which the church operates. Cardinal Pell, in a denial that has been echoed by many bishops but rejected by the recorded facts, resorted to the 'few bad apples' defence stating *inter alia*:

> *I think the faults overwhelmingly have been more personal faults, personal failures, rather than structures.*[5]

Those *'personal faults'* have occurred throughout the world over decades, and this world-wide criminal behaviour by so many Church leaders, supposedly committed to the teachings of Jesus, evidences a systemic and substantial failure in leadership, structure, culture and governance, resulting in the Church's current critical state.

Cardinal Pell's response was typical of the official Church response to clerical child sexual abuse world-wide: an attempt to deny the egregious cover-ups by the Church's leaders

---

[3] See Catholics for Renewal, *Getting Back on Mission* (Mulgrave, Vic: Garratt, 2019).

[4] Former Archbishop of Sydney and Melbourne and former Vatican Prefect of the Secretariat for the Economy.

[5] Royal Commission into Institutional Responses to Child Sexual Abuse, Public Hearing – Case Studies 28 & 35 (Day 159: Monday, 29 February 2016, p. 10.

across the world with the clear knowledge of the Holy See – an institution clearly off mission.[6] The behaviour showed an organisation primarily concerned with a devious defence of its reputation to the point of a universal cover-up. That defence offended gravely against the very teachings of the Church.

The institutional Church is failing to model the teachings of Jesus Christ. The Church's governance is monarchical and autocratic. No organisation can pursue its mission effectively without a commitment to mission based on accountability, transparency and inclusion.

Pope Francis' commitment to synodality as fundamental to the Church's governance offers hope. Francis recognises the institutional Church's failure to listen to the sense of faith of the faithful – the people of God – and the Church's abject failures in governance, leadership and mission.[7] True synodality promotes renewal with concomitant accountability, transparency and inclusion. That inclusion must correct the shameful exclusion of women from ministry and governance in the Church.

The Australian Plenary Council 2021-22 is a test for synodality in the Church, a test that will fail if the Australian bishops reject the learnings of synodality and the imperative of renewal identified so clearly by the faithful and return to 'business as usual'. The current German 'Synodal Path' seems to be a more inclusive exercise and some other national initiatives are underway, but all are handicapped by an established clericalist aversion to engaging with and listening to the people of God. Pope Francis' commitment to a 2023 *Synod on Synodality* is, however, a major opportunity for

---

[6] Catholics for Renewal, *Getting Back on Mission*.
[7] Catholics for Renewal, *Getting Back on Mission*, Part 3: Church Governance.

desperately needed universal reform of the Church if it can overcome that clericalist mindset.

The Church's dysfunctional governance, attuned neither to the People of God nor to the signs of the times, is reinforced by a culture of clericalism – an attitude of clerical superiority that places the ordained on a human pedestal and regards the views of the laity as of limited relevance, implicitly rejecting the very humility modelled by Jesus as a cornerstone of his teaching.

More and more Catholics are becoming aware that the clericalist culture of autocratic control denies the role and the responsibility of the faithful in the Church's pursuit of Jesus' mission, in defiance of the teachings of Vatican II and of canon law (c. 212§3) which requires the faithful to accept responsibility for the state of their Church:

> . . . (*the Christian faithful*) *have the right and even at times the duty to manifest to the sacred pastors their opinion on matters which pertain to the good of the Church and to make their opinion known to the rest of the Christian faithful.*[8]

The clericalist culture must be eradicated, the *sensus fidei fidelium*[9] must be heeded in the Church, and the Church's leaders must adopt an inclusive and accountable approach in their critical role of ensuring pursuit of the Church's mission.

The Church cannot be an effective institution for evangelisation without effective leadership. The Church must become fit for the divine purpose of effectively practising and propagating

---

[8] Vatican II, *Lumen Gentium* – Dogmatic Constitution on the Church (Rome: Vatican, 1965), no. 37.

[9] Sense of faith of the faithful', cf. International Theological Commission, *Sensus Fidei in the Life of the Church* (The Holy See: Vatican publication, 2014), accessed 15 December 2021 at: http://www.vatican.va/roman_curia/congregations/cfaith/cti_documents/rc_cti_20140610_sensus-fidei_en.html

the teachings of Jesus. Good governance as reflected in the principles of synodality is a prerequisite for effective decision-making at every level and on all matters including matters of doctrine.

Dysfunctional decision-making inevitably results in flawed decisions and mission failure. That is the state of the Catholic Church. This paper asserts that the top priority for Church reform lies in synodality, inclusion and good governance.

The Church's mission and synodality

Synodality is a way of being church, based on the idea, the ideal, that all the baptised are walking together with a shared attention to the Holy Spirit.[10]

The Church, the people of God, must 'walk together' in pursuing a God-given mission *'to teach universally and without omission all that has been revealed by God for the salvation and fulfilment of humankind'*[11] – a challenge common to all organisations, ensuring a continuing commitment to mission. Our faith sees no higher calling and moral responsibility than the mission of Christianity,[12] a divine mission demanding the highest level of commitment and expertise in its governance,

---

[10] Cardinal Joseph Tobin, Archbishop of Newark, in a keynote address to the Cathedral Ministry Conference, Chicago. See O'Loughlin, Michael J., in *America-The Jesuit Review*, 'Cardinal Tobin: Refusing to deal with complexity in the church is a form of heresy' 12 January 2022, accessed 14 January 2022 at: https://www.americamagazine.org/faith/2022/01/12/cardinal-tobin-synodality-242186

[11] ARCIC-Anglican/Roman Catholic International Commission (Second), *The Church as Communion* (Rome: Vatican, 1991) n.34, accessed 19 Oct.2016 at: http://www.vatican.va/roman_curia/pontifical_councils/chrstuni/angl-comm-docs/rc_pc_chrstuni_doc_19900906_church-communion_en.html

[12] Robin Gill, *Moral Leadership in a Postmodern Age* (Edinburgh: T&T Clark, 1997), 92.

leadership and people. Pope Francis' call to synodality is a call to good governance to ensure a shared commitment to that mission.

The Church of Jesus is much more than the visible institution, the human means of governing and leading the work of the Church as the people of God. There are many images of Jesus' Church that speak to its Christ-given mission, particularly the People of God, mostly embracing the ecclesiology of communion, in *'communio'*,[13] the Communion of Saints,[14] the Mystical Body of Christ (*'the unity of those who live with the life of Christ'*[15]), the Temple of the Spirit, and even Bellarmine's problematic view of the Church as a *'perfect society'*.[16]

Attempts to describe the nature of the Church distinguish, but should not separate, the concepts of the Church as communion of people and the Church as an institution with human governance. As Vatican II taught:

> . . . *the society structured with hierarchical organs and the Mystical Body of Christ are not to be considered as two realities, nor are the visible assembly and the spiritual community, nor the earthly Church and the Church enriched with heavenly things; rather they form one complex reality which coalesces from a divine and a human element.*[17]

---

[13] Walter Cardinal Kasper, *The Catholic Church: Nature, Reality and Mission* (London: Bloomsbury T&T Clark - Kindle e-book Edition, 2015), loc. 821 et al.

[14] Holy See. *Catechism of the Catholic Church* (Strathfield, NSW: St Pauls Publications, 2000), nn. 946-948.

[15] Belgian Jesuit Emile Mersch quoted in Avery Cardinal Dulles SJ, *Models of the Church* (New York: Image, 2002), 44.

[16] Avery Cardinal Dulles SJ, *Models of the Church*, (New York: Image, 2002), 26.

[17] *Lumen Gentium*, n. 8.

The *'visible assembly'* of the Church – the Church's decision-making structures and practices – is critical to the success of the Mystical Body of Christ in its God-given mission. A failure in the governance of the Church is a failure to use the best of our God-given skills for the Church's divine mission. This paper focuses on that visible assembly that Kasper refers to as *'the juridically constituted form of the church represented by the pope and bishops'*[18] (referred to as the 'institutional' Church).

The governance of the Church refers to how the visible assembly is organised and takes decisions in pursuing the mission of Jesus' Church as the People of God in communion, the *'one, holy, catholic and apostolic (Church), which our Saviour . . . commissioned Peter to shepherd, and him and the other apostles to extend and direct with authority'*.[19]

It is clearly the duty of the leaders of the Church, in *'directing with authority'*[20] with the people of the Church in communion, to ensure that its *'juridically constituted form'*[21] reflects Jesus' teachings in its leadership and governance. The Church must reject institutional practices that prejudice pursuit of Jesus' mission. The adoption of inclusive synodal governance is imperative to that end.

The Church's current model of governance reflects two millennia of survival through many turbulent times, from a struggling community movement to an integral, albeit conflicted, role in the civil government of the Holy Roman Empire, including times when there was *'absolutely no concept of a separation of church and state.'*[22] The Church's governance today still reflects that history of inappropriate governance models.

---

[18] Kasper, 129 (loc. 3550).
[19] *Lumen Gentium*, n. 8.
[20] *Lumen Gentium*, n. 8.
[21] Kasper, 129 (loc. 3550).
[22] Paul Collins, *The Birth of the West* (New York: Public Affairs, 2013), 50.

Good governance: critical to all human institutions

Good corporate[23] governance is critical to any organisation's success; all institutions need to apply the best of human knowledge and skills to their governance. The Church should model best practice governance and human leadership models, ensuring accountability and inclusiveness, and the adequacy of its leadership and decision-making. The Church's governance is key to good decision-making and thus good doctrine and the effective pursuit of its mission.

The OECD Principles of Corporate Governance[24] provide a good insight into best human practice in corporate governance and human leadership. These principles seek to ensure that the leadership of an organisation accepts responsibility for the achievement of the organisation's mission. The principles state[25] that corporate governance

> the process by which organisations are directed, controlled and held to account. It encompasses authority, accountability, stewardship, leadership, direction and control exercised in the organisation.[26]

---

[23] Note the derivation of 'corporate' from Latin *corporare*, 'to form into a body.' The term 'corporate governance' is generally applicable to institutional bodies, including the institutional Church.

[24] OECD, G20/OECD *Principles of Corporate Governance* (Paris: OECD Publishing, 2015), accessed 24 August 2016 at: http://dx.doi.org/10.1787/9789264236882-en and http://www.keepeek.com/Digital-Asset-Management/oecd/governance/g20-oecd-principles-of-corporate-governance-2015_9789264236882-en - . V71AZmW3PFI

[25] OECD, 9.

[26] Joint Committee of Public Accounts and Audit, Report 372, *Corporate Governance and Accountability Arrangements for Commonwealth Government Business Enterprises*, (Canberra, Canprint, 1999), p. 7.

The Cadbury Report of the United Kingdom in 1992 (*'generally considered to be the genesis of modern corporate governance'*[27]) based its key findings on the principles of openness, integrity and accountability. Generally, corporate governance standards are based on ethical standards common to and in large part derived from Christian teaching, including:

> *the protection of fundamental interests, respect for shareholder and stakeholder rights, and the fundamental precepts of fair, honest and transparent conduct of business.*[28]

Without a focus on mission through accountability and associated transparency and inclusion of stakeholders, leaders are more subject to the influence of conflicted and inappropriate influences. In practice, many Church leaders lack both accountability and transparency in decision-making and show scant regard for the views of their 'stakeholders', the people of God. It seems that many Church leaders are simply and happily adopting the naïve teaching of Pius X, rejected by Vatican II[29]:

> . . . *the one duty of the multitude is to allow themselves to be led, and, like a docile flock, to follow the Pastors.*

Much has been written on leadership, Heifetz describing it as *'providing a vision, and influencing others to realise it through non-coercive means'.*[30] Leadership should be transformational, ensuring that socially useful goals *'elevate followers to a higher*

---

[27] Dempsey, 4.
[28] Dempsey, 37.
[29] International Theological Commission, *Sensus Fidei in the Life of the Church*, n. 4.
[30] Ronald A. Heifetz, *Leadership without Easy Answers* (Cambridge, Mass.: Belknap Press, 1994), 15.

moral level'.[31] Lowney develops the leadership role further through a Christian lens in describing the 'four unique values' of leadership from Ignatian spirituality as *'self-awareness, ingenuity, love, and heroism'.*[32] The autocracy, unaccountability, and lack of inclusion in the institutional Church are clearly the antithesis of good leadership.

Leadership also drives culture, and the culture of the Church should be exemplary in reflecting Christ-like values and morality. Good leadership promotes effective means of ensuring that mission is pursued and that values are lived, and that accountability for mission is paramount, an accountability reinforced through inclusive practices which model Jesus' teachings.

Accountability ensures that leaders act as stewards of the organisation's mission, never using their authority for personal benefit or conflicted preferences. Accountability is supported by transparency whereby decisions are informed by the invaluable knowledge of stakeholders.

Human experience teaches us that the best leaders are selected on merit having regard to skills necessary for the demands of the job, without gender discrimination; those leaders are generally not differentiated nor artificially supported by grandiose titles or distinctive dress. In good governance practice, leaders' performance is constantly under scrutiny, ensuring accountability for organisational performance[33] and for their relationships with stakeholders. Senior leaders usually sign fixed terms contracts (3-6 years) that are subject to continual appraisal and often not renewed, sometimes

---

[31] Heifetz, 21.

[32] Chris Lowney, *Heroic Leadership: Best Practices from a 450-Year-Old Company* (Chicago: Loyola Press, 2003), 9.

[33] Heifetz, 125-149.

terminated during the contractual term for perceived inadequacies. Leaders also need continual development and learning.

The Church's clerical leaders are selected, formed and promoted with a strong focus on spiritual, pastoral, and theological matters, but usually with little training and experience in the real world of leadership, made worse by a self-satisfied culture of clericalism.[34] Only males are eligible, pomp and status is central to the maintenance of status and authority, appointments are for life (age 75+) without any required reviews of performance, and there are minimal provisions for development and training – all unsurprisingly leading to a lack of accountability, transparency or inclusion. In practice, synodality has little meaning to our pastoral leaders.

An important development in secular governance has been significant attention to gender balance at all levels of leadership. Western society now accepts that gender equality is not only an issue of equality and justice, but that gender balance contributes to a better decision-making environment and better organisational performance. The *McKinsey Quarterly* in 2015 reported on an analysis of data from 50,000 managers across 90 entities around the world showing correlation between gender balance and business metrics such as consumer satisfaction, operating profit and employee engagement, and concluded that *'teams with a male-female ratio between 40 and 60 percent produce results that are more sustained and predictable than those of unbalanced teams.'*[35]

---

[34] John P. Beal, James A. Coriden and Thomas J. Green (eds), *New Commentary on the Code of Canon Law* (New York: Paulist, 2000), Book II, Part 1, Title III, 'Sacred Ministers or Clerics'. Also v. Canon 378 *'Qualifications to Be a Bishop'*.

[35] Michel Landel, 'Gender balance and the link to performance': Commentary, *McKinsey Quarterly*, February 2015.

With developments in corporate governance has come a strong sense of corporate citizenship largely informed by Christian values, particularly respect/love for others and ethical standards. Corporate citizenship, like personal citizenship, demands social responsibility:

> All companies have economic, social, ethical and environmental responsibilities, some of which require compliance with the law, others requiring discretionary action to ensure that the company does not knowingly operate to the detriment of society.[36]

Good corporate citizenship and high standards of governance are implicit in the teachings of Jesus, far beyond requiring the Church to ensure that it 'does not knowingly operate to the detriment of society'; indeed, the betterment of society is integral to the Church's mission. However, Christ's Church has demonstrably failed the corporate citizenship test, illustrated scandalously in its response to clerical child sexual abuse as shown by formal inquiries throughout the world,[37] with shocking consequences for its reputation, credibility, and capacity to witness to the teachings of Jesus.

Jesus' teachings and good governance

The Gospels and the other books of the New Testament record Jesus' teachings as the primary guidance for Christian living, as guidance for his disciples and his Church on how they should live their lives to attain the purpose of their Creator. Jesus has relied on his Church to proclaim his teaching and

---

[36] Malcolm Mcintosh, Deborah Leipziger, Keith Jones, Gill Coleman, *Corporate Citizenship: Successful Strategies for Responsible Companies* (London: Financial Times Management, 1998), 284.

[37] Note especially Ireland, USA and Australia.

is *'at least in some sense, left utterly dependent on our free human response'*,[38] a response that should be informed by the best use of God-given human knowledge and skills.

The most quoted reference and claim for authority in the Catholic Church is Jesus' statement to Peter:

> *Go therefore and make disciples of all nations, . . . teaching them to obey everything that I have commanded you... (Matthew 28:19-20a)*

Peter is authorised to act only in accordance with the teachings of Jesus: *'whatever you bind'* is not an absolute discretion but is always focused on the witness of Jesus, discerning *'the will of him who sent me'*.

In the early days of the Church, Paul held Peter to account for *'not acting consistently with the truth of the gospel'* (Galatians 2:14a) and *'opposed him to his face, because he stood self-condemned'* (Galatians 2:11b). Paul was challenging Peter on a question of governance in the context of proper authority which must be exercised *'consistently with the truth of the gospel'*. Peter apparently accepted this challenge to accountability and in that acceptance modelled major features of good leadership: humility, accountability and inclusiveness.

The teachings Jesus revealed by his words and example embody principles and values of behaviour, showing us a Christ-like exercise of authority with accountability and inclusiveness. Jesus showed us in practice a 'Christian' culture for his Church. The Church is called to teach *'everything that I have commanded you'*, clearly requiring the Church to become

---

[38] Nicholas King, *The Helplessness of God – Biblical models of leadership* (Suffolk, UK: Kevin Mayhew Publishing, 2014), 14.

'people who take on the attitudes, virtues, and way of life of Jesus'.[39]
'You will be my witnesses… to the ends of the earth' (Acts 1:8b).

Jesus stated that *'all the law'* hangs on his commandments of love, the epitome of inclusiveness[40] and the essence of *'everything that I have commanded you'* (Matthew 28:20a).

Jesus particularly condemned hypocrisy, endorsing openness and transparency, and rejected rules as ends in themselves, setting the highest of governance standards with a constant focus on mission. He explicitly condemned some practices of the Pharisees to show the standards of governance he expected, using harsh language to stress the importance of this message (Matthew 12:5, 23:28, Mark 7: 9).

The lack of humility and of accountability, transparency and inclusion in the leadership of the Church, illustrated at their worst in the Church's response to the clerical child sexual abuse scandal, is shameful in any light but particularly in the light of Jesus' fundamental teachings; and even more damning in the case of clerical child sexual abuse, given Jesus' specific warning about care for children:

> If any of you put a stumbling block before one of these little ones who believe in me, it would be better for you if a great millstone were fastened around your neck and you were drowned in the depth of the sea. (Matthew 18:6)

It is axiomatic that the teaching of Christian values must involve living and modeling those values. On this Jesus was very clear: *'you will be my witnesses. . . . to the ends of the earth'* (Acts 1:8b). The Church's dysfunctional governance and inadequate leadership are failing the teachings of Jesus.

---

[39] Patricia Lamoureux and Paul J. Wadell, *The Christian Moral Life – Faithful Discipleship for a Global Society* (Maryknoll NY: Orbis Books, 2010), 10.
[40] cf. Mark 12:28-34; Luke 10:25-28.

What does the Church say about good governance?

Pope Francis' commitment to synodality could be the most important step towards reform of the Church's governance in the history of the institutional Church, reclaiming in modern terms the practices of the first Christians in their communal governance and worship.

The *Code of Canon Law* and the *Catechism of the Catholic Church* are the major formal sources of the Church's standards of governance and leadership, ostensibly dependent on Church teachings from the Scriptures and tradition as reflected in the documents of the councils and synods, especially the most recent ecumenical council Vatican II (1962-65). Papal leadership is critical.

Institutional leadership should seek to model the highest values, attributes and dispositions to which an institution's mission commits its members. The Church is expected to be a witness to Christian governance in *'teaching (all nations) to obey everything that I have commanded you'* (Matthew 28:20a). The Catechism of the Catholic Church notes that *'Scandal is grave when given by those who by nature or office are obliged to teach and educate others'.*[41]

Canon law, *'the rules that govern the public order of the Roman Catholic Church, . . . our ecclesiastical regulations',*[42] includes helpful instruction on the role of the faithful. Vatican II introduced some key principles on inclusiveness of the faithful in Church governance, later included in canon law provisions.

---

[41] Holy See, *Catechism of the Catholic Church* (Strathfield, NSW: St Pauls Publications, 2000) n. 2285.

[42] James A Coriden, *An Introduction to Canon Law* (New York: Paulist - Kindle e-book Edition, revised 2004), loc.106.

The Vatican International Theological Commission stated in its 2014 report[43] that Vatican II:

> ... banish(ed) the caricature of an active hierarchy and a passive laity... (and) taught that all the baptised participate in their own proper way in the three offices of Christ as prophet, priest and king. In particular, it taught that Christ fulfils his prophetic office not only by means of the hierarchy but also via the laity.

Pope Francis' commitment to a synodal approach reflects the highest level of Church teaching. Further, in *Lumen Gentium* (the Dogmatic Constitution on the Church), the Council taught: '*The entire body of the faithful, anointed as they are by the Holy One, cannot err in matters of belief.*'[44]

In 1931, Pius XI proclaimed the related governance principle of subsidiarity in *Quadragesimo Anno*:

> ... it is an injustice and at the same time a grave evil and disturbance of right order to assign to a greater and higher association what lesser and subordinate organisations can do.[45]

Local responsibility is not only synodal and inclusive, but can ensure organisational responsiveness and inclusion of those affected by decisions. Pius XI applied subsidiarity to '*every social activity*'.[46] Properly implemented, subsidiarity enables informed and inclusive decision-making with accountability and understanding of the *sensus fidelium*. The principle is a feature of all good governance, but its implementation requires

---

[43] International Theological Commission, *Sensus Fidei in the Life of the Church* 2014, n. 4.

[44] *Lumen Gentium*, n. 12.

[45] Pope Pius XI, *Quadragesimo Anno* (Encyclical), 15 May 1931, n. 79, accessed 15 December 2021 at: http://w2.vatican.va/content/pius-xi/en/encyclicals/documents/hf_p-xi_enc_19310515_quadragesimo-anno.html

[46] Pope Pius XI, *Quadragesimo Anno*, n.79.

culture and structures consistent with synodality. That culture and those structures are missing in the institutional Church.

The *Code of Canon Law* explicitly provides some mechanisms supporting subsidiarity, such as diocesan pastoral councils comprising *'members of the Christian faithful . . . that truly reflect the entire portion of the people of God'* (c. 511), and diocesan synods including *'lay members of the Christian faithful'* (c. 463). These canonical provisions are mostly ignored by the Church's leaders.

Canon law includes some specific governance provisions in references to structures, authority, sacraments, executive and delegated power, jurisdiction, discipline, decision-making processes and judicial processes, many ignored by Church leaders. There is no explicit recognition of the importance of good governance to the Church's pursuit of its mission. The most explicit reference to the nature of governance (cc129 and 274) is discriminatory:

> 129 - §1. *Those who have received sacred orders are qualified, according to the norm of the prescripts of the law, for the power of governance . . . §2. Lay members of the Christian faithful can cooperate in the exercise of this same power according to the norm of law. . . . 274 - Only clerics can obtain offices for whose exercise the power of orders or the power of ecclesiastical governance is required.*

The ban on women's ordination (c.1024) thus ensures the exclusion of all women from positions of governance, not just the priesthood. The universal Church is a male dominated autocracy whose celibacy further distances female influence. Canon law legislates the discriminatory treatment of women. Much of canon law is not doctrinal and can and must be changed.

In Australia, the Royal Commission on Institutional Responses to Child Sexual Abuse unsurprisingly criticised the Church's decision-making and accountability, and recommended[47] to the Catholic bishops that that they *'conduct a national review of the governance and management structures of dioceses and parishes, including in relation to issues of transparency, accountability, consultation and the participation of lay men and women'*. In response to that recommendation, the Australian Catholic Bishops Conference established a review *'to be conducted in light of Catholic ecclesiology'*[48] which resulted in a comprehensive report *'The Light from the Southern Cross'*.[49]

That very respectful and courteous, albeit frank, report provides much sound advice on necessary governance reform in the Australian Church, noting importantly that *'(t)here is significant flexibility in canon law to introduce improved governance practices'*. Implementation of this significant report, composed by leading theological and governance minds nationally and internationally, has not been a priority for the Bishops Conference, despite the Report's concern that the *'recommendations deserve immediate attention'*.[50]

The Church's leaders generally appear comfortable with the Church's dysfunctional governance. Recently Archbishop Fisher of Sydney, after paying some lip service to *'collaborative*

---

[47] Final Report, Volume 16, *Religious institutions recommendations*, Rec.16.7, p. 50 accessed 15 January 2022 at: https://www.childabuseroyalcommission. gov.au/sites/default/files/final_report_-_recommendations.pdf

[48] Governance Review Project Team, *The Light from the Southern Cross - A Report and Recommendations on the Governance and Management of Dioceses and Parishes in the Catholic Church in Australia*, May 2020, p.4, accessed 15 January 2022 at: https://drive.google.com/file/d/1TXZd4SP-EBk4VtH9JyB9PMSmjY9Mfj7E/ view

[49] Governance Review Project Team, *The Light from the Southern Cross*.

[50] *The Light from the Southern Cross*, p. 134.

collegial synodal terms as Pope Francis asks', dismissively and simplistically rejected proposed reforms of the Church's governance as *'aping secular models of governance'* and *'reduc(ing) the role of pastors to the ceremonial, while leaving church Governance to boards of Lay experts'*.[51] Fisher warned, without any evidence, of a danger *'of creating new power elites and a new lay version of clericalism'*, finishing his homily with a pious and naïve assertion that *'if we focus on our mission as servants of God, we can be confident by God's grace we will have the right servant leaders going forward'*. Archbishop Fisher demonstrates the effective denial of so many Church leaders blinded by their existing status and authority supported by the toxic culture of clericalism.

Fundamental change to canon law and governance practices must be made if the Church is to be renewed in its mission, noting, however, that the few current canonical provisions for good governance practices are commonly ignored by Church's leaders – a feature of clericalism.

A culture of clericalism

On 20 August 2018, Pope Francis wrote a Letter to the People of God[52] throughout the world acknowledging *'the abuse of conscience perpetrated by a significant number of clerics and consecrated persons'*. Francis stated that *'no effort must be spared to create a culture able to prevent... the possibility of (abuse) being*

---

[51] Archbishop Anthony Fisher Homily, Mass at St Mary's Cathedral, Sydney, 25th Sunday in Ordinary Time – 19 September 2021.

[52] Pope Francis, 'Letter of His Holiness Pope Francis to the People of God', Vatican City, 20 August 2018 https://www.vatican.va/content/francesco/en/letters/2018/documents/papa-francesco_20180820_lettera-popolo-didio.html accessed 28 November 2021

covered up and perpetuated'. Importantly, he invoked a statement by his predecessor Benedict XVI in 2005 before becoming Pope:

> *How much filth there is in the Church, and even among those who, in the priesthood, ought to belong entirely to [Christ]! How much pride, how much self-complacency.*

Culture is at the heart of effective leadership, of an organisation's well-being and performance, and of good governance. Culture refers generally to the nature of relationships and the values shared in pursuing an organisation's goals; it is driven from the top. The Drucker Foundation identifies the culture of an organisation as the owner's *'beliefs, values and basic assumptions . . . transferred to the mental models of the subordinates'*.[53] George B. Wilson SJ offers a complementary definition in the context of priesthood:

> *A culture is a power-filled reality that conditions the ways the people in a given social system will tend to think and behave.*[54]

In the case of the Church, the clerical culture should clearly be formed by the *'beliefs, values and basic assumptions'* of Christ as *'owner'* and be *'transferred to the mental models'* of all the people of God to *'think and behave'* in accordance with the teachings of Jesus, primarily guided by Jesus' teaching of love. When leaders fail to model *'beliefs, values and basic assumptions'* inherent in the institution's mission, culture can become toxic in rejecting an organisation's values. That is the situation faced by the Catholic Church.

---

[53] Edgar H Schein, 'Leadership and Organisational Culture' in *The Leader of the Future*, The Drucker Foundation, ed. (San Francisco: Jossey-Bass,1996), 61.

[54] George B. Wilson S.J, *Clericalism: The Death of Priesthood* (Collegeville, Minn.: Liturgical Press, 2008), 3.

A Sydney parish priest nailed the 'culture of clericalism' in commenting on the scandal of clerical sexual abuse and its cover-up:

> *I have come to realise that the culture of clericalism is responsible for the ongoing tragedy that has left the vulnerable unprotected and unhealed by a leadership too willing to be hoodwinked by the doctrine of a priesthood that places priests above other human beings and what they call 'the good of the church' above destruction of lives.*[55]

Dr Marie Keenan, an Irish psychotherapist who had worked with victims and clerical perpetrators of child sexual abuse for decades, published ground-breaking work in 2012 locating the problem of abuse not just within the individual pathology of perpetrators, but also within the very cultural fabric of their priesthood and the governance structures and practices of the Church.[56] Keenan referred to clericalism as:

> *the situation where priests live in a hermetical world, set apart and set above the non-ordained members of the Catholic Church . . . with a presumption of superiority.*[57]

A culture of clericalism in the Church sustains the lack of accountability and inclusiveness, effectively disempowering the laity in the pursuit of the Church's mission, assigning them instead to the role of meekly accepting directions from the governing elite of the clergy. The laity are thus both prejudiced by clericalism and *'implicated in its continuance'*.[58] The scandal

---

[55] Peter Maher, *No more secrets: A homily for Child Protection Sunday*, Sunday, 9 September 2012.

[56] Marie Keenan, *Child Sexual Abuse and the Catholic Church: Gender, Power and Organizational Culture* (New York: Oxford University Press, 2012).

[57] Keenan, 42.

[58] Wilson, 7.

of clerical child sexual abuse is a tragic and shameful symptom of this fundamental governance failing.

Formation of the laity in the Catholic Church has been driven by that context of assumed priestly leadership and superior knowledge *'in a hermetical world'*, an extension of the obedience context whereby the laity are rarely expected or invited to be involved in decision-making. The 'Catch-22' is that the laity are themselves inculturated by the Church's dysfunctional governance, many accepting their exclusion from matters of governance, and worse, rejecting their responsibility for ensuring good governance of Christ's Church.

This rejection of lay input – the antithesis of synodality – isolates many decision-makers in the hierarchy from the most valuable source for any decision-making, namely the views of those affected by their decisions. Professor Margaret Nutting Ralph notes that *'there appears to be a resistance on the part of ordained Catholic leaders, including the Magisterium, to listen and learn from nonordained people'*.[59]

This clericalist lack of lay engagement is contrary to both the teachings of Vatican II[60] and canon law (c.212 §3). The role of leaders is to constantly seek to establish and reinforce a culture consistent with the organisation's values, a culture that witnesses to the mission.

---

[59] Margaret Nutting Ralph, *Why the Catholic Church Must Change – A Necessary Conversation* (Plymouth: Rowman & Littlefield, Kindle e-book Edition, 2013), loc. 3802 of 4765. Ralph directs the master's program for Catholics in pastoral studies at Lexington Theological Seminary in Kentucky and teaches in the deacon program for St Meinrad Seminary and School of Theology, Indiana.

[60] *Lumen Gentium*, Chapter II, and cf. International Theological Commission (above).

Leadership, accountability and inclusiveness

There are many good clerics in the Church who strive to live and witness to the teachings of Jesus despite the prevalent culture of clericalism. The Church barely survives on the faithful commitment of these leaders, clerical and lay, who model the culture of love and humility taught by Jesus. These leaders are thwarted by the dominating culture.

The Church's autocratic governance structures and culture are reinforced by the clericalist culture of privilege and compliance, involving inculturated loyalty that might be seen as a form of *'blind obedience'*.[61] Vatican II taught that *'(t)he entire body of the faithful . . . cannot err in matters of belief'*.[62] The identification of that *'sense of faith of the faithful'* should be a focus of Church leaders, as both good doctrine and good governance; all leaders need to be in touch with their stakeholders.

Despite the efforts of Pope Francis to promote synodality, the Church's leaders still deny synodality in practice by committing the *'grave evil'* identified by Pius XI of *'assign(ing) to a greater and higher association what lesser and subordinate organisations can do.'*[63] The subsidiarity principle rejects autocracy and requires inclusiveness. Pope Francis' adoption of synodality is fundamental to reforming the Church's governance.[64]

In the pursuit of an organisation's purpose and mission, leaders at all levels are expected to take decisions on behalf

---

[61] See a helpful discussion of this issue in Keenan, p. 223, also 156 and 224.

[62] *Lumen Gentium*, n.12.

[63] Pope Pius XI, *Quadragesimo Anno*.

[64] John L. Allen Jr., 'On Communion debate, Pope Francis opts for decentralization' in *Crux* September 25, 2016, accessed 15 December 2021 at: https://cruxnow.com/analysis/2016/09/25/communion-debate-pope-francis-opts-decentralization/

of the organisation in the best interests of the organisation's mission. The absence of accountability, transparency and inclusiveness in decision-making can result in egotistical, arrogant and ill-informed decisions. Accountability is central to every definition of good governance, and essential to the Ignatian 'four unique values' of Christian leadership: 'self-awareness, ingenuity, love, and heroism'.[65]

Sound selection of leaders is key in all human endeavours. The current process for the selection of bishops, the Church's leaders, is simply inadequate. The canonical process gives a key role to the apostolic nuncio, the Vatican's representative in each country, usually a foreigner often with limited local knowledge. The nuncio prepares a list of three candidates (the 'ternus' or 'terna') for bishop vacancies, in consultation mainly with the current bishops and limited others, to send to the Apostolic See (c.377). The candidate pool is narrow (celibate ordained males), the process is open to improper influence, and there is limited provision for assessing the leadership qualities of the candidates, or even considering the needs of the particular diocese, let alone consulting the diocesan faithful on those needs, and no provision at all for inviting applications, a best-practice process to ensure merit-based selection from the best candidates.

It would seem from canon law provisions (cc. 377-378) and known practice[66] that primary consideration is given mainly to the ill-defined notion of suitability for the episcopate (c. 377),

---

[65] Chris Lowney, *Heroic Leadership: Best Practices from a 450-Year-Old Company* (Chicago: Loyola Press, 2003), 9.

[66] Peter Wilkinson, 'Selecting Australia's Bishops: Finding a Role for All', *The Swag, journal of the Australian National Council of Priests*, Spring 2016, accessed 21 October 2016 at: http://www.theswag.org.au/2016/02/selecting-australias-bishops-finding-a-role-for-all/

with secondary importance attached to 'other qualities' (c. 378), with no specific mention of leadership capacity or specific diocesan needs, but the clear exclusion of females.

The exclusion of women from ministry, and thus from governance and substantial executive decision-making, is a further fundamental defect in the Church's leadership. Beyond the profound issue of justice, the lack of gender balance in the Church's leaders, prejudices considered decision-making and contributes to the Church's governance failures.

The Church must face up to the established fact that a system of governance whereby all senior authority is vested in males, is not adequately able to understand and respond to the social and spiritual needs of communities. The competence of exclusively male leadership should be questioned as to its adequacy in skills, responsiveness and accountability. The negative impact on Church decision-making of exclusively male leaders, limited even in their socialising with women, is immense.

In March 2013, some six months after the death of Cardinal Carlo Maria Martini and his call for the church to *recognise its errors and follow a radical path of change, beginning with the pope and the bishops'*,[67] a new pope was elected. Pope Francis subsequently issued his first apostolic exhortation, *Evangelii Gaudium*, in which he spoke of his 'dream' of:

> *a missionary impulse capable of transforming everything, so that the Church's customs, ways of doing things, times and schedules, language and structures can be suitably channelled for the evangelisation of to-day's world rather than for her self-preservation.*[68]

---

[67] John L. Allen Jr. 'Translated final interview with Martini'.

[68] Pope Francis. *Evangelii Gaudium – Apostolic Exhortation on the Proclamation of the Gospel in Today's World.* (Rome: Vatican/St Paul's Publications, 2013), 28.

One might hope, from this and other statements and initiatives of Pope Francis since his election, particularly his commitment to synodality, that the Pope's 'dream' reflects Martini's *radical path of change* for the Church's governance.

The Pope's 'dream', let alone any *radical path of change*, remains far from realisation. In Australia, there has been little indication that the bishops appreciate even the gravity of a Royal Commission's condemnation of the Church's dysfunctional governance, findings that were no surprise to those who have become alienated from the Church.

Renewal of the Church's governance

No human organisation, including the Catholic Church, can be effective in its mission without accountability, transparency and inclusion, particularly the inclusion and full equality of women. The Church must become fit for purpose, for the divine purpose of effectively practising and propagating the teachings of Jesus. Good governance, informed by a commitment to synodality, is a prerequisite for effective decision-making at every level and on all matters including matters of doctrine. Dysfunctional decision-making inevitably results in flawed decisions, and questions about the adequacy of Church teaching.

The essence of renewal

Renewal of the Catholic Church ultimately rests with those least likely to support the necessary changes: a monarchical and patriarchal leadership complemented by a clericalist culture that fails to model the teachings of Jesus. The inadequacies of decision-making in governance and doctrine can only be corrected with a Church leadership that rejects sexism, autocracy and clericalism, and embraces a Christ-like culture reflected in accountability, transparency and inclusion.

Prior to his current major focus on synodality, Pope Francis had taken a number of steps towards reforming the Church's governance, in public statements and in initiatives such as the Council of Cardinal Advisors, the Synod of Bishops assemblies on the Family, the new Dicastery for the Laity the Family and Life, and the Pontifical Commission on the Protection of Minors. Pope Francis has long indicated his commitment to synodality and the *sensus fidelium*, notably in 2015 in addressing the Synod of Bishops:

> *A synodal Church is a Church which listens, which realises that listening 'is more than simply hearing'* (Evangelii Gaudium, n.171). *It is a mutual listening in which everyone has something to learn.*[69]

The Church's God-given responsibility is to teach through word and example. No organisation can influence the beliefs of others without its leaders and members being seen to model its teachings. The imperative for the Church is to correct the present failures in governance and thereby to ensure the Church's ability to prosecute its mission effectively, that is to provide a sound witness to the teachings of Jesus, 'making disciples of all nations' (Matthew 28:19a).

The Church's governance failures require global changes to the Church's leadership, structures and processes, and particularly the Church's culture. The Church in Australia has

---

[69] Pope Francis, *Address Commemorating 50th Anniversary of the Synod of Bishops* (Rome: Vatican, 17 Oct. 2015), accessed 15 December 2021 at: http://w2. vatican.va/content/francesco/en/speeches/2015/october/documents/papa -francesco_20151017_50-anniversario-sinodo.html

committed to changes in processes for dealing with allegations of clerical child sexual abuse,[70] but has not addressed the fundamental governance failures of the Church, either at the local level, which is within their competence, or at the global level which might be beyond their competence but not beyond their influence.

In a strong statement in 2013 about necessary change in the Church, Pope Francis called on the world's priests to bring the healing power of God's grace to everyone in need, to stay close to the marginalised and to be *'shepherds living with the smell of the sheep'*.[71]

Those in leadership positions who live in a hermetical world without 'the smell of the sheep' are not leaders. Awareness of the *sensus fidei fidelium*, 'living with the smell of the sheep', should be central to the culture of Church leaders, just as effective secular leaders are in touch with their stakeholders.

Accountability and inclusiveness

Canon Law already recognises some need for accountability and synodality in the governance of the Church through the provisions for diocesan pastoral councils (cc. 511-514) – ignored by most bishops – and synods (cc. 460-468), both including the laity. There is also the mandatory provision

---

[70] Truth Justice and Healing Council, Submissions to the Royal Commission, accessed 14 October 2016 at: http://www.tjhcouncil.org.au/royal-commission/tjh-council-submissions.aspx

[71] Carol Glatz, Catholic News Service, 'Pope Francis: Priests Should Be 'Shepherds Living with the Smell of the Sheep'', in *The Catholic Telegraph*, 28 March 2013, accessed 16 December 2022 at: http://www.thecatholictelegraph.com/pope-francis-priests-should-be-shepherds-living-with-the-smell-of-the-sheep/13439

for quinquennial diocesan reports (c. 399) to the Pope, but there is no provision for involvement of the faithful in their preparation, or even for their publication.

Present canonical provisions supporting synodality, accountability and engagement of the *sensus fidelium* have not been embraced by the bishops, evidencing rejection of the critical role of '*the testimony of the entire believing community*'.[72]

The Church's failure to admit, apologise for, and take steps to correct its demonstrably inadequate governance in its response to clerical child sexual abuse has in fact added to its loss of credibility in the world. An organisation that acts contrary to its mission in order to avoid scandal has lost its way and needs to hold its leaders accountable, not just introduce new processes.

There are many means of increasing accountability, but structures in themselves are inadequate without a committed culture. Cultural change is critical to address the Church's governance shortcomings requiring strong leadership modelling the Church's fundamental values. Culture is a '*power-filled reality*'[73] that determines to a large extent common organisational attitudes and decision-making.

Clearly, the present leadership of the Church, both Curial and diocesan bishops heading dioceses throughout the world, do not for the most part recognise the failings in the Church's culture and governance. That is not surprising given the hermetical world inhabited by the hierarchy and the inadequate selection process for appointing new bishops.

---

[72] Richard R. Gaillardetz, *By What Authority – A Primer on Scripture, the Magisterium, and the Sense of the Faithful* (Collegeville, Minn.: Liturgical Press, 2003), 117.

[73] George B. Wilson S.J, *Clericalism: The Death of Priesthood* (Collegeville, Minn.: Liturgical Press, 2008), 3.

A necessary first step in improving leadership in the Church is the full involvement of the faithful, particularly the laity, in the life of the Church. Consultative approaches will in themselves facilitate a greater involvement and interest of the laity in their responsibilities as the people of God and a greater sense by bishops of their accountability to, and understanding of, the *sensus fidelium*; but such reform requires other steps to enable the faithful adequately to undertake such a role.

A proposal

The implementation of real renewal in the Church requires immediate commitment to:

1. synodality at all levels of authority and decision-making in the Church
2. acceptance of the equality of women in governance and ministry, and
3. eradication of clericalism.

The following steps are proposed to reinforce those necessary commitments and ensure reform of the Church's governance, with a particular focus on synodality supported by accountability, transparency and inclusion:

1. Amend canon law specifically to mandate all bishops to:
   a. establish a diocesan pastoral council;
   b. conduct a diocesan synod every five years with agenda determined in consultation with the diocesan pastoral council and with broad participation of clergy and laity;
   c. develop and constantly review a public diocesan plan in consultation with the diocesan pastoral council and informed by the diocesan synods to pursue the mission

of the Church in the unique circumstances and needs of the particular diocese;

d. ensure that quinquennial reports are informed by the proposed diocesan synods and reflect consultation with the diocesan pastoral council, and require the reports' contents to be generally available, saving any justified confidentiality.

2. Reform the selection processes for the appointment of bishops (with appropriate amendment to c. 377-8):

   a. to require nuncios to ensure effective consultation with the faithful, including clergy and laity, at the least involving consultation with forms of voting, with diocesan pastoral councils and public invitations to the faithful to comment on the needs of the diocese;

   b. to publicise explicit selection criteria including leadership skills and experience, and the needs of the diocese in the context of the diocesan plan and the views of the diocesan pastoral council and the faithful;

   c. modification of the secrecy provisions of the selection process so that there is public knowledge of the conduct of the process and its nature; and

   d. consider means of introducing the election of bishops by the people of the diocese.

3. Repeal Canon 129 on the restriction of the power of governance to the ordained;

4. Ensure continuing formation programs for all clerics, particularly bishops, to promote an understanding of, commitment to, and skills in leadership of people, based on Christian values and respect for the *sensus fidei fidelium*;

5. Commit to gender balance in the leadership of the Church at all levels starting, as a matter of urgency, with the appointment of progressive women with appropriate skills

and qualifications to half the executive positions leading dicasteries in the Vatican Curia;

6. Ensure regular turnover in the Vatican Curia appointing leaders, lay and cleric, from throughout the world selected on merit, familiar with *'the smell of the sheep'*[74] and committed to a sound sense of accountability to Christ's mission for the Church and informed by the *sensus fidelium*;

7. Revise canon law to include in the General Norms a section on guiding principles of governance and leadership based always on Jesus' teachings in the context of accountability, inclusiveness and subsidiarity; and Australian bishops should immediately accept their report *'The Light from the Southern Cross'* as a foundation for reform of their governance.

The above steps would lay a new structural foundation in the governance of the Church for accountability and inclusiveness, accompanied by transparency and subsidiarity, and for the reform of the culture of clericalism. Such structural and cultural change needs champions at the most senior levels. There is clearly resistance in the Church at present to substantial change of the nature outlined above and seemingly supported in principle by Pope Francis. A catalyst is necessary to ensure the acceptance of change and the essential cultural shift. That catalyst is now available through the Pope's Synod on Synodality.

Conclusion

The key proposition advanced in this chapter is that the Church's governance structures, practices, culture, and decision-

---

[74] Carol Glatz, Catholic News Service.

making are inadequate and inappropriate to the Church's God-given mission. The Church's current model of governance is dysfunctional and fails Jesus' teachings and best human practice, resulting in decisions and performance contrary to its very mission throughout the world. People are leaving the Church in great numbers and the Church is dying.

The Church's loss of much credibility in the world, and the alienation of so many Catholics, requires a determined and Christ-like response. Good governance, the means of directing human organisations towards the achievement of their mission in accordance with the values demanded by society, is critical to any organisation's success. In the case of the Church, good governance reflecting the values of Jesus is critical to mission. Those values should permeate the Church's leadership rather than the 'long-established pathologies in the clerical culture'[75] at the heart of the Catholic Church's governance failings.

The reforms to the Church's dysfunctional governance proposed in this paper address grave failings; the proposals may be seen as radical or challenging by those wedded to the status quo, but they simply reflect Jesus' teachings and the teachings of his Church. The current governance practices of the Church promote the exercise of authority with minimal accountability and negligible inclusiveness, resulting in much harm in the world and failure to pursue the mission mandated by Jesus; our Church is dying.

We must move beyond the dysfunction; a substantial challenge, but achievable by a Church truly committed to the faith it proclaims. Indeed, that faith cannot be adequately proclaimed until the institutional Church truly reflects that

---

[75] Oakley and Russett, *Introduction*, 9.

faith, modelling the faith in all its work. Synodality, inclusion and good governance will take the Church beyond dysfunction to a true and effective commitment to mission, answering Cardinal Martini's call to *'recognise its errors and follow a radical path of change, beginning with the pope and the bishops'.*

Addressing Trauma in our Lives in an Age of Uncertainty

Maree Stanley

CARE ALERT preface to the article

There is a care alert that written here might be something that triggers an emotional response about your own experiences. I give a series of composite examples that are a snapshot about some of the forms of trauma. Please be kind to yourself by considering your own well-being about whether you wish to read such an article. One of the important aspects of recovery from trauma is to make decisions on your own terms. You do not have to go where you do not wish to go. It is an act of compassion toward yourself to take steps to protect and conserve your own well-being.

Trauma is the problem of evil writ large and stamped upon someone's being, whether the source be war, deprivation or the predatory and exploitative nature of social systems or other human beings. It disrupts identity; the sense of self is distorted so that trust in one's own worth or in how to read or trust others is undermined. It can arise out of the bad luck to just happen to be in the wrong place at the wrong time; to encounter an accident; be subject to a crime or threat. It can arise out of the predatory behaviour of another or of some toward others. It can be sufficient for it to arise merely from being the witness to some event that disturbs, or even upends, the frame of reference by which we make sense of the world.

Fear and Trauma go hand in glove to diminish a person and undermine their capacity to cope with doing ordinary life in a way that is meaningful for them. At worst, it stunts their development and can take a toll on both emotional and physical health. Sometimes, its grip is so intense that it literally is a struggle to find a way to breath.

In other cases, the consequences of trauma may not be readily apparent. Sometimes, it can be elusive to contain its impact precisely because its consequences can be fluid. It can be both pervasive and elusive. It can act like a tide that might suddenly rear into consciousness in certain settings and might recede in other contexts.

The label or diagnosis of trauma only serves a purpose when it enhances the possibility for recovery. It can provide an explanation that can bring some relief and understanding to the puzzle of why someone experiences difficulties or their lives function as they do. It can assist in putting some context or shape around what has happened to them. This recognition can aid diluting the impact of an experience that has undermined their sense of identity.

Trauma doesn't account for all suffering but it takes a toll that can reverberate across decades and even generations. The work of the Vietnam Veterans Counselling Service, now named Open Arms, attests to the impact of war trauma on the children and partners of veterans.[1]

Rather than being defeated by trauma in its many forms, we need to regard it as an ever- present predicament. It is about our world and of its nature. We are indeed very fortunate if

---

[1] http: www.openarms.gov.au website of the formerly named Vietnam Veterans Counselling Service. This has been simply but graphically outlined in the phrase 'I thought it was only Me' which can apply alike to veterans and their families as they struggle to overcome its consequences.

its direct impact remains peripheral to our experience of the world.

When encountered in others or directly experienced, it is a brush with the shadow side of life. To some extent, we are all the walking wounded. Just as with the sword in Jesus' side on the cross, we are all lanced by it. While not wishing to detract from the needless and unwanted afflictions of trauma endured, it is also the case that resilience is not formed in the absence of difficulties and challenges. Nor is the possibility for compassion developed.

Any efforts to restore and recover from trauma is about compassion and justice toward ourselves and others. It is an act of faith to attend to trauma in ourselves and others. Encounter with the Trauma of another can engender fear, touch past experiences of pain and can destabilise one's belief in safety and trust. It challenges certainties. To live with hope and faith in the goodness or godliness in life, we need to approach ourselves and others with tender attentiveness. To listen with our ears not our fears. We all have the capacity to act at some level as a healer for self and others in our world.

To some extent, trauma is in the nature of human life; accidents, bereavements, disappointments, illness, war, dislocation are not uncommon events. To some degree, we all vicariously experience some aspects of trauma every time we watch the news, go for a job we don't get, are overlooked for promotion or get dumped by a friend, a relationship breaks down or we have to move cities and leave behind friends and family. The dust of daily battle has sleights to our sense of worthiness at many turns. At varying levels, life presents us all with problems and we do our best to resolve them or recover from them.

However, significant trauma can bear down upon the person so it obliterates problem-solving abilities. It becomes the all-enveloping narrative around which the person's life revolves and is subsumed. The trauma can overtake a person's sense of self and come to freeze and restrict their capacity to experience anything other than the impact of the trauma. The experience is held so close to their identity that they may not realise trauma is the source of their difficulties; the restless sleep, the feelings of inadequacy, anxiety, even addictive behaviours. The encounters we all undergo of the curve balls and difficulties life presents mean we all possess some comprehension and insight from our lived experience about what trauma is. This is a grounding from which to recognise and respect others' painful experiences. None of us is without the capacity to contribute to healing.

We all get a touch of it entering our lives unbidden – the difficult suffering or loss of a loved one, being robbed, being a witness to something happening to someone else, getting caught up in an accident, becoming ill or getting a disease diagnosis. These might be somewhat commonplace events in the story of humans but nonetheless dramatic in their consequences upon the person involved. Our reserves to deal with this buffeting by life are so variable. As a general rule, the number of more severe events encountered over a period of time the more difficult it is to recover a sense of equilibrium and agency about approaching life.

The impact of any trauma can be dependent upon the intensity and frequency of the events and the prior experiences of the person. While every story of trauma and its impact is as unique as our fingerprints, there are some broad general categories of trauma.

Some categories of trauma

Sexual and/or physical abuse endured in childhood can have profound impacts on the trajectory of a child's life and their capacity to learn or to thrive in any domain. The same can be true of an experience of general neglect. It can often result in complex ongoing problems. The longstanding consequences of prolonged exposure via, for example, inadequate and unstable home life can lead to complex developmental impairment. When, for example, parents have an addiction such as drug use or alcoholism and that addiction overtakes their lives, this often precludes much attention to their children. These conditions of abuse or neglect can create a cascade of complex developmental effects for the child. The child's life is impoverished so that learning is blocked and self-esteem is impaired.

Post-traumatic stress disorder often evolves from an identified event or set of circumstances like war or being witness to or the subject involved in a violent event. The ensuing repercussions also bring self-doubt and suffering that interrupts motivation, ability to think and function and deprives someone of their sense of agency and choice.

Prolonged Exposure to Trauma compounds over time. The steady undermining of repeatedly dealing with a difficult set of circumstances exhausts the mind, body and the spirit. It can seep into most or all aspects of identity. People often become isolated and confused. They blame themselves for not 'getting over it' and feel unworthy and ashamed of both events in their lives and who they are. They take on an unwarranted burden of misplaced responsibility for their condition.

Just watching the news can challenge our sense of well-being. We get large doses of trauma-at-one-remove delivered inside our homes via media, movies and many things we read. For some, the word Trauma has become so commonplace that it is a shorthand for anything upsetting. Sometimes people even quite lightly explain 'I was traumatised' by something difficult or stressful but, when used this way, the word sounds more like a catch-all for general stress rather than a debilitating state.

Many of the actions of Jesus were the acknowledging of people who were sick or troubled.

Deliberate or casual and sustained abuse of the powerless has been a constant feature of what we know of human history. Humans have a great capacity to wreak havoc and make chaos for others.

I suspect nothing much about trauma was foreign to Jesus. Living in a town that was on trade routes, he would have seen the itinerant, the dispossessed and the violence of survival amidst poverty. He would have been aware of the impact of accidents, the contagion and dire consequences of illness with little to abate its impact, and the ugliness of intimidation, raw threat and tortuous punishments. Belonging to a subjugated people, the stoning he challenged, arrest and nailing to a cross were common events of the era in which he breathed.

All around us there is the pulse of trauma in everyday instances such as:

The child newly arrived at a school who is threatened by bigger kids who taunt that they will flush her hand down the toilet. She never tells anyone but endures years of finding ways to avoid going to the school toilets. She always delays getting ready to go to school. She never knows what might happen, nor why they chose her.

The woman whose ex-husband has a grievance against her. He pursues her by turning up unannounced at her home and sometimes is both drunk and angry. She is always trying to defuse his intrusive outbursts. She keeps to herself at work. She is also very guarded about making friends at her children's school. She is terrified he will escalate his behaviour to one day make a scene at school or in her workplace. In spite of the intervention order, she is willing to tolerate his rants at her front door in the hope that by not calling the police he will stay away from outbursts in other more public settings. She takes a calculated gamble to endure the abuse in an effort to placate his sense of grievance. She reasons it preferable to limit the damage of public humiliation he may do at the children's school or her workplace. Thus, she is trapped in isolation as she juggles the continual anxiety. It is the least worst option to withstand private abuse over the risks of inflaming his anger to then take issue with her in more public places.

You are suddenly confronted by an accident that happens in front of you. Afterwards, you find you can't get the images of the event out of your head. This arises especially when you try to relax or sleep; it keeps recurring in your thoughts.

The diagnosis that shatters all your plans. Your mind cannot really take in the words, let alone what they mean. In an instant, everything is changed forever. You notice in someone else, or in yourself, that you are no longer interested in things; a what-is-the-point ennui descends over everything like a deep fog. It can be puzzling as to what has led to this diminished interest. The person lost to this state realises that, for others, it can be draining to be around them so they further retreat from any social supports.

Someone goes to hospital for a routine procedure and they unexpectedly never recover. In the hospital corridor, the partner is returned a few possessions and clutching a pathetic bundle of clothes realise this is all that remains of the beloved person. That very same person they had light-heartedly farewelled at Admissions with a cheery wave. They replay in their mind how they dashed back to the car with no other thought than to be at work on time. They have regrets and feel cheated of the chance for a proper farewell. The hospital clears its records as the partner signs for the meagre parcel. They go home numb and lost. A policeman turns up at your door and has to report an accident or sudden death that shifts your world.

Witnessing a beloved subject themselves to self-destructive behaviour and being at a loss to help or limit the damage.

Awakening every day, holding your breath about the possibility of relapse of a loved one who is struggling to recover from a destructive phase; an addiction or a psychological condition in one person can leave those who care about them both anxious and fairly powerless.

Your home is robbed. It is not so much the objects stolen as the sense of invasion that is undermining. Sometimes, it is the senseless mess made or abusive graffiti on the walls that leaves you most afflicted, denigrated and abused.

Recalling the quiet terror of being a child in a car where a drunk parent is driving erratically. The child strains to see over the dashboard as they veer around the road.

You go to a performance review that stuns you with its criticisms. You feel both caught off guard and humiliated. Afterwards, you regret you didn't defend yourself or think to ask questions that now repeatedly go around in your head. You are left hanging in limbo; devalued and without a clear picture of what exactly were the faults in your work. You have no idea how to correct it. You feel so belittled that you feel unable to seek more feedback to gain clarity about what the problem is, let alone correct or improve it. Thus, you are left powerless to fix things but now cringe at how others at work might regard you.

The child shrinking back as they witness parents fighting and holding the fear of the violence that might or does erupt. Absolutely powerless to prevent the pain around them, they must endure its impact.

Trauma can take a less obvious and even elusive form. It can be a sense that you may have witnessed or been part of something that you did not understand at the time but the memory stays with you; leaving you uncertain about your own perceptions. Did I really remember that correctly? or I now wonder why I went along with doing that, letting things happen. I am confused about my own actions or inaction. Why did I laugh when I felt uncomfortable? Could I have stopped something happening? Why did I not say no? or tell someone else? Why did I stay quiet? What does that mean about who I am? The suspicion or the conviction lurks that there is something very unusual and negative about me that allowed things to happen as they did.

The unsettling realisation that the school camp you enjoyed was a place that, years later, there are now people speaking of how they were abused or bullied there at the very same time. Kids like you, but their experience was so vastly and alarmingly different. Why them, not me? 'I was there and never realised what was happening around me' can be a troubling insight.

Sometimes, Trauma leads to a lack of interest in things or a neglect of self. More stridently, it can emerge in risk-taking behaviour that is oblivious to any regard for personal safety.

You might put on weight or drive recklessly as trauma lodges in the mind and body and then impacts on your behaviour.

It can be indirect or vicarious experience such as that of the child of a war veteran whose dad has episodes of binge drinking or nasty moods where he 'blows up' due to his unacknowledged war trauma. The children are left wondering or assuming it is something about them. They feel implicated in their parent's inexplicable behaviour. The child perceives it as their fault and they blame themselves for the outbursts. There is often no way to discuss it after the parent regains composure. The incidents are never directly mentioned but lurk as a backdrop to a child's life.

A common consequence of trauma is that the experience of safety and predictability is shredded. You don't trust your own perceptions to recognise safety and doubt whether you can read others or situations in your environment. You cannot rely upon your own judgments. It makes you a stranger to yourself and estranged from yourself and others. The world becomes an uncertain place and you are deprived of belief or confidence about your capacity to control anything that happens. It robs you of spirit and deprives you of agency to be an effective actor upon your world.

The story of the brick in the basement - seeking a place to put an experience of trauma

In 2003, I was told an evocative story about trauma by the presenter at a training seminar for psychologists. The presenter, Dr Robert Grant, told a moving story from his previous role as a psychologist working in a veteran's hospital in the U.S.A. I recount here my best recollections of Dr Grant's contact with a patient whose state left the doctors both puzzled and concerned. The patient was unaccountably and dramatically losing weight. In the absence of a medical explanation, he was sinking into death. The psychologist was called to the bedside as a last-ditch attempt to avert what was a physical crisis that had no apparent source. The man lay quietly in bed, listless and gaunt as Grant spoke with the man; while a group of clinical staff surrounded the bed to observe. The exchange appeared to have no obvious impact on the man's condition. In the midst of his colleagues, the psychologist brought no relief or improvement to the man's state. In front of his health care colleagues he was unable to provide a bit of 'magic dust' to alleviate things for the patient.

Later the psychologist, Grant, returned alone and the man then recounted an experience. The man recounted having been held in a gruesome prison camp in a war zone. The prisoners were so desperately hungry that they had eaten grass. Upon his survival and return to civilian life, he had never told anyone about his experience and had gone on to resume his ordinary life.

The body knows

During his war ordeal, he had kept a secret record in minute writing on tiny scraps of paper.

Late in life, something about his hospital treatment for a physical illness triggered once more the near-death trauma experience and his body appeared to shut down into starvation mode. This story displays how psychological suffering and physical expression can be linked and in this case, reached the extreme of near starvation. That the body stores and remembers is a theme articulated by a current author and practitioner in the trauma field, Bessel Van Der Kolk (Van

Der Kolk, B. 2015).[2] The body is alerted to imbalance that can present as less dramatic, but often chronic, symptoms of restless sleep, headaches or anxiety. Sometimes the body knows more than we can put into words.

The minute notes of the patient war veteran had been carefully stored, undisclosed to anyone else, behind a brick in the basement of the patient's home. He had manoeuvred the cement away and placed his miniature diary inside the wall cavity. It was stored in place behind the re-cemented brick. The record was sealed in under his everyday world upstairs. For many, many years, it remained undisturbed. The diary held in an unseen place but remaining both a record and witness. It was a sentinel testament of that deeply traumatic phase of his life. One might describe it as the retention of a shadow memory, stored intact, but separate, that had no place in his daylight world. Yet it continued to exist via his diary as part of his life story.

The lodging of the tiny scraps of story cemented in the basement is a graphic image of what trauma does; it leaves a mark or wound that needs addressing in some way so that it does not subsume the development of the person. There needs to be a space of safety created where it is recognised and contained so its impact is diminished. The man went on to overcome the health and healing crisis that the illness had re-triggered. Recognition of the stored memories was part of the path to the patient returning home in health.

---

[2] Van Der Kolk, B. *The Body Keeps the Score: Brain, Mind, and Body in the Transformation of Trauma*. London: Penguin Books, 2015.

Silence undermines people

Over time, silence about trauma can do a lot of ongoing damage. It smothers the individual whose experience is not seen, heard or even recognised as a feature of their existence. The burden of its impact and meaning is borne alone. Remaining invisible to others and nameless goes hand in hand with shame. There is a lovely image by American psychologist, Brene Brown (Brown, B. 2022)[3] that Shame is like mould – it grows in the dark and needs illumination to disperse or dissolve. The trauma consequences, such as shame, fester in the silence that often surrounds them.

Silence and shame often accompany Trauma

Silence is often accompanied by a sense of shame about oneself and a lack of self-worth. Shame is a corrosive force that provides no impetus to seek support, correct, improve or repair the impact of trauma. You have been shamed and are ashamed of your state. You lack positive self-regard. The attitude toward the self is formed that you are not worthy of being treated respectfully. This in turn leaves you more vulnerable to further manipulation or coercion by others into the future. Subsequent poor treatment is confirmatory proof of the low self-image. It becomes a self-fulfilling prophecy.

You can acquire a distorted sense of self that is based around your shame. Thus, you blame yourself and conclude that it is something about you, rather than the events, from which the fault arises. You are overtaken by the event(s) that you have encountered or that have befallen you. Rather than

---

[3] Brown, B. (2022) http: www. Brene Brown.com/home page.html

it being something you underwent and survived (however costly or damaging), it becomes the defining aspect of one's life and identity. A cycle of belief is established where, over time, the life evolves in recurring spirals of difficulty that magnify the impact of previous trauma. It sets up a treadmill; an emotional burden that has to be carried as a core aspect of identity.

Being ashamed about feeling shame

A destructive cycle is set in train of being ashamed about your inability to deal with the traumatic events and the ensuing vulnerability, doubt, depression or anxiety suffered. You have feelings of negativity about your feelings that compound the sense of unworthiness and low self-esteem. You can be ashamed of being ashamed. Events are viewed as a sign of some fatal inner flaw and innate inadequacy. This further reinforces negative beliefs. These negative beliefs then can be held as a powerful self-fulfilling prophecy. Identity takes the cast of a victim rather than an actor.

Finding a place to put experiences to gain a different perspective

I like the image from the story of the veteran who was Dr Grant's patient as I believe often getting assistance to find a place to put things, to reorientate belief about self is at the core of responding to trauma. The task being how to gain the self-assurance to make an internal place to acknowledge and address, then set to one side, the trauma so it is scaled down as a feature of one's life. To limit its capacity to be an ongoing roadblock that undermines faith in life and yourself.

The aim is to reach a point where the person sees themselves as worthy and their life as worthwhile. To create buttresses to stabilise this belief in self so that it is not dragged down by the undertow of past trauma and its consequences. I am not my trauma experiences. Nor am I at fault for having had these experiences. The trauma needs to be reframed to be something that happened to me rather than a feature that dominates who I am.

The dog with three legs is a remarkable dog: encountering the person rather than identity being defined by a problem

My daughter's first word was dog. This was despite her dad's keen coaching to get that really important word 'Dad' to be first in her lexicon. When my daughter was about age four, we were driving in the car and she burst out that we needed to stop. She was inspired by the sight of a really remarkable dog; she breathlessly said, 'Look, mum. There is a dog who has got three legs and a tail'. It wasn't the missing fourth leg that grabbed her attention, but rather, the way this dog was unique. She was impressed that such a different kind of dog existed. For her, there was no sense of absence or fault in a dog only having three legs. For her, this dog had an extra dimension that was deserving of investigation. It made that dog a particularly rare and exceptionally interesting sort of dog.

Getting out from under trauma needs a shift in orientation. The person needs recognition for who they are. Ideally, the aim is to have trauma recede to be an aspect amongst many of their life story that is to be acknowledged and its consequences addressed. Reparations and legal actions can be significant contributions to this effort. To be able to shrink its impact by turning it into a strand in the fabric of their story rather than the definition of identity. This can be a hard-won shift where a scar often exists and persists but the trauma is not the determinant of capability or one's worth. This can be the realisation of a truth that is freeing from self-blame.

Just as that dog my daughter gleefully noticed was its own unique (albeit with a non-standard leg count) self, its circumstances did not prevent it taking on life as a dog on its own terms. Being the dog it was reminds me of the miracles over trauma that are rarely noticed.

Miracles are out there

If we are all, to some degree, the walking wounded then our defeats and suffering are the story of damage and withstanding it. Alongside all the trauma, there are remarkable signs of hope that are not readily explained or investigated. In work with the children of alcoholics, for example, there is often a child who appears to be able to emerge from a family of dysfunction apparently exceptionally well adjusted and competent. These children are often notable in the way they have persistently performed as the school captain or the academic star while their home circumstances are very difficult. These stories do not receive nearly enough attention. They are not well understood for what capability or some inner spirit of identity that has sustained them so the impact of trauma does not appear to hold back their progress in life.

Another overlooked set of stories are the miracles of those childhood survivors of trauma who don't abuse and refuse to live life repeating what was done to them. This is worthy of more celebration and investigation than it ever receives. How do some, indeed the majority, of those abused or enduring debilitating trauma as children, never go on to perpetrate what was inflicted upon them? This is hope in action; while living with the damage, they appear to be able to hold steadfast in a refusal to replicate the damage imposed upon them. By some quality of instinct, disposition or sense of self (or perhaps grace?), their own behaviour toward others, especially their own children, does not a replicate their own negative experience.

The Trauma of others is amongst us

When I go to the supermarket, I can find myself pondering about the nature of trauma. In any supermarket, there are enough people, workers and customers gathered, that make the statistical odds very likely that trauma survivors are amongst them. At the very least, the chances are high that there will be at least one woman in the aisles who has endured sexual assault at a young age. The likelihood expands when including all the other possible sources of trauma that can be encountered. Yet here we all are, politely and stoically doing the routine things that keep daily life going. On your average day, trauma can exist in quiet proximity around and alongside us all in those we encounter at the cashier or the call centre.

The survivors of trauma are not apart or separate in any way from the majority of us. We all have stories of damage. Every time we watch T.V. news, we are exposed to triggers that can heighten anxiety and vigilance to dangers carried in our memories. I repeat, to a certain extent, we can all be seen as the walking wounded. There is not a category of them and the rest. Their experiences, whether recognised or not, do not make them in some way unusual or foreign to the wider mainstream story of living ordinary life. Trauma is related to all our lives. We stand with trauma survivors at the checkout or beside them taking milk out of the freezer cabinet. We are one in a common humanity.

You don't have to pretend you know more than you do

Realising the commonality amongst us all is a first step toward diminishing the impact of trauma. We do not have to feign knowledge, a professional designation or a capacity to fix a situation. To simply bear in mind, when dealing with others, what we do not know of their experience is a healing approach that aids undermining the impact of trauma. To set aside assumptions that can be so readily made and endeavour to approach others aware of gaps in our knowledge is to engage with a care that validates the other. It is a stance that conveys respect. In this way, we can all contribute to increasing the chances that our encounters help rather than hinder others in their progress through life, carrying whatever trauma they may have endured, as best they are able.

This is not to discount the utility of professional help and specific strategies as very valuable and vital aids to managing and defusing the impact of trauma. Rather, it is to assert the practical worth of awareness and respect to be life-affirming. Some simple but practical things worth considering are outlined below.

Helpful language

To use language that refers to survivors (rather than victims) is recognising our commonality. Just as there is a shift in perspective between describing someone by a medical condition they might have: he is an asthmatic rather than they being a person who happens to have asthma. Like psychological trauma, a physical illness is an unchosen difficulty, yes; but not the defining quality of the person. Just as the dog with three legs and a tail is still a dog. It is not our problems that define our identity.

There is a lot of usage of the word trauma. I would like to put the case for being careful with past tense endings such as 'they are traumatised'. It is not just a fixed event or state that once done cannot be undone or modified. I believe it preferable to use descriptions that speak of someone as active in regard to any trauma experience. To speak of living with an experience of trauma, working at overcoming a trauma, making sense of a trauma or seeking redress about a past trauma is expressing hope. This language implies the possibility of action to recover and respects the agency of the person. God hasn't finished with any of us yet. It also affirms the active courage for people to be as they are in relation to trauma. The person, whatever the state of their scars, has survived to reach this point, to live, to be, in spite of their pain. The person exists independent of what they have been subjected to or encountered.

This is not to presume we know what it has been like for anyone else in their suffering. Rather, it is to adopt a stance of learning and tentative interest. Drawing upon our own experience is a starting point to begin imaginative wondering about what it might be like for another. It does not require sharing and comparing our story to that of anyone else. Instead, it is a brave step out of our comfort zone as well as sometimes pressing upon our own sadnesses. It is a step of approximation toward empathy. It is realising and treating with care what we may not know, alongside the clues that we might possess. Some inklings about trauma from our own lives are not to be cited as a benchmark but serve as a platform on which to tentatively build understanding another. By no means does it bypass the uniqueness of every experience but it is a step to tolerance and acceptance that is an act of love. A stance with some humility about what is unknown of the life of another tempers the rapidity with which others are judged, discounted or written off.

The intent to try to alleviate another's trauma is far better served by our awareness of our limits in understanding. It also takes pressure off ourselves by letting go the pretext that we have the capacity to fix it. When you are mindful of what you may not know, it makes you tread more carefully in respecting and attending to another.

Sometimes less words are more useful

In instances where someone reveals something of their trauma experience to you, finding the words of response can be tricky. Often words can get in the way. When feeling inadequate or uncertain as to how to respond, I invite you to pause to regard the hands of the person. When you watch another's hands, you are respectfully attending. You are not attempting to overtake but are alongside. It is a way to regard and tune into the other without feeling the need to find something to say. The desire to remove suffering can unintentionally diminish another by moving at your pace to solution rather than staying in contact with where the other is at this moment. Just being alongside displays faith that what the other is holding they may find a place to put it, to lessen its intrusive impact.

While it can feel awkward or inept, it is preferable to admit 'I have no idea what to say' or 'I am at a loss as to what that experience must be like' than to paper over or submerge with words what the other is experiencing. Psychologist Brene

Brown characterises this as keeping it awkward, brave and kind (Brown, B. 2022).[4] The drive to fix 'it' or to say the right thing can be well intentioned. However, that is the listener's desire rather than the survivor's and it can get in the way of actually acknowledging another in their state about their trauma experience. To be present by sitting and watching, rather than comment can serve as a respectful bridge. A trusting silence can be powerful. It expresses belief and recognition but does not usurp the other as the expert on their own experience. The self- reproach attached to trauma can be lessened by quiet letting be; concern demonstrated by permitting them to be as they are.

This can be a form of compassion. It is a quality of exchange, of watchful waiting where we accept the mystery; the mystery we are to ourselves and the awareness to respect what we may never know of another's circumstances. To realise our knowing of another is only ever, at best, an approximation.

The wounded healer

The phrase wounded healer is a concept outlined in a modest book by theologian and priest, Henri Nouwen (Nouwen, H. 1979).[5] I find the concept is a helpful one that captures the tension between being attentive to recognising our own wounds and limits and then using them for better attending to others. When one feels let down or ignored by others, a useful question might be to ask how might I have liked to have been

---

[4] Brown, B. (2022) http: www. Brene Brown.com/home page.html.

[5] Nouwen, H. J. M. (1979) *With Open Hands*. (13th Edit.) Ave Maria Press Notre Dame, Indiana 46556.

treated by others. Many of us have had experiences, often after a bereavement, of knowing others intent is well-meaning but their phrases of comfort actually make things worse. It does not help to be told it is 'God's will' or some other cliché such as 'nothing happens without a reason' or 'we are sent nothing we cannot bear' which do not match at all with the state of the person being consoled. None of us is without personal griefs and disappointments. It is a challenge and action of faith to re-work them as reference tools into a constructive approach to others. If trauma is a form of robbery of the spirit, then we need to find and make safe places for affirming and holding the unique spirit of each.

I cannot readily see any purpose in itself of the trauma wrought in people's lives. Accepting I have no explanation is to walk with humility about what I don't know or understand. Humility is not passive meekness, nor does it preclude anger or seeking account or consequences for perpetrators or restorative justice. Rather, humility is a cue for being mindful when relating to others. No one really knows what another has endured nor how an event has impacted upon them. The intent to travel with respect is to place faith in the trauma survivor, whether identified as such or not.

Sometimes as a counsellor I have been both shocked and deeply disturbed about the predatory nature of some human beings and the artful ruses they construct to inveigle themselves into positions of trust to exploit others. Instances of what Grace Tame describes as 'hard wired evil'.[6] I have no doubt that many people of faith have pondered this issue in

---

[6] Maley, J. 'It's much more sinister': The hard truths about sexual assault. *The Age: Good Weekend*, 27 November 2021). p. 16.

light of the behaviour of the Church organisations regarding allegations and convictions on sexual abuse by the clergy.

What Carl Jung might define as the shadow side appears to be an inherent aspect of the human condition. It is a mystery, baffling as are the sorrowful mysteries of the rosary; which essentially were all about the infliction of terrible and senseless trauma and the endurance of the afflicted. The concept of being a wounded healer I find a useful way to tackle recovery and moving beyond suffering. With our wounds, we can all act in faith to attempt to take a stance as healers.

I believe you do have to find a spiritual place to put your wounds. To consider that they may be put into useful service to develop your identity, self and to improve your stance toward others is an act of faith. To work at making a place to put the heartache of suffering and trauma damage is a courageous quest. The core meaning of the word Religion is binding back; return, recognition and renewal of self in relation to the good.

The words of St Scholastica to 'go forward as you can' seem an appropriate edict. It is a case for treading a little more gently in our approach to others. To use our wounds to enlarge our understanding and to see others trauma as on a continuum on which we are all aligned.

Learning to be snow angels

As a young student teacher, I went on a week-long trip to the snowfields with a large group of other trainee teachers. Lots of people struggled with learning to ski and ability levels were very mixed. For some of the physical education majors, in particular, it was unsettling to discover a sport where they didn't readily get the knack of keeping upright. Hopefully in the longer term, an experience of falling hard while learning made them more effective teachers.

Despite being sore from all our tumbles, we were all able to learn to do a delightful snow trick; a display of group mastery of this cool and slippery surface. A lecturer, Marguerite Fry, had taught in snow-bound places in Canada. She lined us up along a reasonably deep snow drift banked upon the side of a road. She then told us to turn away from the snowbank and form a line where we all were facing out to the roadway. Then, following her instruction, we centred ourselves with a breath and as one, allowed ourselves to fall directly backwards. We dropped back into the snow in all its lush wetness. Once we had all fallen into the snowy ground, with arms by our sides and lying face up to the sky, Marguerite told us to settle back into the indentation each had made and flap our arms out to the sides. We pushed outstretched arms up and down, dredging furrows back and forth through the snow. We then helped each other up out of our shallow holes and turned around to look back at our handiwork. There was a beautiful, glistening line of indentations in the snow that Marguerite told us were known as Snow Angels. Upon the snowy surface, our bodies and arms had made shadowed blocks shaped like classic kindergarten drawings of broad-winged angels.

We are all clumsy, awkward and fall backwards but we can still be luminous. Our presence can make a difference. We can use our arms and hands to make a shape that can be a wing that extends support and upholds belief and values. It may apparently melt but the potential to leave an imprint on the lives of others truly exists. While it may appear insubstantial, even invisible, it is not nothing. Like the stone that skips or skims across the water, the ripple effect happens.

Faith is believing that our efforts to respect, acknowledge, appreciate what we may or may not know of someone else is of value. I believe it is a kind of praying to be mindful of how others might have suffered. We tread the earth differently when we are aware of the potential wounds of others.

It is a stance that increases the chances of understanding that enables addressing of trauma. To act in the humility of what we do not know sets the scene for a quality of engagement that can be tender and attentive. This in turn paves the way for constructive trust and healing to occur. To be humble does not mean apologising for yourself or your limits but moving in the world as a sacred space where you are encountering the wounds of others, known or unknown. It contains the seed for empowering others to hold on, to retain the spark to seek to heal and be healed.

This is an approach that counters psychological trauma via quiet responsiveness. To attend to the other as we would wish to be tended in our wounds. Holding faith in the capacity of us to both heal as we attempt to be a healing presence.

From Trauma, to Trust, to Trinity

Berise Heasly

Exploring the Trauma ... the Lived Experience of those afflicted by Trauma.

It is the norm of the human condition to ask when/ where/ why/ what/ how/ which/ and what if? – in relation to the circumstances we meet in daily life. No one can be sure, or completely certain of the answers, the reasons, the problems, the unsolvables in such questions. It is the lonely lot of many of the People of God, the 'people in the pews', to struggle in the face of these many unsolvables which happen often concurrently.

The traumatic sources of suffering facing 21st century living globally are deep, diverse and draining. In our hurt, our uncertainty, our confusion, we have turned to our church to seek comfort, secure in the knowledge of the message of Jesus. In the third millennium, we are not hearing much response from the bishops in Australia or worldwide to the variety of trauma which hits us in our *lived experience*. Where is the leadership of the many Bishops' conferences, the compassionate responses of the various cardinals to each of the sudden challenges that the People of God, the 'people in the pews', face today?

In the *physical* milieu, in the world around us, we find evidence of torture, jailing without due process, slavery, serial sexual abuse, abuse of women, serial and decades-long war, extreme personal abuse, scapegoating, cyberbullying, and highlights within church circles of extreme emphasis on continuing penitential behaviours especially in some religious orders; we find systematic oppression of women domestically, asylum-seekers, violent unnecessary death, violent and institutional racism, serious long-term health syndromes, miscarriage, birth complications, irreversible child illness and death, PTSD with the lifelong nightmares and other mental and emotional outcomes, psychic shock endured by women who are subjected to barbaric physical assault...

'I share Rambo's insight' (says Catherine Keller in the Foreword to Shelley Rambo's *Spirit and Trauma - a Theology of Remaining*, p. ix) 'into trauma's refusal to recede into the past – how it interrupts any theology that would leap right from the crucifixions of history to the hope of resurrection'. I also share this jump as showing inappropriate binary thinking which ignores, as clericalism has done, the middle ground: response needs response-ability, and response-ability leads to responsibility.

In the *emotional* milieu, even in our Church, we find evidence of gender distortion, brainwashing, enforced celibacy, suppression of independent thinking, deliberate promotion of lies, censorship, stalking, cyber-stalking, insistence on perfectionism or its opposite emphasis on sinfulness, requirement to practise false humility, oppression and suppression of female influence, insistence on a priori choice of masculine virtues, values and what counts as ethics in decision-making, premature judgment of emotional intent as a means of control, sudden grief...

'The study of trauma' (says Rambo, p. 4) 'has also moved away from an exclusively individual look at the psyche to a study of cycles of history and the global and political effects of ongoing violence. The study of trauma has expanded to account for multiple levels of trauma: historical trauma, institutional trauma, and global trauma'. I see the existence of historical trauma even in the 20th century wars; I see the institutional trauma in the dreadful consequences of child sexual abuse in almost every major country; I see the global trauma in climate change, world hunger, blatant war-mongering and human trafficking. It follows that all clerics, existing and impending, must have the ongoing opportunity for the span of their seminary studies, and way beyond, to complete a full academic course on consequences of trauma.

In the *social* milieu, within diocesan and parish protocols, we find evidence of callous authoritarianism, clerical and sometimes lay resistance to change, defiance, political and ideological blindness, dictatorial governmental processes, coverup behaviours and corruption, convenient scapegoating by elements of ecclesial government and by often clerical religious figures, harassment of victims especially in Australia where some male Orders are still subjecting their victims of sexual assault to unfair legal trauma, systematic suppression of personal freedoms, interminable or sudden war; we see famine, plagues like mice and rabbits, the despair of Australian farmers, flood, drought, incarceration especially with brutal racial overtones, long-term refugees, loss of career or job or marriage through stress and strains of pandemics surrounding the various nations of the world, colonialism which still haunts so many countries described as third-world economies...

Rambo reminds us: 'The most familiar theological discourse about suffering is known as theodicy, the theoretical practice of reconciling claims about the goodness of God with the presence of evil in the world. While theodicies provide logic for thinking about religious claims about God's nature and human suffering, they do not function effectively to address and respond to suffering. While theodicies might provide explanation, the degree to which explanations are helpful to the healing process is unclear' (p. 5). It becomes obvious to me that here is the very point of the need for massive doses of development of all branches of existing theological thinking in 21st century terms if Synodality is to be born, let alone grow and function. The renaming of Curia departments as Dicasteries, all fifteen of them, does not even get to the starting line of addressing the message of the compassion of Jesus and his radical message.

In the *intellectual* milieu, including scholastic and theological domains, we find brutal silencing of researchers and theologians (who are valiantly trying to define the elements of practical theology fit for purpose in 21st century living conditions), fake news, censorship of so many despite their personal learning and lived experience, lies used to hoodwink the vulnerable and the naïve, suppression or dismissal of consciously careful personal moral decisions, education withheld or manipulated to control the vulnerable, the use of the concept of priestly ontological change (again as a means of control), systematic upending of the Sacrament of Baptism as entrée to the community of the People of God, the 'people in the pews', and the conspiracy and corruption uncovered in money matters ⸰ whether in secular or religious venues ...

'The work of theologians such as Flora Keshgegian, Serene Jones, Cynthia Hess, and Jennifer Beste suggests that trauma poses unique challenges, transforming the discourse about suffering, God, redemption, and theological anthropology in significant ways' (says Rambo, p. 5). She continues:

'Their work testifies to the fact that trauma is not simply a category that can be confined to the fields of psychology and counselling; it has broadened to present profound challenges to epistemology, constructions of the self, and theological understandings of time'. I find the evidence of lived experience of the laity, in managing the horrendous effects of trauma in so many lives, is one glaring reason why so many 'people in the pews' have walked away, why younger generations don't listen because they can't make sense of what the Church is offering, and why ideology has taken over the minds of so many. Until present church authority is wrenched clear of ideology, power and control measures, we will always have fundamentalist ideologies trying to take the place of a reasoned faith based on the message of Jesus.

In the *spiritual* milieu, especially when managing the spiritual life of vulnerable souls, we find entrenched and defiant clericalism, hooked on divorced or gay people's lives – or its partner: fundamentalism. We see extremism, minimalism, exaggeration weaponised for religious control especially in the attempt to deny some Catholic politicians reception of Holy Communion, blatant colonialist attitudes used to subdue and suppress the vulnerable through fear and brutal dictatorship – both secular and religious – clerical duplicity used as a control measure (even in scalding censorship), interference in marital matters of virtue, values and ethics, dominance over marital decision-making by distant disrespectful celibates whose ignorance is laughable, and interference by clerical decision in the relationship between any individual and the Cosmic Mystery we call God...

Rambo makes these interlocking issues clear: 'The dynamics of traumatic experience press Christian discourse beyond the site of the cross to think about what it means to live in the aftermath of death. Studies in trauma suggest that trauma has a double structure: the actual occurrence of a violent(s) and a belated awakening to the event... This phenomenon in different ways, but the nature of trauma is such that an inability to fully process an event means that it returns... Suffering is what, in time, can be integrated into one's understanding of the world. Trauma is what is not integrated in time; it is the difference between a closed and an open wound... The experience of survival is one in which life, as it once was, cannot be retrieved' (p. 7). It is patently obvious that the first demand of Wijngaard's Ten Commandments for Church Reform is a requirement, as he states that theologians and other scholars must be allowed to develop research into these interlocking areas of deep concern. It makes the existence of clericalism and the depth of shallow piety look ridiculous.

No wonder Pope Francis is pleading for people to do away with pride, in favour of deep listening, referring variously to our institutional church as a 'field hospital' or as needing to get close to the people who are suffering, to feel 'the smell of the sheep' – after all, the Gospels did have Jesus say 'Feed my lambs, feed my sheep' in favour of promoting Synodality, a concept which approaches the educational concept of tensegrity .

In the face of such massive challenges, we acknowledge the depth of suffering in each and every one of the sets of circumstances listed above. Unless we are currently suffering one or more of such serious challenges, we do not know how severe the degree of desperation, nor the urgent need for relief can be. Every possible person, every imaginable effort will be needed to address the magnitude of suffering faced by every person, whether within the community of the Christian faith or otherwise circumstanced. The Covid pandemic has taught us this much already. And the advent of authoritarian regimes bent of control of huge populations through deprivations in every area of existence is the ultimate in trauma for the people of God, the 'people in the pews' – whether secular or religious in nature.

How do we trust?

In theory, it is possible to wish to help, and we all feel intimidated by the depth and diversity of suffering by the People of God. Perhaps if we are able to listen deeply enough, as our respected Miriam-Rose, our wonderful Aboriginal leader, has taught us, and to expose the brutal resistance and indifference behind such circumstances, working together, praying together, planning together, we can first make a difference to the degree of pain. But it does mean everyone – prelates, People of God, 'people in the pews' – acting to effect restorative justice rather than punitive legal punishments. In such a way, we need the courage and the strength to keep on keeping on! We begin by modelling daily the truthful, supportive patience needed to help all with long-term illnesses. We try always to model honesty and accessibility and sustainability in our daily lives, so that trust will be possible, and suffering can be mitigated.

What do we mean by *Lived Experience* of trauma? The uncomplicated answer is probably to indicate that lived experience of any sort must involve problems, paradox, dilemma – and these are not synonymous terms. Faced with such hurdles, we must make decisions: sometimes impulsive, hesitant, ignorant, sometimes in denial, or careful, hasty, irresponsible, or reasoned – based on the best available option, or faulty, circumstantially based, or nuanced...

Consequences of personal decisions, intentional or impulsive dismissal of consequences, even dismissal of personal or institutional decisions may occur in order to protect non-accountability or the identity of the decision-maker. Personal decision-making is hard enough to recognise when overwhelmed with trauma, but the overlay of institutional decision-making complicates and deepens the trauma. Inability to recognise value and significance of possible options, or identification of double jeopardy considerations may therefore lead to deliberate reliance on authoritative decisions made by people with responsibility for the well-being of the People of God, the 'people in the pews', without compassion, or as revenge, or duplicity – and the *lived experience* of such trauma is hidden and dismissed. In countries all over the world, the result has been identified in various Commissions into Child Sexual Abuse, in which hierarchical figures have featured in pandemic proportions – the latest being the research into the Irish question by Derek Scally (2021).

Refusal to learn from mistakes, refusal to practise responsibility for brutal decisions despite evidence of serious injustice inflicted on children or vulnerable people, all this is dismissed because it is so often invisible. Fear of accepting restorative justice as a 21st century virtue, or dismissal of restorative justice as a community value, is to devalue that same traumatic suffering which can be a lifelong sentence. Using apathy and inaction, stonewalling as a means of power and control over vulnerable and injured minorities, leads to the same lifelong sentence.

Dismissal of the process of maturity in individuals within the clerical and lay apostolate – who don't/ can't/ won't recognise the significance of the arc of response – response-ability – responsibility; or who prefer the disengaged framework of moral and political norms as a way of building a moral compass, is the process which leads to dire suffering as *inescapable lived experience*, and affects women, children, co-dependent relationships, and oppressed minorities. The devious nature of this dismissal means that the victim will always feel reduced to the status of a non-person, whose suffering means nothing, no matter how many times in a homily, a victim hears a clerical figure talk about love, compassion, and the message of Jesus.

It seems that we need to understand another virtue called resilience as a 21st century response to uncertainty, to anxiety, to fear, to torment and torture, to wars of invasion, to injustice which crushes the soul and silences the victim's channel to hear the voice of a compassionate God. As mature adults, members of the laity are already familiar with patterns of trauma, even that of religious trauma, and we gradually learn through our *daily lived experience* to recognise how to manage mistakes, to learn response-ability as skills of reasoned response to enduring the unendurable! BUT it helps when that lived experience of maturing individuals directs us to recognise the comfort and support of Sophia-Spirit, whose gifts we receive at the start of puberty in the sacrament of Confirmation, and which we articulate in every Eucharist that we share.

Working, searching for authentic trust ...

What seems to be needed is a mixture of action, planning and praying. In each personal sphere, in all institutional milieux, we need to systematically explore in 21st century terms the simple ways to understand the complexities of all the elements of trauma: the physical, the emotional, the social, the intellectual, the spiritual. In the spirit of parrhesia, we face the knowledge of where imperfect knowledge or lack of action has embarrassed us by highlighting the lack of leadership by the supposed hierarchical leaders.

We know that many of the laity with relevant expertise are fully committed to Social Justice work all over the world. We know the terrible exhaustion which precedes the realisation that the only way left is resilience. We know also that many priests have been as fully committed as their lay partners in managing huge daily enterprises within that daily lived experience. But we need more. The Australian Plenary Council can be a counting house, performing a valuable service of initiating the various planned actions needed to set up further dedicated processes so that experts can go into action with immediate outcomes for the vulnerable and the suffering.

However, if fear of change, rigidism as an ideology, or demand to keep positions of status, prevents our leaders in governance from learning to model accountability, actual leadership and transparency, we are doomed to become a belittled group known to the world around us for lack of courage. Not a comfortable outlook! As Paul Collins (2022) indicates: 'For sure, there has always been a tension between a broad, open vision of Catholicism rooted in living experience, and a static, sectarian view of faith... the narrower vision is a revival of what's called "remnant theology"'. Not a way to look beyond the present either!

For the People of God, the 'people in the pews', we need to own that our own *response* is to recognise that somehow, we must find the strength and courage, to find the compassion of Jesus, to feel the support of Sophia-Spirit as we cling to the first threads of hope and translate that hope into resilience. We discover in our lived experience that resilience promotes socially strong networks as aid in times of trauma, in order to address fear and uncertainty, remembering our personal moral principles. Resilience leads us to recognise and overcome the overwhelming effects of trauma, enough to allow ourselves to glimpse the strength, courage and clarity to respond as adequately as possible, i.e. *response-ability* – to the changing situations we face, even if we can't monitor or change those fearful conditions. Then the realisation that the partnership with our Cosmic Creator, our Compassionate Jesus, our Sophia-Spirit will carry us forward as we take up the *responsibility* to ourselves, to others around us, and to the lived experience of trauma whenever it appears.

It is never a matter of returning to 'normal', because there is no longer a measure that can be normal. Consequently, we search for that which promotes a positive adaptation, i.e. responsibility – often including an instinctive protective capability as well. (Nuala Kenny, *La Croix*,15 September 2021: 'Ritual, Resilience and Recovery'). Resilience is a gradual development of understanding how to gather strength, knowledge, courage to act for our own survival, despite adverse lived experience. It springs gently out of hope as a better personal outcome, as a relief from trauma. By degrees, a second outcome is the tiny seed of trust in a compassionate God, who walks with us as we grow in mature understanding of the reality of our own lived experience. That trust is also the blossoming of a belief that the God who walks with us is a Mystery; that the God who walks with us is present in the innermost recesses of the soul; that it is possible to listen with our heart, and cautiously begin the process of walking coherently with our God.

Resilience allows us to glimpse recovery. The various scientific disciplines which bolster that journey of recovery need to be couched in 21st century terms, rather than reliance on idolatrous medieval ideologies like patriarchy and clericalism. The concept of synodality which Pope Francis is emphasising is built on the separate and precise concept of tensegrity, which allows for the development of alliances, in preference to comfortable ecclesial communities of conformity. Alliances allow for the coming together of groups of the People of God, the 'people in the pews', who are working on particular issues and considerations, where conformity is alien to the solving of problems and where restorative justice is mangled by efforts to control outcomes before full understanding of difficult terrains are seen to be manageable.

And by degrees, too, the warmth of God's love infuses us with a strengthening of that resilience, and Trust recovers, and responds by blooming ever stronger. We are conscious of a deepening of nearness, of the tiny light of hope, of presence – and trauma recedes, even if it does not disappear. There is comfort in that! As we age, we are conscious of the invitation to know God more nearly, more intimately, more strongly.

For those baptised into the community of the Lord, that maturing element allows for a continuing conversation as we test the ideas that inspire us towards trust in the significance of our bond and prompts the deepening of faith and belief in the God of Jesus, the Cosmic Trinity. That awe-inspiring Presence we are beginning to discover as Creator of the multiverse that 21st century scientific discoveries show us.

Eventually, Sophia-Spirit causes light-bulb moments to strengthen us on our journey. As that trust solidifies, we find ourselves able to admit that our anger and frustration with a defiant institutional Church can be turned into mature action. And perhaps many light-bulb moments later, Trust emerges again, and we find the path of faith in our Trinitarian Godhead, whom Jesus taught those around him to trust and proclaim. Only then can we seriously, through daily lived experience, reveal to others our certainty of the love and understanding of our God.

However, we must include in our considerations the massive re-organisation of Roman Curia departments, now to be known only as Dicasteries:

' <u>Reorganisation of Curia departments by Pope Francis: the long road to Reform and Co-responsibility.</u>'

(Accessed through *National Catholic Reporter* 20 March 2022).

'All departments are now titled as Dicasteries. In the order of significance:

1. Evangelisation
2. Doctrine of Faith
3. Service of Charity
4. Eastern Churches
5. Divine Worship and the Discipline of the Sacraments
6. Causes of Saints
7. Bishops
8. Clergy
9. Institutes of Consecrated Life and Societies of Apostolic Life
10. Promoting Christian Unity
11. Interreligious Dialogue
12. Promoting Integral Human Development
13. Legislative Texts
14. Communication'

It will be interesting to discover whether this will be followed through structurally, or whether the stonewalling familiar over the centuries will prevail! Noticeable here also is the imposition of boundaries which force a false stopping point within a hierarchical structure, which has survived intact, even though changing names and job descriptions per Dicastery means a form of change!

Before Trust can be established, it will be a very interesting and possibly painful transition if we are to follow the Ten Commandments for Church Reform, published recently in succinct and honest language by John Wijngaards:

'**10 Commandments for Church Reform**' – John Wijngaards, Institute for Catholic Research

(Accessed through Root and Branch Synod: 'Your Voice at the Vatican' 17 March, 2022.)

'Dear Pope Francis,

We members of the international Catholic Community submit for your consideration the following Ten Commandments for Church Reform.

We urge that these principles should be enshrined in Church Law and faithfully implemented on all levels.

1. Allow theologians and other scholars unrestricted freedom of research without fear of consequences.
2. Recognise that a pastoral leader's first priority is caring for the people, not upholding ecclesiastical institutions.
3. Select perceptive administrators in the Roman Curia, not narrow-minded bureaucrats intent on blocking reform.
4. Appoint open-minded pastoral bishops not hardline traditionalists.
5. Abandon the misguided repression of sex, based on the assumption that any sexual act not geared to procreation is sinful.
6. Grant parents freedom to plan their families responsibly.
7. Give women full access to holy orders.
8. Allow priests to benefit from the support of a loving spouse.

9. Respect the God-given dignity of every member of the community – treating grownups as adults.
10. Update church doctrine and practice after listening to the advice of independent competent scholars, pastoral councils and experienced pastors.'

It is important right here to highlight the significance of the last publication of the late Bishop Geoffrey Robinson because his legacy is not only a beautiful view of a courageous, scholarly and compassionate pastor and bishop. Whether he knew it when he wrote 'Human Misunderstandings of God' (*Towards the end of my days*, pp. 4- 5), he has left us with a mandate to recognise how to channel our journey as Church, as Community, as People of God, as 'people in the pews'.

He says: 'To promote growth, we must move ...' (p. 4). He highlights various perspectives of how humans visualise their God, and asks us to move **from** an outdated or mistaken view **to** a deeper understanding of that God.

I highlight some of his transition channel to make the familiar journey – **from** – **to**:

1. *From* a God we struggle to find words to describe, *to* a 'stunned awareness of an 'otherness' beyond the reach of words – through stretching our wonder and awe at the Cosmos, as Science is teaching us;
2. *From* a God described in a book *to* a God 'who cannot be contained by any created thing' – through the lived experience of our God who is a God of compassion and mystery;
3. *From* a God that 'religious authorities believe they can contain' *to* a God of 'infinite surprise' – through courageous development of comparative theology, of experimental metaphor, of feminine compassion, and beyond;

4. *From* 'limited human ideas' to be stretched beyond all limitations, *to* a God who is neither male nor female – through an expansion of the infinite variety emanating from Sophia-Spirit/Holy Ghost the repository of God's Wisdom;

5. *From* a God 'who should always agree with our ideas' *to* a God who constantly challenges our ignorance' – through the pursuit of lived experience, through the work of scholars in all of today's disciplines, through the humble recognition of all we don't know;

6. *From* 'a God greatly concerned with glory and majesty' *to* a God 'caring passionately' for us as individuals, as community – through the story of Jesus, through the aegis of the Holy Spirit, through the mystery of the Creator of what lies beyond what the human mind can contain.

There is so much more that Bishop Geoffrey has given us, as a deeply committed son of our God he served so well in Australia. The title of his book highlights the accumulated wisdom, lived experience and interior bond between himself and what we call the Blessed Trinity. *Towards the end of my days* is a legacy which covers so much of what the Australian Plenary Council did not fully address, but may do so in the Implementation step now in operation. This content allows us to visualise what a Bishop can do to deliver the best of what was proposed at the Vatican ll Council, distilled into manageable sections and reflections, allowing us to approach what it means to trust once again. As we learn, as we meld this content with our lived experience, as we find ourselves deepening our own interior bond with the Blessed Trinity, that Trust will flower again.

And now to Trinity...

One of the legacies that I find very valuable as a consequence of the long gestation of studies in my PhD thesis has been the work on understanding of the concept of auto-ethnographical writing, and the critical thinking and personal honesty and integrity needed to put this form of academic research and inquiry into action. Spearheaded at the time by W-M. Roth (2005) and Mary Beattie (2009) – both Canadian academics – they saw and researched the value and significance of the *lived experience* of people in their own milieux. One outcome of this form of learning has, for me, been the gradual dawning of the serious recognition and knowledge we need to appreciate in the lived experience of the People of God, and particularly those 'people in the pews', identified in *Call No One Father* and also modelled in *We too: the Laity speaks*.

During our lived experience of life's journey as members of the Christian community, there are signposts: Baptism, Eucharist, familiarity of the stories which tell us of the teachings and message of Jesus. The meanings and coherence of these matters in our own lives need expert scholarship and deep commitment to authenticity and historical relevance, so that the emergence of the substance and sustainability of our trust is not smashed by ignorant and shallow homilies. Consequently, we query why Dicasteries in Rome seem so distant from the lived experience of the People of God, the 'people in the pews'. Or, more uncomfortably, we also query why there are significant silences, and apparent stonewalling taking place, as the prevailing opinion seems to indicate that the Reform-ers will run out of steam, and then the institutional church can proceed as they have always done!

Mired in medieval concepts and ideologies of patriarchy and clericalism, the output from Dicastery offices and from the Australian hierarchy (Fewtrell, 2022) currently does not reach the ears of those in need, in so many countries, where deprivation and unnecessary suffering makes a mockery of churchy and clericalistic language used to highlight status of the author(s), regardless of the recent moves made by the present Pontiff. I can't help returning to the breadth of research outlined in Uta Ranke-Heinemann (1991) which was highlighted in 'Towards Regeneration and Reform' section in *We Too: The Laity Speaks* (2020) as she showed the extraordinary and brutal treatment of women over the centuries by the Catholic leadership.

Other recent research by Dyan Elliott (2020) has highlighted the convenient and subtle change in the working meaning of celibacy: the term began as an abstention of sexual behaviours with anyone; it became 'adjusted' to mean an abstention of sexual activity with women; in practice, it became a convenient substitution to claim that sexual activity with young males did not contravene the ban, and it was considered no sin, 'whoever has carnal knowledge of handsome boys does not commit a sin' (Elliott, p. 235).

Ilia Delio states clearly that Bonaventure 'views the world as sacramental. It is a symbolic world and one full of signs of God's presence. The world is created as a means of God's self-revelation so that it might lead us to love and praise the Creator' (2021, p. 70). Not much of Bonaventure shows in the research that Uta Ranke-Heinemann (1991) discovered. Nor in Dyan Elliott (2020), Frederic Martel (2019) and John Cornwell, Derek Scally and others brave enough to address appalling questions about the double standards of some of the priestly caste over two millennia. We are left with authentic research which confronts us, shames us, and confuses the good pastors who honestly tried to carry the good news of a compassionate

Jesus to us, in our own lived experience. So normal became soiled, and abnormal became the norm!

We must, and are desperate, to guard our trust – in the existence, the majesty and the mystery of our Trinitarian God. It is the acceptance of this mystery, of all that we don't know, which comforts us in our trust, and which deepens our faith in that Trinity – despite clericalism, betrayal, trauma, and deep suffering. And gradually, the internal conversation with God becomes a realistic reverence for the existence of personal faith. It becomes a grateful *response* for all the support we have experienced on our journey; it becomes an acknowledged *response-ability*, couched in knowledge and faith, that we accept the personal *responsibility* to grow into our identity as partners, as co-creators with God, in the journey of those around us – those we love, those who are our neighbours, our communities. We look back then on trauma, recognising the times when we could not see our way because of overwhelming suffering. We name also with gratitude those significant others who were inspired by Sophia-Spirit to support, prompt, lead us in our time of woe.

In a paper for the education journal, *Discourse and Communication for Sustainable Education* (vol 12, issue 2, 2021), titled 'Edu-tensegrity: an expanded Integration of 21st Century Education' (pp. 76-95), I highlighted the trilectic (or in religious terms: trinitarian) elements of the interlocking concepts within education. It is patently obvious that this treatment models *going-beyond* established boundaries and allowing for integrated and developed understandings which can now be extended into Theo-tensegrity – a conceptual device that gives us a channel to allow methods of logic, reason and change to emerge as we evolve urgently towards 21st century melding of sciences, religions, cosmology, archaeology towards trust and hope in an expanded recognition of who and what our Trinitarian God really is. It is beyond understanding that several Popes were able to salve their consciences by rejecting what they called modernity as though somehow whatever they thought modernity was, it was intrinsically evil. Such an intransigent stance enabled evil influences in the secular and the religious world of 20th and 21st century history to emerge, evolve, overwhelm, and certainly not be addressed ethically. We face the appalling consequences today.

This is beyond the end point of recognising the mystery of understanding fully the wholeness of the Divinity, which is beyond the outer boundaries of humankind, but may not always remain so distant. To delve into the wonders of creation, through the lens of science and cosmology today, allows us to recognise what Delio is highlighting: 'Matter has a drive towards spirit, but only one who is matter and spirit can unite the material world of God. It is for this reason, Bonaventure states, that the role of the human person is to lead creation back to God' (ibid. p. 70). Deplorably, there is no sign that women, the channel of creation for new souls to enter human form, are included in the appalling discoveries identified by Ranke-Heinemann, whose documentation is authentic in its sources and in its conclusions.

I am again indebted to Delio (2021), as she pursues how Teilhard de Chardin delved into the deepening realisation of the power of the Creator of the cosmos: 'Here is an amazing insight that both Francis of Assisi and Teilhard realised: the power at the heart of matter, of a leaf, for example, is the same power at the heart of my life – it is the power of God.'(ibid. p. 157). It is with admiration that I note Delio's own response to the contemplation of Creation and the metaphor of Trinity: Creator/ Lover/Spirit as she concludes that 'contemplative vision is the heart of the Christian life by which we are brought into a new reality, connected through the heart to the whole of life, attuned to the deeper intelligence of nature, and called forth irresistibly by the Spirit to creatively express our gifts in the evolution of self and world' (ibid. p. 167).

No sign is implied here that the harsh interventions of clericalism, hierarchical power and theocratic control, that is uncovered in the lived experience - 'the troubles' of the small island and its tightly-gripped fortunes of the Irish, as we follow Derek Scally's epic research regarding the fate of Ireland, including his autobiographical (auto-ethnographical also) emphasis. He is careful to identify the significance of the research which covers the appalling cruelty, the callous clericalism, the distortion of the message of Jesus, endured by generations of Irish in what really was an unannounced theocracy. The power of the hierarchy overwhelmed the government and the culture, because no one was capable of overcoming their fear, being bullied into submission by those who railed against modernity. It is difficult to recognise differences between the documentation Scally examines of the role of the Catholic Church in Ireland, and other documentation of Nazi Germany, regardless of religious or political beginnings being of different origin. Scally attempts to address this traumatic history of Ireland in his Epilogue (2021, pp. 303-308).

I have derived a certain relief in the opportunities to study as much of the sciences as I can possibly undertake. The emergence of studies in space research, of the importance of secure understanding of deep space introduces us to the vastnesses of multiverses, has also allowed experimental theology by brave theologians, despite likely silencing by faceless individuals wielding Curial power. We are indebted to remarkable and mystical theologies by theological experts well versed in the disciplines which surround human efforts to try to understand God's unlimited power as Creator of multiverses, not just the universe; of the mystery invisible to humankind in the actual role of Jesus as Lover, and the insistent presence of the Holy Spirit who is not a Ghost, as was the title of the 1940 -50 theology of my youth.

We are introduced to the majesty of the understanding of First Peoples and their recognition of the mystery of ancient times, ancient history, and the immanent presence of the Creator of all, regardless of their creation stories being different from our own cultural narratives. All of this content we wonder, we wrestle with for meaning, and eventually we arrive at the point at which we acknowledge that Energy, Space, Rainbow Serpent, and many other names for the God of all as beyond the human mind to totally understand. At that point, I find myself recognising faith in the unknown 'I AM' who I really know as Creator, Inspirer and Wisdom in my life, beyond the trauma, beyond the confusion, beyond boundaries being imposed by others.

This is my attempt to discover a process, a channel, a pathway to address the overpowering lived experience of trauma today. No amount of pontificating, sloganeering, sermonising in moralistic mode will address the requirement of learning the skills needed – that response-ability – to achieve relief for the People of God, the 'people in the pews', who are drowning, in suffering, in deprivation, in need of compassion. We obviously must go 'beyond' what applies now (Chittister, 2022). Taking up that responsibility to participate, in authentic trust, in integrity, in conscious faith, means actively working and praying for restoration, regeneration and renewal of the early Christian communities, with compassion, respect, and understanding – for Jesus' sake and for our own sake. Lord of the Cosmos, show me how!

References

Armstrong, Karen, *The Case for God: what religion really means* (London: The Bodley Head, 2009).

Armstrong, Karen, *Fields of Blood: Religion and the History of Violence* (London: The Bodley Head, 2014).

Barton, Julie S. & Constant J. Mews (1995) *Hildegard of Bingen and Gendered Theology in Judeo-Christian Tradition* (Monash University Centre for Studies in Religion, 1995).

Beattie, Mary, *The Quest for Meaning* (Rotterdam: Sense Publishers, 2009).

Bourgeault, Cynthia , *The Wisdom Jesus* (Colorado USA: Shambhala Publications 2008).

Boston Globe Staff, *Betrayal: The Crisis in the Catholic Church* (London: Profile Books, 2002).

Brennan, Frank, *Acting on Conscience* (St Lucia: UQP, 2007).

Brennan, Frank et al, *Refugees, Morality and Public Policy* (Melbourne: David Lovell Publishing, 2002).

Bruteau, Beatrice, *The Holy Thursday Revolution* (Maryknoll, NY: Orbis Books 2005).

Camara, Dom Helder, *The Church and Colonialism* (New Jersey USA: Dimension Books 1969).

Castley, Paul F., *A Time To Hope* (Melbourne: Coventry Press 2019).

Chan, Mark, LY and Roland Chia (eds), 'Beyond determinism and reductionism: genetic science and the person' *ATF Science and Theology* , Series Four (Hindmarsh SA: ATF Press 2003.

Chittister, Joan, *An Evolving God, an Evolving Purpose, an Evolving World* (Melbourne: John Garratt Publishing 2022).

Cleary, Ray, *A Time To Speak* (Melbourne: Coventry Press, 2021).

Collins, Paul, *Recovering the 'TRUE CHURCH'* (Melbourne: Coventry Press, 2022).

Cornwell, John, *Church, Interrupted* (San Francisco: Chronicle Prism, 2021).

Crawford, Evelyn, *Over My Tracks* (Melbourne: Penguin Books, 1993).

Davidson, Robyn, *Tracks* (London: Bloomsbury, 2017).

Davies, Paul, *The Mind of God: Science and the Search for Ultimate Meaning* (London: Penguin Science 1992).

Delio, Ilia, *The Unbearable Wholeness of Being: God, Evolution and the Power of Love* (Maryknoll: Orbis Books 2013).

Delio, Ilia, *The Hours of the Universe* (Maryknoll: Orbis Books 2021.

Doherty, Beth, *All The Beautiful Things* (Adelaide: ATF Press, 2020).

Elliott, Dyan, *The Corrupter of Boys* (Philadelphia: Penn, 2020).

Faggioli, Massimo, *Vatican ll: The Battle for Meaning* (Mahwah, NJ: Paulist Press 2012).

Faggioli, Massimo, *Sorting Out Catholicism* (Collegeville MN: Liturgical Press 2014).

Faggioli, Massimo, *A Council for the Global Church* (Minneapolis MN: Fortress Press, 2015).

Faggioli, Massimo, *Joe Biden and Catholicism in the United States* (New London CT: Bayard, 2021).

Fewtrell, Terry, 'When bishops play dirty' in *The Swag* , Vol. 30, no. 2 - 2022).

Gaillardetz, Richard R, 'A promising roadmap for ecclesial reform and conversion' Accessed *La Croix International* 4/6/2020.

Gallagher, Brian, *Set Me Free* (Melbourne: Coventry Press 2019).

Gates, Melinda, *The Moment of Lift* (Sydney: Pan Macmillan, 2019).

Goosen, Gideon,*Clericalism* (Melbourne: Coventry Press, 2020).

Grant, Adam, *Think Again* (London: The Bodley Head 2020).

Halik, Tomas, *Patience with God* (New York: Doubleday 2009).

Halik, Tomas, *Night of the Confessor* (New York: Doubleday Religion, 2012).

Heasly, Berise Therese, *Towards an Architecture for the Teaching of Virtues, Values and Ethics* (Bern Switzerland: Peter Lang, 2015.

Heasly, Berise, *Call No One Father* (Melbourne: Coventry Press, 2019).

Heasly, Berise & John D'Arcy May (eds), *We Too: The Laity Speaks* (Melbourne: Coventry Press, 2020).

Heasly, Berise, 'Edu-Tensegrity: An Expanded Integration of 21st Century Education' in *Discourse and Communication for Sustainable Education* , Vol.12, issue 2, 2021.

Hill Fletcher, Jeannine, *The Sin of White Supremacy* (Maryknoll: Orbis Books, 2017).

Levitsky, Steven & D. Ziblatt, *How Democracies Die* (New York: Broadway Books, 2018).

Lipton, Bruce H., *The Biology of Belief: Unleashing the Power of Consciousness, Matter and Miracles* (Sydney: Hay House, 2008).

Lohfink, Gerhard, *Prayer Takes Us Home* , 2nd Edition (Minnesota: Liturgical Press, 2020).

Loughrey, Glenn, *On Being Blackfella's Young Fella* (Melbourne: Coventry Press, 2020).

Mackay, Hugh, *The Art of Belonging* (Sydney: Pan Macmillan 2016).

Mallon, James, *Beyond The Parish: Divine Renovation* (Melbourne: John Garratt, 2020).

Martin, David, *The Future of Christianity: Reflections on Violence and Democracy, Religion and Secularization* (Surrey: Ashgate Publishing 2011).

Martin, James, *Learning to Pray* (London: William Collins, 2021).

McCabe, H. & Rizvi, J. (eds), *Untold Resilience* (Sydney: Penguin Life, Random House, 2020).

McNamara, James, *The Power of Compassion* (Mahwah NJ: Paulist Press, 1983). Nuzzi, Gianluig, *Merchants in the Temple* (New York: Henry Holt and Company, 2015).

Pope Francis, *Laudato Si'* (Strathfield NSW: St Pauls Publications, 2015).

Pope Francis, *Gaudete et Exsultate* (Strathfield NSW: St Pauls Publications, 2018).

Pope Francis, *Fratelli Tutti* (Strathfield NSW: St Pauls Publications, 2020).

Rambo, Shelly, *Spirit and Trauma* (Louisville KY: Westminster John Knox Press, 2010).

Robinson, Bishop Geoffrey, *For Christ's Sake* (Melbourne : John Garratt Publishing, 2013).

Robinson, Bishop Geoffrey, *Towards the end of my days* (Melbourne: John Garratt Publishing, 2022).

Robinson, Ken, *Creative Schools* (London: Penguin Books, 2015).

Roccas, Nicole M. , *Time and Despondency* (Chesterton IN: Ancient Faith Publishing, 2017).

Rohr, Richard, *What the Mystics Know* (New York: Crossroad publishing, 2005).

Roth, Wolff-Michael, (ed.), *Auto/Biography and Auto/Ethnography* (Rotterdam: Sense Publishers, 2005).

Rush, Ormond, *The Vision of Vatican ll: Its Fundamental Principles* (Collegeville MN: Liturgical Press Academic, 2019).

Stockton, Eugene, *The Deep Within: Towards an Archetypal Theology* (Lawson NSW: Blue Mountain Education and Research Trust, 2011).

Tacey, David, *Edge of the Sacred* (Melbourne: HarperCollinsPublishers, 1995).

Tacey, David, *Beyond Literal Belief; Religion as Metaphor* (Melbourne: John Garratt Publishing, 2015).

Tanner, Kathryn, *Christ the Key* (Cambridge: Cambridge University Press, 2010).

Thomas, Gordon, *Desire and Denial: Sexuality and Vocation – A Church in Crisis* (London: Grafton Books, 1986).

Treston, Kevin, *Opening Doors* (Melbourne: Coventry Press, 2019).

Treston, Kevin, *The Wind Blows Where it Chooses* (Melbourne: Coventry Press, 2018).

Walsh, Chris, *Over My Tracks* (Evelyn Crawford) (Melbourne: Penguin Books 1993).

Warhurst, John, *Wrestling With The Church Hierarchy* (Melbourne: John Garratt, 2021).

Williams, Rowan, *On Christian Theology* (London: Blackwell Publishing, 2000).

Wilson, George B., SJ, *Clericalism* (Minnesota: Liturgical Press, 2008).

Zagano, Phyllis, *Women: Icons of Christ* (Mahwah NJ: Paulist Press, 2020).

Epilogue

Beyond the boundaries

Part 1

Janette Bredenoord Elliott and Berise Heasly

Updating theology for the 21st century

Cameo 1: Dicastery in Rome on Artificial Intelligence: development of theology of the person – when? Because modernity was outlawed, it is possible to ask which newly titled Dicastery will become responsible for developing expertise in all areas where artificial intelligence is contributing to current living. Ethical questions can not be addressed until experts in salient areas of this remarkable industry are recognised in the science arena, before they are given responsibility to work within a Dicastery as part of the institutional church. In the medical field so far, the use of numbers of digital interventions that lengthen human life, push us theologically to ask when serious theologians will be 'allowed' to develop understanding of such matters. We will, therefore, also be thankful for the ABC tv investigative program ('The Great Accelerator', 8 May 2022), tracing historical development of the first transistor in 1947 through all the expansions into 21st second decade information of users' brains today perhaps changing towards 'scattered thinking' rather than 'analytical and critical thinking skills'.

Cameo 2: Climate Change conference in Glasgow: development of theology/moral norms for care of our planet – when? The violence of the climate events and the state of the north and south icecaps of our planet are providing serious and deadly threats to humankind. The lack of voices from the Dicasteries of the institutional church is so obvious. When teenagers and others can only take to the streets, and global financial conglomerations stick to their greed, which Dicastery is going to field experts who know how to marshal the enthusiasm of all those who recognise that action is needed? No amount of nicely enunciated statements or responses to questions in media conferences is going to change this very dangerous position. Unless, those unctuous statements need to be accompanied by immediate and continual action, no matter the cost!

Cameo 3: Professor Greg Craven interview with Geraldine Doogue during the first Plenary Council sessions (and his statement during the second session) : development of theology of the cosmos is needed so that the church has the expertise and skills to converse reasonably with the current three generations, rather than harking back to pre-medieval times, or trying to pin a false accusation on 'the reform-ers'. Accusations of conspiracy can not stand up to scrutiny. It seems that it is more comfortable to defy what is real today than it is to recognise the possibility that the Holy Spirit is present in the work of reform-ers. So which Dicastery is going to appoint experts whose sociology is current, is balanced, is non-judgmental and is capable of collaboration with existing young leaders to resolve some of the nasty and narcissistic putdowns so easy to trip of the hierarchical tongue?

Cameo 4: That letter... It seems that there has been the audacious appearance in the last few months before the second session of the Plenary Council of a letter with a pseudonym rather than a name: Demos. This letter, addressing the cardinals assumed to be those who will attend the next conclave (after Francis has been harassed enough to go to God!), requests the cardinals to vote in a new papal person who will reverse every change and development sponsored by Pope Francis. The request also asks the cardinals to find a person who will return the church to 'NORMALITY'!! Does normality include the hypocrisy that Frederic Martel found in the Vatican? Does normality include what Ute Ranke-Heinemann's research showed us on the brutality of institutional church treatment of women? Does normality include the recent extraordinary research of Dyan Elliott, about the way clerics behaved towards women, and treated boys so brutally, smashing their psyches on a regular basis? Does normality include the theocratic behaviour of Irish Catholicism of the last centuries researched by Derek Scally, when harsh and criminal behaviour and secrecy regarding punishment of victims of sexual misbehaviour and resultant deaths were regular occurrences? Does normality include the financial crimes researched by Gianluigi Nuzzi, when an underground financial empire was built, and seemingly still exists?.....

Cameo 5: Re-imagined definition and identity of the Laity.

Having been formed in the wisdom and breadth of Benedictine Spirituality, in which an understanding of what it means to be 'lay', bridges the apparent 'Twin-Towers' of ordained vs. laity, many questions arise regarding the often-unhelpful dichotomy of these terms. These questions are at the proverbial tip of the iceberg in relation to the expectations, desires and hopes for the Plenary Council. For already, the hopes of the laity are being dashed against the fortress of the long-standing, in-built systems that protect, favour and bias the ordained, hierarchical mode of leading the Church. The balance is tipped to favour those with the power to invite consultation, but not necessarily the will to act on what the laity – with courage, long-suffering and hope – hear the Spirit calling today's Church to. I honestly wonder if the ordained ever sense the prison-like nature of their fortress, their tower, their constrictive systems that bear too much prescriptive, limiting, non-life-giving fruit.

This is not to disparage individuals who recognise what a pivotal moment this is for the Church in Australia and abroad. Yet in our own backyard, the systemic dynamics of the collective reality that is symbolised by the metaphor of fortress lead more to despair and cynicism, than real hope for birthing an open, inclusive, transparent, accountable, compassionate and prophetic Church. And why can't there be a more inspiring term than 'laity' that does not lock the laity into a concept or category that is by these structures and systems the lesser half of the Church? Are the laity placed in the same category as the woman defined as that taken from man? Is the laity by definition only a derivative of another body – collective and/or individual?

Surely there can be a better term for the extraordinary body of baptised people in the Church that shows genuine respect, authentic care, empathetic witness, and empowering encouragement. Surely there is a better term that allows laity and ordained to labour alongside each other equally in the vineyards the Lord calls us to. Surely there is a better way of understanding what it means to be laity in the Church that doesn't harness us to infantile behaviour as regards seeking permissions, approval from the top, rather than in listening to each other – lay person to lay person – as well?

The Laity is not the same as it was pre-Vatican II; it is made up of a plurality of groups carrying out good works, Bible study groups, prayer groups, reform groups, those simply content to live a life of quiet faith and devotion, those who cling to the old comfortable ways, those also who deny the scandal of sexual abuse and still expect their priests to be 'God's voice' to them – often in ways unhelpful and unhealthy. Then, of course, there are the cohort of laity employed by the Church in parishes, in education, and a range of professions, plus the profoundly generous volunteers who give hours to Boards and Committees, Parish Councils and parish initiatives.

John Warhurst recently noted this demographic within the laity registering its significance as well as its vulnerability. Among all these groups representing the laity today are those we can never, ever forget – the marginalised who are still deeply wounded and scarred by Church scandals, and also by apparent Church indifference to those whose expression of faith is judged invalid due to their LGBQTI A+ declaration. In all the questions regarding the laity, I had first thought about what could possibly unify us all, enabling and empowering the laity. My thoughts went first to the Plenary Council, but the deeper question that engages me more is that of the re-imagination of the term laity which respects baptismal identity and forms us for response-ability as Christians for today's needs in our fragile, broken Church and world. As Gideon Goosen noted in his article 'The Catholic Church: who needs reform?' (*SWAG*, Summer 2020): 'Reform is more than politics, it is inclusive conversion'.'

Cameo 6: The question of Spiritual Redress

'Spoiled identity' is a term used by Kathleen McPhillips to describe the impact of Institutional stigma on boys especially who suffered sexual abuse in the Church. (See 'Traumatic Isolation: Institutional Stigma and the Australian Royal Commission into Institutional Responses to Child Sexual Abuse'[1]) As the result of 'particular organisational mechanisms that induce isolation,' this 'traumatic isolation' means that there are hidden in our midst, absent from the pews – and they are not alone – absent from our gatherings, absent even from our consciousness, a body of God's beloved children aching for spiritual redress. Yes – **spiritual** redress. It is a sobering and soul-aching undertaking to spend time reading the Case Studies and Narratives of the published Final Report of the Royal Commission into Institutional Responses to Child Sexual Abuse.

So we cry, we rage, we despair, we grieve and we perhaps even choose to walk away from the Church in disgust. All these reactions are completely understandable. The empty Church pews witness to the travesty of both those who suffered abuse and continue to live with the aftermath of the trauma, and those who literally can't stomach the knowledge or thoughts that in the very place of worship and communion, their trusted priest(s) carried out such abhorrent acts on such innocent and vulnerable children.

The human mind – as we know after two years of navigating COVID with its lockdowns and the need to re-think all our public actions around personal hygiene – can only bear so much and remain healthy. Such wounding of the innocent is

---

[1] *Health and History*: Australian and New Zealand Society of the History of Medicine, Vol. 20, No. 2, 2018, pp. 75-90.

humanly speaking too much to bear indeed, and especially in the context of Church. Yet, that body of people – our brothers and sisters – precious to God as much as we are, remain hidden, absent and invisible outside of the court cases, the 'breaking news' in the plethora of digital and printed media, Government rulings and other initiatives to address Child Sexual abuse in Church and society. So the Royal Commission handed down Recommendations which rightfully address financial compensation or the redress scheme, changes to Church governance structures, to formation of the ordained and religious, training for lay ministries and mandatory supervision for those in all forms of ministry involving care of children and vulnerable adults. These are not only good, but absolutely necessary. Who could deny that?!

However, if we listen closely to the voices of the boys and girls in the narratives which are the testimony of their abuse – often and significantly for the first time – a deeper cry can be heard for spiritual redress. What do I mean by this term? I am referring to addressing the unseen need for spiritual nourishment, communal embrace, a simple smile of welcome, the 'sign of peace,' the experience of singing together and all the other signs of inclusivity that normally go with coming together as God's people to worship God, to encourage one another and to share the sorrows and joys of life as we live in God's presence.

As for victims of CSA – the silencing by them of perpetrators, the shame of the abuse, the robbing of innocence and dignity and self-worth, the fear of further*Janette Bredenoord Elliott and Berise Heasly* abuse, entrapment, and, tragically, even the cooperation, manipulation or blackmailing of family, police, schools and even other religious – have all served to isolate this body of God's beloved. Living as those shunned by all the horrid and evil dynamics of this kind of abuse, the victims have become cut off from the love and affection of the community, access to spiritual nourishment and imprisoned in their 'spoiled identity' through institutional stigma.

Initiatives such as LIFEBOAT founded by Fr Kevin Dillon are magnificent. We need so many more to enable awareness if not visibility, and spiritual redress initiatives to infiltrate the dark, hidden places where victims and survivors of abuse may know their real worth and dignity as beloved of God and be respected as such.

Part 2

Janette Bredenoord Elliott

In my opening remarks, I referred to meeting the Easter Christ on the shores of hope and healing, awareness and forgiveness, mercy and grace, of courage and of justice. As we now conclude, we look also to the Holy Spirit, the Advocate who is *with us*, who is *in us*. The gifts of wisdom and of courage are ours to claim in abundance for this phase of our journey into maturity within the Australian Church. For the re-building of trust that needs to take place requires courage, wisdom and great love as noted by Berise Heasly in her introductory words. To embrace trust beyond trauma invites the Maker, the Protector and Lover (Julian of Norwich, Long Text 4), that is, God the Blissful Trinity as Julian of Norwich understand God. Julian wrote that we are all enclosed in the Trinity, and the Trinity is all enclosed in us. So that we would understand that we are accompanied through life in the Trinity, she expands on this understanding:

The all-powerful truth of the Trinity is the Father, who created us and keeps us within him. The deep wisdom of the Trinity is our Other, in whom we are all enfolded. The exalted goodness of the Trinity is our beloved Lord: we are held in him and he is held in us. We are enclosed in the Father, we are enclosed in the Son, and we are enclosed in the Holy Spirit. The Father, the Son, and the Holy Spirit are enclosed in us. All Power. All Goodness. All Wisdom. One God. One Love (*Long Text* 54).

Berise Heasly

The third book in this trilogy has addressed the anomalies that arise in the responses of diverse form which emerge as the People of God, the 'people in the pews', do their best to arrive at reasonable and carefully managed decisions as Catholic Christians today. There is a certain element of aloneness which accompanies the confusion caused by the events of the 20th and 21st centuries in the institutional church, as well as the blurring of boundaries in religious and secular milieux.

Our initial brief was to invite contributors to look beyond the boundaries that seem to close off opportunities to use our God-given imagination today. So much new information, knowledge, expertise has been disfigured by unethical and criminal behaviour in certain parts of the institutional church, that the freedom to express their inner thoughts was the starting point for each author. No other requirement was expressed. It is delightful to recognise then, that their various and magnificent chapters model the inner tensegrity that allows diverse and sometimes painful topics to be addressed.

Certainly, the uncomfortable position which accompanies the use of parrhesia makes writing in some areas a very sensitive and scary experience. The remarkable autobiographical content, sometimes openly expressed, sometimes informing the expertise and knowledge displayed, is a tribute to the integrity of the writers and the editors are sincerely grateful to each one for the bravery and honesty that has been displayed.

About the contributors

Morag Fraser (B.A. Hons., M.A., Dip. Ed) is a writer and one of Australia's most experienced social and literary commentators.

After teaching English, drama and literature for 15 years, Morag edited Eureka Street, the Jesuit Magazine of public affairs, the arts and theology (1991 -2003). She was Adjunct Professor in Humanities and Social Sciences at Latrobe University (2003 – 2009). She has been a Member of the Kildare Education Ministries Board since its inception, and actively engaged in Brigidine education for three decades. In 2004, Morag was made a Member of the Order of Australia, for services to journalism.

Morag resides on the lands of the Wurundjeri peoples of the Kulin nation.

Hugh McGinlay was born and educated in Scotland. He has post-graduate degrees in Theology (Gregorian University, Rome), Scripture (Biblical Institute, Rome and Jerusalem) and Religious Education (Dundalk, Ireland). He has worked in publishing in UK and Australia, including twenty years with the Uniting Church's publishing house, where he was responsible for that Church's Adult Education programs and liturgical resources. He currently works as Acquisitions Editor for Coventry Press in Melbourne. Hugh is married to Andrea, and they have two sons and four grandchildren.

Hugh lives on the land of the Wurundjeri people.

Janette Elliott is a PhD candidate at the University of Divinity and works for Jesuit Services in Melbourne. She has been praying and working with the writings of Julian of Norwich – the subject of her PhD thesis – over a thirty-year period. Originally a teacher, and formed strongly in Benedictine spirituality, Janette seeks through her writing to empower others – as Julian did.

Janette lives on the land of the Wurundjeri people.

Gideon Goosen

Gideon Goosen is a Sydney-based theologian who lives in the Blue Mountains, NSW. He holds doctorates in Philosophy and Theology. He has taught theology for many years at the Australian Catholic University and the Irish School of Ecumenics at Trinity College, Dublin, and was Chair of the Theological Commission of the NSW Ecumenical Council as well as working with local ecumenical groups. He is a member of ACTA (Australian Catholic Theological Association), CTSA (Catholic Theological Society of America) and ESCT (European Society of Catholic Theologians). He is the author of a number of books and journal articles. His latest book is Clericalism: Stories from the Pews (Coventry Press, 2020).

Gideon lives on the lands of the Dharug and the Gundungurra peoples.

Ian Hamilton

Ian Hamilton is a cradle Catholic who has spent his working career within Catholic secondary education in NSW, South Australia and Queensland. In addition to his work as an English teacher, he has often taught Religion and Ethics and the Study of Religion. His leadership roles within schools included being Director of Spirituality, Director of Mission and

Liturgy. Initially completing an Arts degree and Diploma of Education at the University of Newcastle, he later undertook an MA in English Literature at Sydney University. Later still, he completed the Graduate Diploma in Theological Studies, followed by the Masters degree in Theological Studies at Adelaide College of Divinity (Flinders University).

Ian lives on the land of the Turrbal people.

Adrian Hubbard graduated as an Osteopath in 2001 after five years of fulltime study. He holds both a Bachelor of Science and a Masters degree in Osteopathy. Adrian's treatment approach is Neuro-Musculoskeletal; he uses specific neurological pathways to influence the body structure. This methodology recognises that some symptom patterns may be impacted by factors outside the musculoskeletal system. His objective is to apply treatment to effectively restore musculoskeletal function and reduce discomfort, as well as teaching people how to optimise their functional movement patterns to both prevent recurrence of dysfunction and improve overall wellbeing.

This approach is wholly in harmony with Tensegrity principles.

Adrian lives on the land of the Wurundjeri people of the Kulin nation.

Michael Elligate AM
Michael spent forty-eight successful years in parishes in the Archdiocese of Melbourne, thirty-five of them as Parish Priest of St Carthage's University Parish, Parkville, in Victoria. A graduate in Social Sciences and Education, he is Chair of Human Ethics Research (Social Sciences) University of Melbourne.

Michael lives on the land of the Wurundjeri people.

Naomi Wolfe

Naomi is a Trawlwoolway Aboriginal woman with Jewish, German, and Irish heritage, who lives and works on Wurundjeri country (Melbourne, Australia). She is an Academic at Australian Catholic University where she teaches Indigenous and Ancient histories. Prior to her transfer to the Faculty of Education & Arts, she was the Academic Coordinator of Jim-baa-yer Indigenous Higher Education Unit at ACU. Naomi is also the First Peoples Coordinator at the University of Divinity. She has the great privilege of being the Academic Dean for NAIITS Australian programs. NAIITS: An Indigenous Learning Community, is an international community of Indigenous and non-Indigenous peoples, who deliver Indigenous designed, Indigenous led, and Indigenous delivered theological education. NAIITS is an accredited ATS member. Naomi has a love of history of all types and will take any opportunity to bore people silly with discussions of history and theology. Luckily, she now has her nephew living with her to distract her from such pursuits.

Peter Johnstone OAM

Peter is Co-Convener of the Australasian Catholic Coalition for Church Reform and a member of Catholics for Renewal. He gave public evidence on Church governance to the Royal Commission on Institutional Responses to Child Sexual Abuse.

Peter has worked at all levels of government in Australia in many chief executive roles. He is a former chair of Jesuit College of Spirituality and VincentCare Victoria, and was foundation Chair of Jesuit Social Services, the Council of Catholic Social Services Victoria and Catholics for Renewal. He has qualifications in corporate governance and theology.

Peter resides on the land of the Wurundjeri People.

Maree Stanley

Maree worked as a psychological counsellor for many years in community and private practice settings. She has also conducted training workshops about communication, counselling skills and ethics. Over a number of years, she taught in various post-graduate courses about counselling and ethics in several universities. She regards it as an honour and a privilege to have heard the stories her clients have revealed and entrusted to her.

Maree lives on the land of the Wurundjeri people.

Berise Heasly

Berise spent thirty-six years teaching secondary students in Humanities, English, Ethics and Religious Studies. She holds a PhD from Victoria University, Melbourne, and a Graduate Diploma of Theology from Catholic Theological College, University of Divinity, Melbourne. She is the author of Call No One Father (2019) and a co-editor of We Too: The Laity Speaks (2020). She has been an active member of St Carthage's Parish, Parkville, and is a founding member of Women's Wisdom in the Catholic Church (WWITCH).

Berise lives on the land of the Bunurong Boon Wurrung and Wurundjeri peoples of the Kulin nation.

Lightning Source UK Ltd.
Milton Keynes UK
UKHW041933101022
410228UK00004B/38